BUSINESS
WRITING
With Heart

BUSINESS WRITING

With Heart

How to Build
Great Work Relationships
One Message at a Time

Lynn Gaertner-Johnston

Syntax Training, Seattle, Washington

Business Writing With Heart: How to Build Great Work Relationships One Message at a Time

For information about this title or to order other books and/or electronic media, contact the publisher:

Syntax Training LLC
7332 16th Avenue NW, Seattle, Washington 98117-5415
www.syntaxtraining.com
info@syntaxtraining.com

Library of Congress Control Number: 2013952284

ISBN: 978-0-9778679-0-5

Printed in the United States of America

To my parents, Ed and Louise Gaertner,
who live on in my heart

Contents

BUSINESS WRITING
With Heart

Introduction

When you think of establishing business relationships, what comes to mind? Perhaps you imagine schmoozing at trade shows and conferences or listening attentively to new clients. Maybe you see yourself shaking hands with new employees during their first-day tour or smiling at them in videoconferences. If your business is strictly online, perhaps you envision uploading new-customer offers on your home page. Those are a few easy steps in initiating relationships.

But once begun, the challenge is building and maintaining those bonds. How do you maintain individual relationships with coworkers, employees, customers, industry peers, donors, board members, citizens, and others? How do you protect professional relationships from fading due to lack of attention or cracking under fast-paced, high-pressured communication? How can you cultivate relationships to support your success and gain a competitive advantage?

> **Writing With Heart =**
>
> Writing with respect and positive intent, using language that makes those feelings clear.

The answer to those questions is the promise of this book: You can build and maintain great work relationships one message at a time, by writing with heart—that is, with respect and positive intent, using language that makes those feelings clear.

More than ever before, writing is the lifeblood of business relationships. If you are like most professionals, you email or text more than you talk on the phone or meet in person. You may have long-distance relationships with people you never meet and rarely speak to, although you write to one another regularly. You may email or IM (instant message) people who work in the next building (or even the next cubicle), rather than walk over to talk with them. Even if you do meet with colleagues, customers, and clients, written messages are likely to keep you connected between meetings.

With this focus on writing comes much risk to relationships. It's very easy to derail work relationships by what we say and how we say it. Hastily written messages, cryptic brevity, clumsy wording, boilerplate language—even punctuation—can unintentionally send the wrong message. After all, readers can't see your sincerity and good intentions on the page or screen. And as a writer, you unfortunately can't see their puzzled or frowning faces to instantly fix the situation.

Applying the lessons of this book, you will be able to minimize writing risks and protect your professional relationships. You will not come across like a soulless suit, a beleaguered or bullying bureaucrat, a self-effacing shadow, a saccharine adolescent, or a [fill in the blank with your fear about undermining your relationships]. Instead, you will be able to communicate authentically and considerately with people in writing, even in awkward and challenging situations.

Business Writing With Heart is for you if you want to build and sustain your business relationships while meeting the challenges of high-speed, high-demand communication. It shows you how to write relationship-building messages rather than relationship-neutral ones. It gives you concrete tips and examples to help you in your work in any industry, from high tech to nonprofits, from manufacturing to government, from finance to consulting to education.

No matter what your job is, if your work involves relationships and the communication challenges that flow naturally from them, this book helps you meet those challenges. Whether you are a corporate communications specialist, an administrative assistant, a vice president, a human resources manager, a sales or customer-service rep, a team leader, a teacher, a contractor, a consultant, an entrepreneur, or another type of professional, you will find the right words and messages in this book to create win-win communications. If you don't have a job because you are self-employed or between positions, *Business Writing With Heart* helps you connect with people in positive, natural ways that lead to sales, contracts, interviews, and job opportunities.

With clear sample messages, before-and-after examples, easy-to-apply dos, emphatic don'ts, and memorable stories, *Business Writing With Heart* helps you:

- Add heart to your messages so they intentionally nurture rather than unintentionally ruin your relationships.
- Send brief messages that come across as efficient yet friendly—not brusque and thoughtless.
- Cultivate relationships with thank-yous, congratulations, positive feedback, and condolences that sound sincere instead of smarmy.
- Avoid unconscious email habits that injure and end relationships.
- Choose the perfect words and tone to communicate bad news without fostering bad feelings.
- Disagree without destroying initiative and damaging relationships.
- Give constructive feedback to improve performance and reinforce relationships rather than make everyone feel embarrassed and defensive.

- Stay connected during your job search without feeling like a bother.
- Say no clearly, courageously, and courteously, without guilt or foot-dragging.
- Apologize in a way that redeems a situation and makes everyone feel better.
- Deal diplomatically with angry messages and transform your own anger rather than enlist in a verbal war.
- Choose warm yet professional ways to begin and end your letters and emails. (Hint: You don't need to use *!!!!* and *xxoo*.)
- Send holiday messages that strengthen your business relationships rather than spam your contacts.
- Write quick, thoughtful messages that introduce others, enhancing your network and expanding theirs.
- Build productive, respectful partnerships—not strained, unsettling relationships—with associates around the globe.

People around the world inspired me to write this book. They asked thorny questions on my blog, such as "How do I deal with a peer who criticizes me in an email and copies other people?" They brought their people issues to my business writing classes, things like "Should I refer to my female coworkers as *ladies, women,* or *girls*?" They emailed me in search of solutions to relationship challenges and opportunities at work, for instance, "What can I do to develop real relationships with people I meet at professional conferences?" *Business Writing With Heart* offers something for all of them—and for you.

Follow this roadmap for ways to build your business relationships and solve communication problems that threaten them:

1. **Read Part One, The Essentials.** It gives you immediate writing tools and tips that reinforce relationships and reduce

misunderstandings. It also cautions you about the huge relationship dangers that lurk in email for unsuspecting users.

2. **Dive into one or more chapters in Part Two, The Opportunities.** The often overlooked messages covered in these chapters can jump-start and supercharge your relationships. Just follow the expert guidelines. Your personal introductions, thank-yous, congratulations, condolences, positive feedback, and holiday greetings will immediately take your relationships to the next level. In a job search, your updates and other networking messages will open doors you had not anticipated.

3. **Review Part Three, The Challenges, when you face a communication problem.** Whether you are challenged with offering an apology, sharing bad news, saying no to a request, disagreeing, reminding someone, dealing with anger (perhaps your own), giving constructive feedback, or communicating with people from other cultures, these chapters give you specific examples and advice to meet the challenge and preserve your relationships.

4. **Create an action plan and deepen your understanding in Part Four, Take Action.** This section helps you develop an action plan to make relationship-building messages part of your routine, no matter what your profession is.

5. **Use For Your Reference when you need more information.** Review Recommended Resources when you want to learn more about building and nurturing your work relationships and dealing with relationship difficulties. Use the other reference sections for answers to your questions about rendering

names and titles in greetings and on envelopes. You can also find suitable greetings and closes for all your messages, even for complicated situations.

The content of *Business Writing With Heart* helps you with spoken communication too. Although its focus is written messages, the book also provides you with the right words to use in many challenging interpersonal situations such as saying no, disagreeing, dealing with anger and insults, and sharing constructive feedback. It compares effective and ineffective wording, and it gives you neutral *I* statements to replace *you* statements that can layer a message with blame and attack. It helps you recognize that words like *sweetie* and *hon* can change a communication from friendly to hostile, even when you have good intentions. It includes practical lessons you can apply in all aspects of your life.

Business Writing With Heart does not cover the topics of writing clearly, concisely, and correctly. It doesn't cover grammar, usage, or punctuation. Although those topics are essential to your success as a writer, this guide focuses on writing with a respectful, positive intent and using tools to communicate that intent unerringly.

Many of the communication principles and methods I advocate in *Business Writing With Heart* apply around the globe. However, most of my experience has been in building business relationships with people in the United States and Canada by writing with heart.

How I Learned About Writing With Heart

Over 20 years ago, I began working as a career counselor with a large outplacement firm. My job was to help people bounce back from a job layoff, hone their job-search skills, and find a new career or position. It included helping them to improve their cover letters and resumes. Maybe because I was new to this work and was coaching people at a higher job level than mine—managers, directors, and vice presidents—I was trying hard to prove myself. To show that I knew what I was doing, I made extensive written comments on what needed to change in clients' resumes and letters, from punctuation to sentence length to content. Then somewhere on the page, I would jot a positive but general remark like "Good job."

My barrage of constructive comments was not intentionally heartless. But as I wrote suggestions and corrections, I was oblivious to the damage they could do to newly out-of-work executives.

I soon recognized that something was wrong with my approach. I noticed that clients would blanch when they saw the annotated pages I pulled out of their folders. I observed that they would appear resigned and deflated. And it was obvious that I was doing something wrong when executives would argue with seemingly every point I made.

I quickly tried new strategies, many of which appear in this book. Sometimes I balanced my positive and constructive comments, making sure that both were specific. At other times, I wrote only positive comments on resumes and talked through those points one by one. Then I would use supportive language, such as, "Let's make sure every entry here presents you as positively as possible," to talk the client through the areas to improve. Sometimes I wrote no comments at all (although I had made private notes to myself), and the client and I would review the resume or letter line by line together, citing both what was strong and what needed additional oomph. When I added or changed punctuation, I described it as "helping the reader get the point quickly" rather than as "correcting a punctuation error."

My new ways of communicating led to much better results and excellent relationships with clients, whose responses to my feedback were markedly more positive. They sat up straight, and they were animated, engaged in the process, and receptive to feedback. They sought my opinion on a letter rather than bracing to learn my reaction to it. When they incorporated my suggestions in a revision, they admired their handiwork rather than begrudgingly admitting it might be better than the original. They began to seek my input on thank-you letters and ways to handle difficult interview questions, and they talked with me about their interview hits and misses. They saw me as a trusted partner in their job search rather than as a know-it-all taskmaster.

I learned a valuable lesson about writing and oral communication at the outplacement firm: If you communicate with care and attention to the feelings of the other person—not just to your own short-term goal or the task at hand—your relationships will be more successful, productive, and satisfying. Since then, I have applied, refined, and expanded the lesson I learned in my work with outplacement clients. I have continued to be sure that what I write (or choose to talk about rather than put in writing) communicates with respect, warmth, and tact. I have learned to write in a way that creates partnerships with others so that I achieve results with people who feel supported rather than in spite of people who feel undermined. Being in business as a consultant has required those communication skills, and I am happy to say that the lessons I have learned have helped my business thrive. This book shares those lessons.

My experience suggests that writing with heart yields a positive return on investment (ROI). I believe that communicating with heart leads to new clients, repeat customers, referrals, partnerships, jobs, contracts, and other satisfying business dealings. However, if you would prefer evidence of ROI that is more tangible, consider these hypothetical situations. They deal solely with the investment of time, but you can imagine the investment of other resources.

Time Required Without Applying the Tips and Principles of Writing With Heart	Time Required as a Result of Not Applying the Tips and Principles	Time Required to Apply the Tips and Principles of Writing With Heart
To write an email to a new assistant telling him everything he did wrong on his first day: 5 minutes.	To hire a new assistant to replace the one who quit in discouragement after reading the critical email: 1–2 months.	To write an email to a new assistant telling him what he did well and what you would like him to do differently tomorrow: 10 minutes.

To write a hasty, impatient response to a client who has misunderstood a contract provision: 2 minutes.	To win back a client who has canceled a contract after reading the insulting reply: 1–3 months.	To compose a tactful, considerate response to a client who has misunderstood a contract provision: 15 minutes.
To not compose constructive feedback for a virtual employee who is doing part of her job incorrectly: 0 minutes.	To redo a virtual employee's work when she repeatedly does it incorrectly because no one has informed her of a problem: 3 minutes a day, day after day, week after week.	To compose thoughtful, constructive feedback for a virtual employee who is doing part of her job incorrectly: 10–15 minutes.
To bang out a sarcastic email in response to a frustrated employee on another team: 2 minutes.	To repair the relationship with the employee who received the sarcastic reply: 2 years.	To stop by the employee's desk to talk, or to write an empathetic email reply: 15 minutes.
To not write an email to introduce to the organization a new employee in a new position: 0 minutes.	For people in the organization to realize there is a new employee and figure out what he does and why: 2 months to 2 years.	To write a company-wide announcement welcoming a new employee and explaining what he will do in a new position and why: 15–20 minutes.
To not write a sympathy message to a customer whose spouse has died: 0 minutes.	To win back the customer, who has begun work with your competitor because of not feeling connected with you: a long time, if it is even possible.	To write and mail a thoughtful sympathy message to a customer: 15 minutes.
To not write an email to people in your network, updating them on your job search: 0 minutes.	To find out about the "hidden" job openings that people in your network know about but do not inform you of because you haven't stayed in touch: a long time, if it is even possible.	To write an email to people in your network, updating them on your job search: 20–30 minutes.

Writing with heart does require investing time, normally just a few moments or minutes per message. However, that investment saves huge amounts of time, effort, and money that are otherwise required to salvage situations that have suffered because of insensitive communication or no communication at all. But regardless of the savings and other quantifiable benefits, perhaps you, like me, will simply feel great connecting with others in ways that are positive, respectful, and diplomatic.

Even with the ROI scenarios, you may feel doubtful about the "heart" and relationship focus of this book. Let's look at some of your possible reservations.

"I am here to work—not to develop relationships."

Effective work relationships help you get your work done, whether you work in a corner office, a cubicle, your car, or your basement. According to social network theorist Karen Stephenson, our informal work relationships are just as important as our dotted-lined reporting relationships at work. In her essay "Trafficking in Trust: The Art and Science of Human Knowledge Networks," Stephenson wrote, "Knowledge ebbs and flows down hallways, in meetings, and in private conversations inside and outside the office. The key to the way that knowledge travels lies in the relationships that can bypass the standard organization chart. . . . Relationships are the true medium of knowledge exchange, and trust is the glue that holds them together." I believe Stephenson's theory applies not only to employees, but also to consultants, contractors, and others who work on the fringes of companies, and those who work outside organizations. Relationships help. Applying the writing tips and principles in this book helps you build trust and develop valuable work relationships.

"I don't want to be a Pollyanna."

Writing with heart does not require that you be unreasonably or foolishly optimistic, if that's what "Pollyanna" means to you. It just requires that you communicate with respect and positive intent. When I adjusted my critiques of client resumes and letters at the outplacement firm, I was not a Pollyanna. I simply got better results and developed much better relationships using a balanced approach than a negative one. Is it possible that your results and work relationships would improve if you communicated differently?

"This is just a part-time, temporary job, so positive relationships don't matter to me. I'm just passing through."

All of us are just passing through in one way or another. I worked part-time at the outplacement firm for five years while I developed my business as a trainer and writing consultant, and I worked with most of the clients there for just a few days, weeks, or months. Yet a client with whom I worked briefly on his job-search documents recently referred me to the training manager at the energy company where he now works, and I am teaching writing classes there—20 years after he and I worked together. If I had regarded myself or my outplacement clients as just passing through and had not taken the time to communicate supportively with them, I would not be enjoying the benefits of long-lasting relationships.

"I work alone. I don't think I need to be concerned about relationships."

You work alone, but do you ever need to rely on other people? Do you ever need a job reference, some quick advice, an introduction to someone, or a bit of information that just one person has? If your answer is yes, work relationships matter to you.

"I don't want to coddle people. They're adults. Why can't I just tell it like it is?"

Here's the problem with telling it like it is: If *it* only includes the negative stuff, people will not listen, as I learned. They will resist, argue, and produce less. If you were giving an employee written feedback on a sales call, for example, even if the employee handled the call badly, she would need to know what she did right as well as what she did wrong.

If you focused on only the negative, you would come across as biased and condescending. Why would anyone pay attention to a biased, condescending boss or coworker? As Rick Maurer wrote in *Feedback Toolkit: 16 Tools for Better Communication in the Workplace,* "Don't inflict feedback. . . . Once you exceed what others can handle . . . you risk never meeting your goals."

"Communicating with heart seems phony."

What is phony about communicating respectfully and positively? If you don't feel respectful and positive toward people with whom you work, why not act as though you do? That is not phoniness—it is a sincere effort to succeed on the job. Otherwise, your feelings will function as barricades to your success.

"Our company culture is to win at all costs. Relationships? We take no prisoners."

Your company may fight to win contracts, cases, clients, and talented employees. But we live in a small world—tomorrow your competitors may be your clients, and your adversaries may be your partners. Winning those clients and partners requires that you have communicated—and continue to communicate—with professionalism, courtesy, and a positive attitude.

"I am not a good writer. How can I possibly worry about another thing?"

Not to worry! You will find dozens of effective relationship-building messages throughout this book. You can easily adapt those models to your situations. You will also find lists of helpful and harmful expressions to help you choose the right approach to solve many communication problems. And you will have at your fingertips plenty of phrases that transform unintentionally harsh comments into remarks that build goodwill.

"We always razz each other. We wouldn't recognize one another if we were nice!"

Communicating with heart is not about being nice. It's about being strategic. It involves intentionally supporting work relationships rather than weakening them. Give it a chance. Spend a week communicating respectfully and positively with one another in writing and in your spoken interactions. Then look for differences in people's performance and attitudes. Especially notice people who are new to your group, on the fringes rather than part of the in-crowd, typically the target of the razzing, or in a minority of one kind or another among the group members (gender, race, age, etc.). You may recognize new confidence, participation, and enthusiasm when you limit the teasing and instead focus on supporting and building up your coworkers.

"This takes too much time. I am maxed out as it is."

Consider the alternatives. Would you rather invest the minutes upfront to communicate with care and courtesy? Or would you prefer to take hours, days, and weeks later on to resolve conflicts, repair relationships, win back clients, replace staff, and so on?

"I need to communicate efficiently. This approach seems complicated."

I show you how to make communicating with heart very efficient, with simple language and small, specific shifts in your writing. Once you get the hang of it, it will take little effort for you to communicate with balance rather than harshness, and sensitivity rather than indifference. This book helps you make relationship-building choices that solve problems rather than create them.

"Won't I be walked on if I come across as nice?"

Communicating with heart does not involve being a doormat. It does not mean you will let people walk on you to get where they are going.

Writing with heart involves treating others—and yourself—with respect and positive intent to build relationships and get results. It means being smarter about the power of your words. Adding heart to your writing is an advantage, not a risk or a weakness. It helps you communicate politely and powerfully.

The positive results of writing with heart increase over time. Since beginning my blog, Business Writing, in 2005, I have earned thousands of fans around the globe who have come to value my thoughtful, relationship-building commentary on business communication. In many years of self-employment, I have developed a long list of repeat clients who think immediately of me when they need to develop better business writers on the job. Why? Because through the emails, letters, referrals, reminders, thank-yous, condolences, congratulations, and holiday greetings they have received from me, they have come to know me well as a reliable, caring business partner.

About the Details

Throughout the book, you will find examples of relationship-building messages, many that I wrote and some that others contributed. For messages that I wrote as examples, I made up names for the recipients and the senders. If the made-up names match those of real people, the match is coincidental. For messages that others wrote and contributed, I identified the writers by name with their permission. Rather than identify certain companies and organizations, I have used fictional names such as ABC Association, LMNOP Inc., and XYZ Company. These names do not refer to any real alphabet-named organizations.

The examples show a variety of ways to format, begin, and end your messages. For guidelines on greetings and closes and rendering people's names, consult the sections on those topics under For Your Reference.

The survey on business writing and relationships, cited throughout the book, included the input of 686 adults working in the United States, most of whom subscribe to my monthly e-newsletter, *Better Writing at Work,* or read my blog, Business Writing (www.businesswritingblog.com).

Each chapter ends with a brief Personal Reflection and Next Step suggestion. They are intended to be painless, practical applications of the chapter content. Use these to move forward, solving communication problems and enhancing your work relationships, one quick step at a time.

Keep in Touch!

I look forward to hearing your stories about how writing with heart has helped you solve problems and nurture rewarding business relationships. Write to me at lynng@syntaxtraining.com.

PART ONE

The Essentials

CHAPTER I

Add Heart to Your Writing One Message at a Time

I teach business writing to people at all levels in organizations, from vice presidents to mechanics, from auditors to security officers. When security managers and officers attend classes, they stand out—not just for their calm, commanding presence but also for the way they communicate. They write and say things like:

Request denied.

Negative.

Cut the fluff. I want the facts.

They don't have to like it. They just have to do it.

When I suggest a more positive approach, they often announce, "I'm ex-military. This is the way we communicate." If another ex-military individual is in the room, that person nods agreement.

When ex-military individuals communicate with others like them, pronouncements like "Request denied" are likely to be clear, effective, and familiar. But when these individuals communicate beyond their group—for instance, to the assistant in accounting or the intern in public relations—"Request denied" comes across as brusque and machine-like—not a communication that builds relationships.

Like the military veterans who attend my writing classes, you may say at one time or another, "This is the way I communicate." But is your way effective? Does it build relationships? Bring in business? Develop new employees? Inspire commitment?

Does it have heart?

My guess is that if you are reading this chapter, you have acknowledged a need to improve the way you communicate. Maybe you have been told you need to change your tone, or you want to help others make changes. You have already moved from "This is the way I communicate" to "How can I communicate better to build business relationships?"

Luckily, for those who want to be better at building relationships through writing, the process of adding heart to your writing is not difficult, as this chapter reveals. The process involves using positive, relationship-building language; having positive intent; and warming up messages so they don't sound abrupt or bureaucratic.

Use Positive, Relationship-Building Language

A first step is to use words that make others feel acknowledged, understood, respected, and valued. Once you start thinking about positive language, it is easy to recognize it. In each of these pairs, which sentence builds relationships?

> You can't use the conference room until my meeting ends.
>
> As soon as we wrap up the meeting, the room is yours.

Adding Heart =
Adding relationship-building language, having positive intent, and warming up the message.

What could make this decision more workable for you?

I don't care if you like it. Make it work.

You are a day late for the special promotional pricing. Sorry.

I will review our pricing to make sure you are getting the best price possible.

The relationship-damaging sentences are obvious when you pay attention to them. "You can't use the conference room" focuses on what you *can't* do—until *my* meeting ends. (It's all about me, right?) "I don't care if you like it" says "I don't care about you." "You are a day late" says "Loser!"

Each of the other sentences in the pairs supports the business relationship by communicating positively and indicating that the reader is important. The sentences say or imply "The room is yours," "This decision can be more workable for you," and "You are getting the best price possible."

The table of Relationship-Busting Statements vs. Relationship-Building Statements provides more comparisons. The relationship-busting statements use negative words and phrases: *no, cut, crap, complaining, wait, cannot, problems, confusion, misunderstood,* and *a lot to be desired.*

The relationship-building sentences focus on the positive with these words: *yes, wish, possible, let's, thank you, sharing, be glad to, first thing, your concerns, just, like to, opportunity, let you know, clarify, creative, fresh, ways to strengthen,* and *support.*

An easy first step to creating a relationship-building message is to eliminate words with negative connotations. Whenever possible, cut negative words and phrases such as these:

absence	hesitate	no idea
complaint	impossible	no way
confusion	late	problem
deny	limited	refuse
difficult	loss	stupid
fail to	misunderstand	unreasonable

Relationship-Busting Statements	vs.	Relationship-Building Statements
Negative. Request denied. The answer is no.		I would like to say yes—let me explain why I can't. I wish that were possible. Here's what I *can* say yes to.
Cut the crap.		Let's focus on the facts.
You don't have to like it. Just do it.		Let me explain why this task is required.
We received your letter complaining about our service.		Thank you for sharing your comments on our service.
You will have to wait. I cannot meet to discuss your problems until Monday morning.		I will be glad to meet with you first thing Monday morning to discuss your concerns.
You cannot open an account with such a small deposit.		It takes just $100 to open your account.
Some of you have expressed confusion over our policy on telecommuting.		I would like to take the opportunity to let you know about our policy on telecommuting.
You misunderstood what I said in my email.		Let me clarify what I meant in my email.
Your ideas are interesting, but your methodology leaves a lot to be desired.		Your ideas are interesting—very creative and fresh. Let's talk about ways to strengthen your methodology to support your ideas.

Use positive words to create a positive feeling, even when conveying bad news. This approach is akin to the "sandwich method," which involves communicating the bad-news meat of the message between two positive layers. When used sincerely (not sarcastically), positive language expresses your positive intent like a handshake and a smile.

Maintain strong business relationships by adding these positive words to your messages:

admire	glad	pleased to
an honor	grateful	pleasure
appreciate	gratified	profit
assist you	happy	satisfied
benefit	happy to	saving
brilliant	help you	terrific
delighted	inspire	thank you
enjoy	joy	thoughtful
feel free	like to	understanding
gain	looking forward	value
generous	please	welcome

Have a Positive Intent

Positive words make a big difference in the tone of a message. But they aren't everything. As a writer, you also have to have positive intent, the desire to communicate positively with your customer, vendor, employee, manager, member, client, patient, or other reader.

I received this brief message from someone I will call Amelia, who unsubscribed from my free e-newsletter: "I teach a professional writing class at work, and I thought this newsletter would give me additional tips or writing skills we were not already teaching. It didn't." Do you think Amelia had positive intent? Was her desire to communicate positively with me, a stranger and fellow writing teacher?

Consider these situations: Imagine you were out shopping in a boutique. If you did not find anything you wanted to purchase, would you say to the shop owner as you left, "I thought I could find something unique to buy here, but I could not"? If you decided not to eat at a restaurant after reviewing the menu in the entrance, would you say, "Sorry. Nothing sounds good on your menu" before you walked away? Of course not!

We can't know what Amelia's intent was. She may not have realized that her comment would come to me, the writer of the newsletter. Nevertheless, I experienced the comment as a putdown. In the small world of business writing teachers, my potential relationship with Amelia ended before it could develop.

Compare Amelia's comment to one from a reader named Beverly, who also unsubscribed from the newsletter: "I'm just trying to reduce the amount of email I get. I can read Lynn's excellent material on her blog. Thanks."

Beverly's positive intent came through in the words *excellent* and *thanks*.

Think about your intent, your purpose in writing, before you write. Be sure to consider your overall, big-picture purpose. For example, imagine you received a request for information from a customer within your organization or outside it. Your purpose in replying would be to supply the information requested. But your larger purpose would probably be to maintain or enhance the relationship and pave the way for future business.

The way you think of your purpose affects the way you write your message. A message whose purpose is merely to respond to a request has a different approach and feeling from one that is to maintain or enhance the relationship.

Let's say you are responding to an unreasonable complaint. Although your purpose in writing may be simply to manage the situation, your larger goal is probably to maintain a good long-term business relationship or at least to protect your company's reputation and your own.

At all times, strive to focus on the big picture, the higher goal, and the long term when you write. While it might feel good to put down or get the best of another person in writing, resist that temptation. You cannot know when having a good relationship with that person would benefit a current project, your company, or your career.

Let me tell you about a time that I considered my purpose—and then wrote a different message.

I was teaching Business Communications for Leaders in the MBA program at University of Washington–Bothell. The first assignment, a one-minute self-introduction, was due on Thursday night. On Thursday morning I started my day with this message in my email inbox, from Steve Teixeira, a student in the class and a talented communicator:

> Hi Lynn,
>
> If it's okay with you, I'm planning to deviate slightly from the "one-minute introduction" assignment tomorrow. I plan to briefly introduce myself and then deliver a mini-speech on communication. I'm trying to challenge myself to engage and motivate but to also be extremely brief. I've rehearsed it down to under a minute as long as I don't flub it.
>
> Steve

I was checking my email while drinking my first cup of tea. Because I was not completely awake yet, I drafted a response that sounded something like this:

> Hi, Steve. The assignment is a one-minute self-introduction so that the class and I can get to know you. Please do not deviate from that assignment. You can use the topic of communication for one of the later assignments.
>
> Lynn

Before I clicked Send, I had the good sense to think about my intent. Was I hoping to prove a point? No, I didn't think so. Did I want to be sure the class assignments were done *my* way, the way I had planned? I wasn't sure. Did I want to frustrate one of the class's informal leaders by denying his first request? No, that would be disastrous during the first week of classes. Did I want to stifle creativity? No, definitely not.

Here is the email I sent to Steve after I realized my purpose was to get off to a good start with the class and to encourage creativity and initiative:

> Steve, thanks for asking about your plan. In response, I believe I have an idea that meets your needs and the expectations of the class.
>
> Do the required 1-minute introduction. Then when everyone is finished, do the introduction you already prepared that challenges you to engage and motivate. Doing both will satisfy the requirements of the class and your desire to stretch.
>
> Giving only your hybrid introduction wouldn't meet the expectations or needs of your audience. The reason is that we want to learn more about you. And we are expecting and prepared to give you feedback, with specific criteria, on a one-minute personal introduction.
>
> So I invite you to do both tonight. However, if you want to give a motivating speech on communication, that would be a perfect topic for next week's presentation to inform or explain.
>
> I look forward to being in your audience.
>
> Lynn

Steve gave both presentations in class. When I asked him later how he had felt about my response to his email, he said that it was fine and made perfect sense to him.

Although the first message I drafted was not a disaster, it wasn't a relationship builder. It contained no positive, supportive language, and it did not communicate a positive intent. In contrast, the message I did send communicated appreciation, a solution, an invitation, and anticipation with words such as *thanks, meets your needs, engage and motivate, satisfy, invite, perfect,* and *look forward.*

I am so happy I woke up enough to recognize my real purpose in writing! I hope you too will recognize your larger purpose in each message and communicate positively with your readers. If your experience is like mine, your efforts will lead to near-term positive outcomes and long-term solid relationships.

Warm Up Your Messages

People who attend business writing classes often tell me they have been accused of being abrupt in their messages, specifically in their emails. They say their style is to get to the point, but other people view them as abrupt.

If you have a job or your own business, you work against deadlines. You have to write quickly, even when the documents and messages are complex and somewhat delicate. It would not be surprising if you, like the people who attend my writing classes, were to come across as abrupt at times when you thought you were simply being efficient. This situation is especially common in email.

Coming across as brusque is a liability when it comes to building relationships. Perceived gruffness can stretch out the time it takes people to realize that you are a fine person, just abrupt. When a sensitive message comes across as brusque, it can take hours, days, or weeks to resolve misunderstandings, heal hurt feelings, and rebuild relationships.

Apply these simple ways to warm up your writing and reduce the risk of seeming abrupt:

In an email, text message, or note, include a greeting. According to my survey on business writing and relationships, 45 percent of people prefer that the emails they receive (individual messages, not group emails) include a greeting and their name; 49 percent don't care. Many respondents commented that an initial email should include a greeting, but when email becomes a back-and-forth discussion, the greeting can be dropped. I agree with that view.

Which of these greetings suit you and your messages?
Hello, Tonya.
Hi David.
Good morning, Dr. Bryne.
Greetings, Fran!
Greetings, team.
Dear Brigitte,

Use the person's name in your message. It may seem sufficient to write "See you next week." But when you include the person's name in the sentence ("See you next week, Sidney"), you acknowledge him or her as an individual. It's a simple gesture that can change the feeling from curt to considerate.

Use your own first name. In email, people often use automatic signatures with their full name. Others use no name at all—they just end the message. Whether you use a full signature or not, type your first name at the end of your message. Using your first name warms up the message, creating a connection between you and the reader. Note: Another way to include your first name is through a screenshot of your handwritten first name, which you can add to your automatic signature block.

Expand on fragments and very short sentences to avoid sounding cold or sarcastic. Even "Thanks" or "Thanks a lot" can sound sarcastic, especially in delicate messages. Instead, write "Thanks for handling this. I really appreciate it." Rather than "See me" or "We need to talk," write "Let's talk soon. I'd like to hear your thoughts on this question."

Include words and phrases that communicate warmth and connection. Any message without positive language can seem cold and abrupt. Use the words and phrases listed earlier in this chapter for a warmer tone.

Avoid cold, canned language. Some phrases, such as "I look forward to meeting you," may be canned, but they aren't cold. Others are canned *and* cold, for example, "Thank you in advance for your cooperation in this matter." To warm up your messages, write as though the reader is a friend or valued colleague, with statements like these: "I appreciate your help, Jonas" and "Thanks so much for considering this request."

Be explicit when you are agreeing with the person. In a quick exchange of messages, you may be tempted to write a simple sentence repeating what the other person has already written. But this action may lead your reader to think *That's exactly what I said!* To avoid such a response, write, for example, "I agree that Auda is great for the job" (rather than just "Auda is great for the job"). That way, you avert this response: "Did you read what I wrote? I was the one who recommended her!"

Read your message aloud—exactly as it is on the screen or page—without adding warmth in your voice. Reading aloud helps you recognize how your writing may sound to others. You may have crisply stated a fact when you wrote "Handling the Gordon account is your responsibility." Reading it aloud, though, you may notice a hint of criticism or doom that you did not intend. Adding a phrase such as "I'm very glad," if appropriate, at the beginning of the sentence may eliminate that hint.

Avoid the words *immediately* and *now* when you are writing with a request or assigning a task. Your reader may have several other immediate jobs, and your request may seem pushy and unthinking, even if you are the boss or owner. If a task must be done immediately, phone, text, or email to ask whether the other person is available. Assume that the other person is as busy as you—even busier.

Think of your reader as a friend. Often gruffness is accidental. But sometimes it comes across because of the writer's underlying feeling of resentment or irritation. So make the reader your friend, at least while you are writing.

In business writing classes, participants sometimes write their case study assignments to imaginary readers. They creatively write "Dear Pain in the Neck" and "Dear Constant Complainer." I advise them to try the opposite: "Dear Favorite Coworker" and "Dear Person Who Pays My Generous Salary." Making that positive shift, changing your reader to your dear friend or respected associate, helps you glow rather than glower. It helps you choose language that comes across as warm rather than chilly.

Use exclamation points—sparingly. Exclamation points can do a wonderful job of expressing warmth and enthusiasm. They communicate the voice inflections you would likely use if you were talking on the phone or meeting in person. Compare these examples:

> I appreciate your hard work.
> I appreciate your hard work!

> Wonderful.
> Wonderful!

> See you in Vegas.
> See you in Vegas!

> Thanks, Yvette.
> Thanks, Yvette!

> Welcome, Sales Team.
> Welcome, Sales Team!

The secret to using exclamation points is restraint. If you pile on several exclamation points in a row (!!!), or use them in every other sentence, you run the risk of coming across like an adolescent girl, or as *Chicago Tribune* writer Rex Huppke remarked, "an overcaffeinated glee club."

Exclamation points help to build relationships when they express positive emotions, not rude commands. If you catch yourself typing "I need it now!" you might want to breathe slowly and deeply and think again about communicating with positive intent.

Start and end with a smile. Before you click Send or Print, make sure your message starts and ends positively.

Do Smiley Faces Communicate Heart?

Speaking of smiles, you may have noticed that smiley faces (such as ☺) did not appear in my list of ways to warm up a message. I encourage choosing the right words to bring a smile to a communication.

Nevertheless, I recognize that smiley faces do warm up emails and other online messages. That's their whole reason for being. The question is: Do readers use and approve of them? Below is part of a discussion that took place on my Business Writing blog.

Margaret Elwood, a technical training supervisor, uses smiley faces purposefully, as she explained:

> I use smiley faces occasionally in internal email messages to clarify and add warmth to the tone. In our company we have typically great longevity of employment, and the strength of my relationships with other employees simply helps me get my job done efficiently and well. While I don't rely on emoticons, I use them now and then when writing a coworker, because I think they confirm my friendly tone in case there is any question of it. I also use them—sparingly—in response to a message that has used them liberally, so that my response does not appear unfriendly by contrast.

A reader named Tony voiced a similar view: "In a business environment, when discussing a difficult issue via email, the emoticon conveys that while you may be looking for resolution to the issue, you are not seriously upset about it." Tony used the example of reminding an employee who has forgotten to do something: "You send them the reminder to get resolution. You include the smiley face. Without the smiley face or some additional wording that may be awkward, they might think that you are upset about their forgetfulness."

John, another reader, disagreed: "I believe that the smiley face can mean too many things. A smiley could mean the writer wants resolution on a point but is not upset, a phrase was meant to be humorous, an expression of warmth and candor, a clue that something is meant to be a sarcastic or ironic remark, a magnification of an emotion expressed in the sentence, or a mark to indicate that a phrase is something for one to ponder or think about. To me, this is becoming too much for one poor smiley face to do."

I agree with John that the smiley face has been stretched thin with the many expectations placed upon it. Except in rare, informal situations, I prefer words to the smiley face and other emoticons. These words express a range of sentiments:

I am glad.	I'm joking.
I am happy.	I'm being silly.
I'm excited.	How frustrating!
I'm so pleased.	What a pain!
I am proud.	I hated it.
Terrific news!	I was disappointed.
That's a brilliant idea!	I was devastated.
I agree completely.	I am sad about it.
You are wonderful.	I'm stressed out.
You are the best.	I'm satisfied.
Thanks so much!	I'm anxious.
I'm kidding.	I am not at all upset.

I am being sarcastic.	I'm bored.
I am serious.	I like it.
I mean it.	I love it.
I'm exhausted.	I love it!
I'm overwhelmed.	

Were all of those clear? Yes. Would the smiley face, frowning face, or another emoticon have been as clear? Probably not.

Regarding the decision to introduce a smiley face or another emoticon in an email, I offer the suggestion of a woman who attended one of my business writing classes: "Don't use a smiley face in a message to a client or customer until the person uses one in a message to you. That way you will know the person likes smiley faces too." I recommend applying that good advice to anyone you need to impress as a professional—hiring managers, CEOs, donors, citizens, patrons, and others.

If you do use smiley faces, use them frugally, never more than one per message. And do not use a smiley face as a regular sign-off. Heather, who posted to the Business Writing blog, provided a reason for this guideline: "I have a team leader who uses :o) all of the time, in every single email I have received from her. It loses its meaning if you overuse it and can often come off as condescending when used during an email discussion or disagreement."

Does *XOXO* Communicate Warmth?

XOXO radiates huggy-kissy warmth, which makes its use too intimate for nearly all business messages. Because the *x* stands for kisses, the *o* for hugs, you should use them only rarely and only with people you kiss and hug when you see them in person—or you would kiss and hug if you had the opportunity to see them. (Talk to your human resources department before taking such a step!) As I was finishing this book, *x*'s and *o*'s in various combinations were juicily appearing, mostly in women's messages. Citing researchers at Georgia Tech, Carnegie Mellon, and Stanford, authors Jessica Bennett and Rachel Simmons wrote in *The Atlantic,* "Among Twitter users, 11 percent of women xo in tweets, compared with only 2.5 percent of men."

For their article "Kisses and Hugs in the Office," Bennett and Simmons asked me to speculate why people added *x*'s and *o*'s to their business messages. They captured me saying, "It's much faster to type the four-stroke xxoo than 'With warm wishes' followed by a comma." True, but don't do it for that reason! Only use *x*'s and *o*'s in your messages to business associates who are very dear friends or becoming dear friends. If your messages are likely to be forwarded, uploaded, or subpoenaed, stick with "Warm wishes." Do not make *xoxo* part of your automatic signature, or everyone will be talking about you—not in the way you want.

Is It Possible to Change Your Writing Style?

This chapter began with a reference to military veterans whose style is brusque, probably through their training and experience, perhaps through natural inclination. Is it possible for them to change their writing to create and nurture business relationships? Is it possible for you, whatever your communication style, to build success by communicating your respect and positive intent in every business message?

The answer to both questions is yes! Just remember these points from the chapter, and incorporate them into your daily business messages:

- Use positive, relationship-building language—words and phrases such as *pleased, opportunity, happy to, thank you,* and *looking forward.*
- Have a positive intent in each message. Think not only of the message's practical purpose, such as to respond to a request. Think also of your overall purpose, for example, to establish and sustain a relationship with the reader.
- Warm up your messages simply, by using a greeting, your reader's name, and your own first name. Avoid canned language that comes across as cold. Think of your reader as a friend.

You *can* change your writing style and enhance your work relationships—one message at a time.

Personal Reflection

- ▸ Do you have business relationships you might strengthen by considering your true, larger purpose when you write?

- ▸ Can you afford taking time to add positive language to your messages before you click Print or Send? Can you afford *not* to?

Next Step

- ▸ Choose a message you sent recently. It may be a letter, an email, or a memo. Look for opportunities in it where you might have added positive language and warmed up the message.

CHAPTER 2

Protect Your Relationships by Avoiding Bad Email Behaviors

W hen I first planned this book, I did not intend to include a chapter on email. It seemed to me to be a medium rather than a message. But when I shared the outline with my friend Melissa Thirloway, she questioned the absence of a chapter devoted to email. She said, "Think of all the serious damage done to relationships in email, especially with ccs and bccs."

Melissa was onto something. In my survey on business writing and relationships, I learned that 55 percent of respondents had received an email that seriously damaged their work relationship with the person who wrote it; 14 percent said it had happened a few times. Melissa's comment and the survey data made me recognize I had to single out email—with its extraordinary, swift power to create animosity, foster mistrust, and kill relationships—for its own chapter.

This chapter will help you protect your relationships by controlling the destructive power of email and avoiding email behaviors that threaten relationships. Let's start with a true story whose details have been changed.

Rochelle, who worked in a technical support position at a large software company, had gathered a lot of valuable data in her work on a project. She learned that the data might be useful to another project, so she offered it to Dennis, the project supervisor. Her email to him included a statement something like this: "Let me know what type of format you would like the data in." When she did not get a response, she decided to be helpful. She created a sample format for the data, filled it with some "garbage data," and emailed Dennis again with a message like this: "Here is a format for the data. Will this work?" She went home for the night, pleased with having taken initiative in offering the data and creating a sample format.

Dennis's reply the next morning stunned Rochelle. In it, he berated her for proliferating incorrect data and implied that she was incompetent. He copied his manager on the email, along with everyone on his project team.

Dennis had mistaken Rochelle's garbage data for the real thing.

Mistakes happen. What killed Dennis's relationship with Rochelle was his behavior after his mistake. Instead of taking the time to ask Rochelle about the data by email, by phone, or in person, he hid behind a swift, careless email attack. He sent copies to other people, making them witnesses to the attack.

Eventually everyone understood what had happened, and Dennis emailed a stumbling apology to Rochelle, noting that he had acted too hastily. Nevertheless, his relationship with her was ruined. And people on his project team may have become wary of Dennis because of his rash judgment and rude action.

Here is another true story illustrating the destructive force of email. I have changed its identifying details.

Henry sang in a volunteer choir. He had joined the choir for many reasons, among them that it would give him and his partner, Jon, an opportunity to sing solos and get exposure for their singing and leadership skills. But when the choir director, Rory, went outside the choir and hired someone to sing a solo, Henry was disappointed for two reasons: (1) he had thought the choir policy was not to bring in and pay soloists, and (2) he had thought Jon would be perfect for the part that had been offered to the paid outsider.

Henry sent an email to Rory requesting clarification of the choir policy and asking what he and Jon could do to be considered for future solos. He received an email reply and a clarification, with advice for him and Jon. However, Rory copied the entire choir on the reply and included Henry's original email.

Henry and Jon took a leave of absence from the choir. Why?

By copying all the choir members on his reply, the choir director embarrassed the couple. What should have been a private reply to a private inquiry became a public humiliation. When broadcast to all the other choir members, Henry's email looked like a whining complaint rather than a straightforward request for information. Rory's advice for the pair exposed their limitations to everyone. As a result, the choir lost two excellent singers.

What did Rory do that severely damaged relationships? He copied the choir on an email that should have been a private message. Rory's simple decision to send a group email rather than an individual one destroyed trust—not only for Henry and Jon. Every choir member who read the email could imagine himself or herself being publicly exposed in a similar email.

Let's give Rory the benefit of the doubt. He probably thought it would be beneficial for all choir members to read his clarification of the policy on solo parts. If that was his goal, he should have sent a private message to Henry, then followed up with an email to the choir. That group email might have started like this:

> I would like to review the policy on auditioning for and getting solo parts. Because I have hired a soloist for the Bach cantata, I thought it would be helpful to clarify the policy and answer any questions you may have.

An effective message would leave out lines such as "Some of you might be upset" or "It has come to my attention that some of you are disappointed . . ." Rather than suggesting a negative, his message should simply clarify.

In the story below, which may be familiar to you, the email writer did not copy others on his emails. Nevertheless, countless people read his messages and mocked them.

A college journalism student phoned and emailed Apple's media relations department with a question about the use of an Apple product in higher education. She received no reply. Because she needed the information for a journalism assignment, she emailed Apple's then CEO, the late Steve Jobs. According to news reports, Mr. Jobs's three emails to the student in an email exchange with her comprised the statements below.

Our goals do not include helping you get a good grade. Sorry.

We have over 300 million users, and we can't respond to their requests unless they involve a problem of some kind. Sorry.

Please leave us alone.

How do I know what Mr. Jobs's emails said? Because they were all over the business news, with the third email drawing ridicule.

When I blogged about Mr. Jobs's unfortunate relationship-busting emails, a training coordinator named Claudia Amaya commented: "This is certainly a wake-up call to all dealing with customers. A thoughtless line in a single email can ruin the image a company has built. . . . This annoying student could be the CEO of their best customer later on. Who knows?"

I agree with Claudia. One email—never mind three!—can ruin a customer relationship. And who knows how important that customer is or may become?

Environmental engineer Matt Charles, another blog commenter, took up the issue of the student's email: "I found that the student's email was lengthy and focused on the benefits that Apple's reply would provide to her (a good grade), rather than identifying any compelling reason for Apple to provide the requested quote."

I have read the student's emails, and I agree with Matt. The student's emails may have lessened her chances of getting the response she wanted. But as in the late Mr. Jobs's situation, we are not accountable for the effectiveness of the email we receive. We are accountable for the email we send.

My guess is that none of the men wanted to destroy business relationships. No sane person would. Yet Dennis's, Rory's, and Steve Jobs's mistakes show how easy it is to trash relationships with email: Just compose, click Send without thinking, and relationships disintegrate.

Risky Email Behaviors

You can rein in the destructive power of email by avoiding these specific dangerous behaviors:

Do not put anything in an email that you would be embarrassed to see on the TV program *Good Morning, America* (where I learned about Steve Jobs's email), in your city's newspaper, or on everyone's computer. Always recognize that your emails may be forwarded and might even be subpoenaed. Any negative comments or innuendos about others revealed in your emails can kill relationships instantly. A writing class attendee recounted an email thread in which she found a reference to herself as the "accounting Nazi." The reference damaged her relationship with the writer *and* the person who forwarded the message.

Email evidence of improper behavior can kill or maim careers and marriages. Just think of Harry C. Stonecipher, former CEO of Boeing, and General David Petraeus, former director of the Central Intelligence Agency, who are both "former" in the wake of indiscreet emails.

Do not send a confidential email to a printer unless you are within 5 feet of the printer and can grab the page as the machine rolls it out. Otherwise, that confidential message can become distressingly common knowledge.

Never cc others or use Reply All on an email in which you criticize someone. Dennis's and Rory's messages illustrate the dangers of this approach. Even though Rory, the choir director, was giving constructive feedback—not harsh criticism—to Henry and his partner, his feedback embarrassed the pair, as did the public airing of Henry's original request.

Avoid copying someone's boss on a negative message. Do not cc someone's manager to get action. A woman in an email class told a story of an external consultant who harangued her for not responding to his earlier messages—and copied her boss on the message. He had to apologize shamefacedly to both of them when it was discovered that he had mistyped her email address on all the earlier messages, so the woman had never received them.

Even if the woman had not responded to messages she *had* received, the consultant did not have any information about why she was not responding. A phone call to her would have been the right choice to clarify the situation.

Don't scold (or flame) anyone for any reason in email. Because email is not two-way communication, you can't get instant information from the other person or gauge his or her reaction. A training manager told me about the time she scolded an employee in email for not showing up at a training session. Only later did she learn the employee had had a motorcycle accident on his way to the training. Although she had not copied anyone on the email, she had presented herself to the employee as someone who is quick to judge without checking facts. That behavior does not build relationships.

Do not communicate when you don't have the time or inclination to do it well, especially with a customer or potential customer. Think again of Steve Jobs's situation. Not answering the journalism student's emails would have been wiser than complaining "Please leave us alone."

Many people look back in embarrassment on their hastily written and sent messages. I once received an email reply from a potential client, a reply that was obviously not intended for me. The email said, "I thought you might want to take a look at this before I just summarily blow her off." (I was the *her* in the sentence.) The writer soon emailed me a brief apology explaining that he had meant to forward the email to his colleague to ask her if she had any interest in meeting with me. To the detriment of our potential business relationship, he had unfortunately clicked Reply instead of Forward and made himself look foolish. The lesson: Never shoot back a thoughtless reply.

Don't be stingy with your replies, especially if you are a manager. When an employee spends an hour or more doing research and writing it up for you in an email, don't respond cryptically in five words or less, if you value the employee and your relationship. Here is an example of what a manager should *not* do, shared in a writing class:

An employee researched venues for an important offsite retreat. She narrowed the possibilities to two venues. She sent her manager an email, briefly describing the benefits of both venues and asking whether the manager had any preference: Would the manager prefer the South Street Retreat Center or McMillan House? The manager replied simply, "Sounds good to me." Ouch! The 4-word email diminished the employee's work and made the manager look silly.

Taking just another moment to notice what type of response the employee needed would have made all the difference. Here is a reasonable 12-word reply: "I have no preference. Both sound fine. Thanks for your thorough research." Even a 7-word "Both sound fine. Thanks for your research!" would provide the polite response the employee needed and maintain the work relationship.

If you are thinking that the original email may be to blame—perhaps it was too wordy or disorganized—you may be right. But remember: We are normally not responsible for others' emails, only our own. If you are a manager who receives long, unorganized emails from your employees, coach them or send them to a writing class.

Don't be thoughtless or downright rude. A writing class attendee told me about her supervisor: "My boss never says 'please,' 'thank you,' 'hello,' or anything nice in email. He just tells me to do things. For instance, he'll send an email that says 'Don't forget to include these figures in the proposal' or 'Be sure this goes out in today's mail.'" When I asked her whether she thought it was simply a style difference between her and her supervisor, she said, "Maybe, but it's very rude."

This employee is not alone. A full 70 percent of individuals prefer that a written request include the word *please* or similar polite language; an additional 10 percent feel disappointed, irritated, or angry if such language is missing, according to my survey on business writing and relationships.

Coming across as a rude boss does nothing for your work relationships or your reputation. To guard against that perception, you can take a few seconds to spread a little kindness. I timed myself typing the words below on my laptop. Notice how little time it takes to communicate kindness and consideration. Even if you are typing on your smartphone, *please* and *thanks* should not take more than a few seconds each, especially if your phone offers typing-completion suggestions.

Please. (2 seconds)	Hello. (2 seconds)
Would you please (3 seconds)	Good morning. (3 seconds)
Thanks. (2 seconds)	I hope you had a great
Thank you! (3 seconds)	weekend. (6 seconds)
Thanks very much. (4 seconds)	Enjoy your lunch.
I appreciate it. (4 seconds)	(5 seconds)

Even if you type slowly, I believe it is worth it to invest the time to raise an employee's morale and build a good work relationship. Don't you?

Avoid accidentally sending a message before you have reviewed it for tone and accuracy. It is too easy to have a thumb or finger slip, accidentally sending a message in an unedited, raw form whose tone can wound recipients. To avoid this mistake, in Outlook type a bit of gobbledygook (for example, *adadf*) on the To, Cc, or Bcc line. It will stop the message from going out. With other email programs, leave the To line blank until you are satisfied that the message is ready.

Avoid demanding (or seeming to demand) that others jump to action. Emails with the red exclamation point indicating high importance, or with the words *urgent, immediately,* and *now,* can irritate people and weaken relationships, especially with repeat occurrences. Rather than jeopardize your bonds with colleagues, call them when a deadline is urgent and explain the reason for the urgency.

In a discussion of email at an investment firm, a new employee complained that people did not respond promptly to his emails. I asked him what *promptly* meant to him. When he said, "Within a few minutes," the other people in the class roared with laughter. The new employee had few meetings to attend and did not yet have many assignments. To him, a few minutes was a reasonable time frame. For others in the class, *promptly* meant within 24 hours.

To preserve your good relationships, place as much value on others' time as you do on your own. Ask, "Do you think you can track down this information today?" rather than stating, "I need this by the end of the day." Ask, "Does a Friday deadline give you enough time to finish this?" rather than stating, "I want to get this to the client by Friday."

Avoid using the bcc (blind courtesy copy) function to communicate secretly. Think twice, then think again about sending a blind copy to someone who should not receive the information. An attendee in a writing class, a man I will call Joel, reported that a friend used to copy him regularly on information he should not be reading. Then one day the friend forgot it was a blind copy and wrote, "Mary, please handle this action item. Kaj, please take care of this. Joel, this is FYI, as usual." Seeing Joel's name, everyone found out he was receiving the information. According to Joel, both he and his friend learned an alarming, embarrassing lesson.

Another class participant I will call Mark told a story of a colleague who contacted him to express her sympathy about a difficulty Mark was having. The only problem was that the colleague should not have known about Mark's situation. How did she know? She had received a blind copy of an email Mark's manager had sent to him. Mark felt his manager had betrayed him.

Follow this guideline: If you feel even a hint of guilt or doubt about sending a bcc, do not send it. Anytime a little voice tells you that you may regret sending blind copies, don't do it! And never use blind copies to damage another person's reputation.

Here is the relationship-building approach when you need to include others: When you need other people to know about a situation but you know that the primary recipient would be distressed about those people receiving a cc or bcc, instead email a *summary* of the information to others. If the primary recipient asks, "Did you copy anyone on this message?" you can honestly say no. And you can add something like this: "However, I did need to summarize what happened for Patrick and Rayleen, so they would be aware of the situation."

Of course, you can always bcc yourself. Unless your smartphone saves sent email, you will want to send yourself a bcc of any important messages you send by phone.

Avoid displaying various individuals' email addresses because of *not* using the bcc function. Cyndy McCollough, director of marketing technology at a law firm, explained when and why the bcc makes sense:

> When sending an email to multiple recipients from different companies, put addresses in the Bcc field. Your audience

will appreciate the fact that you are cognizant of protecting their privacy.

I recently received an email from a conference organizer that was sent to the 12 speakers lined up for the next day's agenda. I blanched when I saw all recipient email addresses in the To field. In listing our addresses in this manner, the sender put our information at risk of being scooped up by anyone desiring to grow their contact database.

Although Cyndy came across calmly, some people explode when they see their email address, along with many others, displayed for everyone to see and for opportunistic people to add to their email contacts.

Avoid using the Read Receipt function. The Read Receipt function on email programs asks recipients of your email to click a link to indicate they have received your message. It irritates many people. They dislike it because it reveals when they have read the message, which they feel is not the sender's business. It makes them feel as though Big Brother (of George Orwell's novel *1984*) is watching them.

If you truly must know that employees have opened an email, use the Read Receipt, but know that it can hurt relationships. A better choice may be to include at the top of the email "Please reply with the message 'Got it' to let me know you have received this important message."

Avoid sarcasm—and avoid or be very cautious with jokes. We have all had the experience of someone misinterpreting our email. Perhaps we were sarcastic, and our reader viewed the message as serious. Maybe we thought we were being funny, and the other person read us as angry. I often need to ask my own husband, who is my business partner, what he meant by a particular quip in an email that he thought I would understand. This type of miscommunication happens often in email—perhaps more often than we realize. Frequently we wonder how other people can possibly have gotten our message so wrong. Were they reading too fast? Not paying attention? Having a bad day?

Researchers Justin Kruger, Nicholas Epley, Jason Parker, and Zhi-Wen Ng looked at the role of our egos in miscommunication. They published their study findings in the *Journal of Personality and Social Psychology* in an article titled "Egocentrism Over E-Mail: Can We Communicate as Well as We Think?" Here are some of the findings:

- Email writers consistently overestimate their readers' ability to distinguish sarcasm from seriousness. In one test, writers estimated that their readers would recognize sarcasm 78 percent of the time. In fact, their readers were correct only 56 percent of the time—no better than chance.
- Email readers consistently overestimate their own ability to recognize sarcasm. In the test just mentioned, although they were correct only 56 percent of the time, they estimated their accuracy at 90 percent!
- When it comes to identifying emotion in email, there is no difference, statistically speaking, between the accuracy of strangers and friends.
- Writers overestimate the degree to which their readers will find their humor funny—especially when the writers have had a rich experience with the humor (seeing it performed on TV, for example).
- Emoticons do not improve understanding.

For the trait that causes both readers and writers to overestimate their ability to handle the subtleties of email, the researchers use the term *overconfidence.*

Here are the lessons to take from the research: Do not be over-confident. Even if you are an extremely upbeat, confident person, assume that the worst may go wrong with your message. Know that your reader will assume he or she is correct—just as you do. Avoid sarcasm. Label your emotions. Pick up your phone or meet in person when the situation is awkward. Do not reply with that zinger you think is so clever and amusing. Know that when you email a joke, your reader may not find it as funny as you did.

Avoid "letting them sweat." Cynthia Clay, who runs a training company, told me about a negotiating technique I was not aware of. Perhaps you have experienced it.

Cynthia had prepared a proposal at the request of a prospective client. Shortly after Cynthia emailed the proposal to the client, all communication from the client stopped. Emails from Cynthia's staff received no reply. Phone calls were not returned. Cynthia was worried that something had gone wrong—until another client told her she was simply on the receiving end of a negotiating technique being touted these days.

The technique is to let the other person sweat. For instance, let her sweat when her email gets no reply. If she worries enough about what might have gone wrong with the proposal, that worry will make her less confident and more eager to negotiate.

Letting them sweat is a perfect way to weaken relationships. When prospective clients do not reply to my emails or phone calls, my concern is not what I might have done better in the proposal but whether I really want to work with someone who is noncommunicative and perhaps stressed out and disorganized. Rather than making me feel more eager to negotiate, I cool off, wondering where I might tighten my proposal to make working with a potentially difficult client more rewarding.

Cynthia waited it out without sweating. Eventually the prospective client contacted her. Then everything became a rush to meet the client's goals, which had been put on hold during the sweating time. The win-lose mentality of letting them sweat is a sure relationship weakener. Wouldn't you rather work with efficient, communicative people than with manipulators?

Avoid terms of endearment. A woman in one of my business writing classes said she hated terms of endearment. She explained: "It's words like *dear, hon,* and *sweetie.* I don't like them in email and other business communication. I would like to respond to people who use them, 'I'm not your dear. I'm not your hon.'" I asked the woman to speculate why individuals used words like *dear* and *hon* (short for *honey*) at work. We decided that people, especially older workers, may simply want to be friendly.

But using a person's name is much friendlier than using a generic term. I remember visiting my then-96-year-old cousin in a New Jersey hospital. When I arrived, she had been in the hospital an entire week, yet every worker except her doctor called her *hon* and *dearie* instead of her name, Mrs. Wallace. The terms sounded impersonal and condescending rather than friendly and nurturing.

Save *hon, sweetie,* and *dear* for your spouse or sweetheart, children, grandchildren, nieces, and nephews. Use it with people who would not even think of responding, "I'm not your hon." If you want to come across as friendly in your email, say *hi, hello, good morning, please,* and *thank you.* Use people's names and sometimes say, "Have a great day!" This recommendation applies not only to coworkers, but also to patients, customers, clients, members, visitors, citizens, and others.

Three Golden Rules

With all the bad email behaviors to avoid, you may be hungry for rules to follow to nurture your business relationships. Here are three:

Always give others the benefit of the doubt. Recognize that there is a good possibility that you are wrong or are simply misinterpreting a message. (Think of Dennis's incorrect assumption about Rochelle's data.) Then, before you can damage yourself or others in an email, ask tactful questions to understand a situation.

Copy people on a message only when doing so will lead to something positive for everyone involved: understanding, teamwork, inclusion, enjoyment, shared credit, etc. When a cc'd email will have a negative outcome for someone, find another way to communicate. (Learn from Rory's message that wounded two choir members.)

Present your best self in email, the one you would be pleased to see on the evening news. (Learn from Steve Jobs's brief, unfortunate messages.) Think beyond the purpose of the email you are writing. Ask yourself, "Why am I in business?" and "Why am I on the planet?" Asking such big-picture questions will help you make the right choice as a writer and a human being in every message you send. It will help you preserve your valuable work relationships.

Personal Reflection

▸ Would adjusting your email behavior help you improve certain business relationships?

Next Step

▸ Review the email behaviors to avoid and the three golden rules. Choose one or two as guidelines to make changes in your email.

PART TWO

The Opportunities—Powerful Messages That Often Get Overlooked

CHAPTER 3

Write Mighty Thank-Yous

If you were to do a cost-benefit analysis of writing thank-you notes, I am betting they would come out as the best business writing investment possible for building and sustaining relationships. These short, happy messages are typically easy to write, and they reap benefits for both sender and receiver long after the receiver smiles at the grateful words. This chapter helps you recognize opportunities to write thank-yous, and it shows you how to take them from polite to powerful.

In my survey on business writing and relationships, 81 percent of people said that a thank-you note they received had a definite positive influence on their decision to do business with a company or an individual again. These comments capture respondents' views:

> I appreciate companies that recognize the value of a personal connection and relationship.

> It adds a personal touch to the business relationship.

> I can't tell you how much of a difference this makes!

On Business Writing blog, inspirational speaker and author Josh Hinds illustrated the power of the thank-you this way: "Just the other day I received a card from someone whose project I had participated in. It was a simple thank-you card (along with a little gift card)—nothing too fancy. But the next time I find myself looking for the type of service this person offers (for myself or a referral for someone else), you better believe they're going to be at the top of the list for that business."

Thank-yous encourage people to continue to work with the sender, whether they include a small thank-you gift or not. For that reason alone, you should invest in writing thank-yous to business associates of all kinds. Thank-yous are one of the easiest tasks in business writing, and the payoff can be huge. There is no excuse for not tapping the relationship-building power of the mighty thank-you.

You have a chance to say thank you anytime someone has:

- Delivered particularly good service.
- Gone beyond the job requirements for you.
- Been especially thoughtful, prompt, or efficient.
- Given you an opportunity (an assignment, an interview, a referral, etc.).
- Given you a gift or treated you to a meal.
- Been a special pleasure to work with.
- Been helpful to you in a stressful moment.
- Bought your product or service.
- Consistently met or exceeded expectations.
- Made your day in one way or another.

Tips for Writing Powerful Thank-Yous

Very little can go wrong in a thank-you when it is sincere and specific. Just follow these tips to help you write from the heart easily and effectively:

Write promptly. Although a sincere thank-you is welcome anytime, writing promptly makes the writing easier because the details are fresh in your mind. In this sample email to a coworker, Jamie refers to specific details he might have forgotten in a few days:

> Dear Suneetha,
>
> Thank you for all your work on today's web conference. It could not have happened without you.
>
> Your attention to detail was evident throughout the program. Your transition between the segments was very smooth. Also, I appreciated the tactful way you handled my problem with the microphone. Because of your efforts, we presented a professional image to potential clients.
>
> Thanks again for your work on this event.
>
> Best,
> Jamie

Sending a thank-you note promptly shows enthusiasm and appreciation. In Keith Ferrazzi's book *Never Eat Alone,* he mentions people who write to thank him the same day, telling him how much they appreciated meeting him at a conference or after a speech. Ferrazzi says he remembers most the people who write first, before many others write. That's one big vote for being speedy when writing to a prestigious person—the message gets noticed.

Say thank you sincerely and specifically. In the previous example, Jamie named specific things he is grateful for. That kind of thank-you has much more power than an empty "Good job. Thanks." When he noted that Suneetha's efforts helped to convey a professional image to potential clients, he pointed out the importance of what she did.

Whenever you can, mention the positive effect of the person's contribution, as Mary Bennett, a manager in a public utility, has done in the message to her colleague Margaret Elwood. The personal details of Mary's message make it a gem of a thank-you.

> Subject: ITSM Contribution
>
> Margaret,
>
> Thank you so much for your contribution to the training success for the Incident management project. I was entirely overwhelmed with the action item of Training when it was assigned to me. Being able to work with you for the development of the course was wonderful! The course outline creation, combined with walking us through how to engage the participants and encourage the hands-on learning, was fantastic. It was a huge benefit to the project to have someone with your expertise guiding us.
>
> On a more personal note, I appreciate your support and encouragement for my presentations. Being the trainer definitely put me out of my comfort zone! I found it super helpful to have you in my corner making me feel better about it.
>
> Thanks again,
> Mary
>
> Mary Bennett
> Manager, ITS Infrastructure Support

Being sincere means saying thank you in your own personal style and voice, as Mary Bennett did. You want your thank-you to sound like you—not like something canned you took from an etiquette book. Tell your own story. Use your own language.

Say thank you warmly. Always use the other person's name and the personal pronouns *I* and *we*. For instance, write "Olga, we appreciate your artistry"—not "Your artistry is appreciated." I sent the following enthusiastic message to our original web designer, Diane Varner, when she completed our site. The eight *we-our-us* pronouns and eight *you-your* pronouns help create the feeling of warmth and connection.

> Dear Diane,
>
> Thank you for the creativity, patience, and hard work you brought to completing our website. The site is exactly what we wanted—in fact, it is much more.
>
> We especially appreciated your feedback on our content, and the way your design complemented it. We also are very grateful for the marketing and search engine insights you shared. We had not realized that a web designer could offer so much solid advice, and we know your efforts will pay off in a site that brings us business.
>
> Thank you for your beautiful work.
>
> Warm wishes,
> Lynn and Michael

Say thank you without saying please. When you say thanks, do not ask for anything. Asking detracts from your thank-you and suggests that gratitude is not the real reason for your message. Imagine how out of place a request for changes in our website would have sounded in the previous message to our web designer.

The following generic letter to "Dear Business Owner" illustrates what *not* to do. It is a request partly disguised as a thank-you. It starts off badly with a nonspecific greeting. Writers should use the reader's name whenever possible.

Dear Business Owner:

Thank you for your past contributions to our annual auction. We are very grateful for your generosity.

This year's auction takes place on Friday, October 19. Can we count on you again?

As a past supporter, you know that all our auction proceeds go to underserved children and families in our community.

One of our procurement specialists will phone or stop by your business in the next few weeks. We thank you in advance for your generosity.

Sincerely,

Nonprofit Organization

In contrast, the personal, specific thank-you to Mr. Austin includes upbeat information on the success of the auction. What's more, it asks for nothing! The recipient will be delighted to receive it.

Dear Mr. Austin:

Thank you for contributing the one-year corporate club membership to our auction. It was a generous gift and a popular item, and we are very grateful for it.

We are happy to inform you that our auction brought in $95,300. Since our goal was $75,000, we are very pleased with the results. It is because of generous donors like you that we exceeded our goal.

Since ticket purchases covered auction expenses, the full $95,300 will be used to meet the needs of underserved children and families in our community.

Your contribution has made a difference. Thank you for your generosity.

Sincerely,

Janice Green
Executive Director

Notice that in the thank-you to Mr. Austin, only the greeting and first paragraph are personalized. That level of personalization makes the letter successful, and it makes the job of sending out the many thank-yous doable.

Match your effort to the reason for the thank-you. An offhand thank-you that does not match the situation will come across as insensitive. For instance, a two-word thank-you is heartless in response to a 10-page report. A two-sentence thank-you might seem stingy to a person who spent hours helping you finish a proposal.

This simple thank-you to a presenter is appropriate from a member of the audience:

Dear Jonathan,

Thank you for your excellent, inspiring presentation today at the breakfast. I had to leave promptly at your conclusion, so I wanted to let you know by note that I appreciated your moving content and high-quality presentation. I learned a lot!

I wish you much success with your new book.

Warm regards,
Deborah

This more elaborate thanks is appropriate from the meeting organizer:

> Dear Jonathan,
>
> THANK YOU for the fabulous presentation you made this morning. To be riveting at 7:30 a.m. is a huge challenge, and you rose to it. You were outstanding!
>
> Thank you for making our association look good. Feedback from attendees was extremely positive, with comments such as "Bring this man back for a longer session!" and "Jonathan's information was practical AND powerful!" People raved about your slides and your story.
>
> Please accept my thanks and high praise on behalf of the association. If you would like a testimonial or a letter of reference, just let me know.
>
> Best,
> Natalie

Let gratitude multiply and spread. When you thank someone for excellent work on the job, send a copy to his or her supervisor and to the human resources department, if appropriate. (You can even tweet your thanks to the world!) When you thank a supervisor directly, mention the group, like this: "I appreciate the commitment your entire team showed in getting this order out on time." The supervisor can post your note or forward it to the group and may add his or her own thanks to yours. Some businesses save and post thank-you notes on their bulletin boards, gather them in scrapbooks, or post them online. The good feelings engendered live on indefinitely.

Email, Electronic Message, Letter, Note, or Card?

You have so many ways to send thank-yous that it can be tough to choose one. Do not let worrying about the medium get in the way. Use these guidelines to help you decide how to express your thanks:

Email or an electronic message through Facebook, LinkedIn, etc., is right for someone who is regularly on a computer. And the speed with which you can write, send, and forward electronic thank-yous makes them an easy choice. They may be any length, from one or two sentences to several paragraphs. An electronic thank-you may not stand out as special, though, and it may be perceived as informal.

When I sent out my monthly e-newsletter with the featured article "12 Ways to Build Work Relationships Through Writing," I received this thoughtful thank-you by email from a subscriber:

> Hi Lynn,
>
> I've been benefiting from your knowledge-sharing articles and tips for quite a long time now. I can't afford to take your paid classes but the kind of information you share in your free articles has been very helpful in sharpening my skills.
>
> I'd not have thought about thanking you, had I not read this article today. I thought of you while reading the first two lines of the first point of the article.
>
> So thank you very much for sharing this enormous and invaluable information. God bless you.
>
> Kind regards,
> Rahul

Because few subscribers send thank-yous, Rahul's message stood out. That is the power of the mighty thank-you: It helps the writer stand out, and it opens the door to new work relationships.

A typed letter or memo is suitable for acknowledging a donation or contribution (like the thank-you to Mr. Austin for his donation). It also fits well to thank someone for significant help or great customer service, and it is the right choice when the thank-you may end up in a personnel file. Because of the way it looks on the page, it must be at least two paragraphs.

A handwritten card or note communicates a personal touch. It is the perfect response to a meal, flowers, gift, or personal help. It's short, typically from two sentences to two paragraphs.

Many people swear by the personal note, as does Jeannette Paladino, a social media writer and blogger. She explained on my blog: "A simple thank-you note will do more for you and your business than a lengthy presentation. It shows you care about the other person. It's also good manners. Dashing off a perfunctory email doesn't begin to measure up."

In this thank-you message I received from my marketing mentor, Marcia Yudkin, you will notice the indented paragraphs, which are standard in handwritten notes.

> Lynn—
>
> In this season of Thanksgiving, I wanted to let you know how much I appreciate having you as a member in Marketing for More.
>
> Thank you especially for the empathy and caring that you show to other members.
>
> Looking forward to seeing you again in Maui!
>
> Yours,
> Marcia

Marcia's lovely card stood out because she was specific in her thanks, noting and appreciating my efforts to empathize with others. I renew my membership in Marketing for More each year, and Marcia's thank-you reminded me of the relationship we have that makes membership worthwhile.

Because I want our webmaster, Margery Squier, to know how much I value her work, I regularly send thank-you cards to her. I pay her invoices by check, and I enclose the check in a beautiful or amusing card. This is a typical brief message:

Margery, thank you once again for your creative, careful work on our website. We appreciate your promptness, good humor, and excellent customer service!

Lynn and Michael

If you send handwritten notes and cards to customers, consider brief messages like these:

For restaurant customers:

Thank you for dining at our restaurant. It was a pleasure serving you.

We hope to see you again soon!

Dante Osorio, Executive Chef

You can easily personalize the message to make it specific and more memorable:

Dear Spiro,

Thank you for dining at our restaurant. We hope your Kobe steak made your birthday celebration even more memorable. It was a pleasure serving you on your special day.

We hope to see you again soon!

Dante Osorio, Executive Chef

For real estate customers who have sold their home:

Dear Mr. and Mrs. Gardner,

Thank you for your patience and flexibility during the process of selling your home. I hope you will be very happy in your new community.

Warm regards,

Angie Tamrind

For jewelry store customers:

> Dear Nicole,
>
> Thank you for the opportunity to help you choose the gold locket for your mother's 75th birthday. I hope she enjoys it as much as you enjoyed purchasing it for her.
>
> I look forward to serving you again the next time you are looking for jewelry for an important person—including yourself!
>
> Abby Loos, Wright Jewelers

For customers of a clothing store:

> Dear Louisa,
>
> Thanks for shopping with us. It was fun helping you choose new pieces for your spring wardrobe. I hope you feel wonderful every time you wear them!
>
> If I can help you in any way, just call me at [phone number]. I hope to see you when you need something new.
>
> Jesse Ward

After we purchased a violin for our teenaged daughter, we received a small box of delicious, locally produced organic chocolates. It was accompanied by a small piece of card stock that said, "A special thanks from Olsen Violins." The small box and brief message made a huge positive impression on us.

Consider how you want to communicate, whether it be by letter, note, card, card and gift, email, text, or even Twitter. But do not let the options get in the way of sending a message. Send the thank-you!

Thank-You Messages for Job Interviews

In my survey on business writing and relationships, 78 percent of people who have hired or recommended hiring indicated that a thank-you note has had a definite positive influence on a hiring decision; 20 percent said this has happened many times. One respondent described the thank-you as a relationship-starting communication:

> Many of the people I've hired throughout my career were the ones who sent a follow-up or thank-you note after an interview. Similarly, I've been told that a follow-up that I sent made the difference in a hiring decision when all other qualifications were considered equal. It all comes down to relationships, and this type of note is often the first step in the relationship you'll have with a new employer. Even if you're not hired, you did the right thing by sending something positive forward.

Another respondent commented this way:

> I've been in human resources for many years and am amazed at how few job applicants think enough to send a thank-you note after their interview. It is so rare—it really stands out in a positive way.

To an employer, a thank-you for a job interview indicates an applicant's enthusiasm for and understanding of the position, ability to observe social norms, and writing aptitude (proofread carefully!). Unlike other thank-yous, the job-interview thank-you often includes details to remind the potential employer of the applicant's strengths and fit for the position. Note those details in this example, sent by email:

Subject: Thank You for the Interview

Dear Felix,

Thank you for the chance to interview for the position of administrative assistant. It was a pleasure to learn about your business, and I would welcome the opportunity to work for you.

As a detailed-oriented "bean counter," I would relish keeping track of your accounts, managing the shopping cart, updating the websites, and coordinating your calendar. The 8–3 schedule would be ideal for me, and walking to work would be a dream come true.

Again, thank you for the opportunity to meet. Please let me know if you need any other information to make your decision.

Sincerely,
Galen Howard

Several respondents to my survey expressed a strong preference for a handwritten interview thank-you. This brief thank-you could be sent in a classy thank-you card:

Dear Ms. Joseph,

Thank you for interviewing me today and letting me observe your class. In that short time, I learned a lot just watching you relate to the students. Each one got your respect and your full attention. Your caring and high standards were obvious.

It would be a privilege to assist in your class. I hope you will consider me for the position.

Best wishes,
Fiona Greenman

One challenge after a day of interviewing is to say something different and sincere to each of the people you have met. The secret to successful thank-yous in this situation is to key in on the interviewers and the conversations you have had with them. These four emailed thank-yous—all for meetings at the same organization—show the variety you can bring to your thank-yous.

Subject: Interview Thank-You From Lassie Elbert

Dear Dr. Mitchell,

Thank you for interviewing me for the position of career counselor. It was a pleasure to talk with you and learn about your goals for the center. I also enjoyed meeting the other team members and learning about their expertise.

I would love to have the opportunity to work at the center. I believe my experience in several industries, my graduate work in counseling, and my love of working one-to-one would help me be successful as a member of your team. I also feel very much in tune with your vision for the center.

Thank you again for talking with me. Whatever your hiring decision, I wish you and the center continued success.

Sincerely,
Lassie Elbert

⌒

Subject: Thank You for Meeting With Me

Dear Dr. Weiss,

Thank you for talking with me today about your work at the center. I appreciate your sharing so much helpful information about the client population, the testing you do, and the many aspects of supporting the clients throughout their search for meaningful work. You gave me a very good sense of what working at the center is like. I appreciated the articles too!

I would love to have the opportunity to work with you. I believe my desire to help people find their path in life, along with my work experience and graduate studies in counseling, is a good fit for the center, and I hope you think so too.

Again, I appreciate your talking with me today, and I hope to have the chance to be a part of the center.

Best wishes,
Lassie Elbert

⌣

Subject: Thanks for Our Talk Today

Dear Tina,

Thanks so much for talking with me today. I loved learning about your background and all the twists and turns that brought you to the center. Your life is a fine example of how career paths are no longer straight.

I would jump at the chance to work at the center. It feels like a place where I could contribute my skills and experience well, learn a lot, and be a member of a productive team that understands work-life balance. It is terrific that the center has corporate season tickets to the Storm. That's my kind of place!

Thank you again for the great conversation.

Lassie

⌣

Subject: Thank You for Welcoming Me

Dear Justin,

Thank you for welcoming me today at the center. I really appreciate your taking the time to show me around, introduce me to the staff, and make me feel comfortable on interview day. You are very adept at reducing an applicant's anxiety!

I enjoyed meeting you and your colleagues at the center. I hope to have the opportunity to work with you.

Again, thank you!

Lassie

That last message serves as an example of an important rule: Don't forget the receptionist!

You may be wondering whether it is necessary to send a separate thank-you to each person at a company who interviews you, whether you have individual meetings or a panel interview. Use this response as a guideline: The more you want the job, the more effort you should put into your thank-yous and every other aspect of the interview process.

If You Do Not Want the Job, Say Thank You Anyway

You present yourself as a polite professional when you send a thank-you, even when you don't want the job. Sending a message like this one can make a positive impression that leads to other opportunities:

Dear Helen,

Thank you for interviewing me for the position of event coordinator. It was fascinating to learn about the wide range of events your company manages. I admire the way you juggle so many plates at once (literally and figuratively!).

Based on the amount of travel we discussed, I do not feel this position would work for me. However, if a position with minimal travel opens up, please consider me for it. I would enjoy applying my skills as an event coordinator at [Company name].

Best wishes,
Lee Chin

Remember: A thank-you for an interview is a professional message. Do not be casual. A senior human resources (HR) professional told me she did not invite a job candidate back for a second interview because of the person's emailed thank-you note. Why? Because it included an animated smiley face. That blinking emoticon moved the HR director to decide the candidate did not have the good professional judgment the job required. That is the only time I have heard of a thank-you going wrong. And yet the HR director's decision was probably perfect; she and that candidate would not work well together.

Thank-You Messages at Thanksgiving

In the United States, Thanksgiving Day takes place on the last Thursday in November. Canada celebrates Thanksgiving on the second Monday in October. Because Thanksgiving is a national holiday not allied with a particular group or religion, it is a perfect occasion to remember customers, clients, and others. Your message will stand out much more at Thanksgiving than at Christmastime, when your contacts are likely to be buried in holiday messages. Since most people take a holiday from work on Thanksgiving, be sure to send your messages several days early.

Here are samples of brief thank-yous to customers. Those with indented paragraphs would be handwritten messages or typed notes—not emails.

Dear Friends at LMNOP,

In this time of gratitude, we give thanks for you. We value your patronage and appreciate your confidence in us. Counting you among our customers is something for which we are especially grateful.

On behalf of all of us at XYZ Company, we wish you a very happy Thanksgiving.

Sincerely,

Jack and Victoria Jepson

Dear Dan and Reese,

Thank you for being our valued customers. We are grateful for the pleasure of serving you and meeting your printing needs.

We wish you a beautiful Thanksgiving and a joyous year's end.

Warm wishes,
Karl and the team

Dear Carlos,

In this time of Thanksgiving, I must express my thanks to you. Working with you over the past two years has been an amazing opportunity for me. I appreciate your high standards, consistent focus, and fine sense of humor.

Thank you, Carlos, for the pleasure of continuing to work with you. I wish you a wonderful Thanksgiving filled with all good things.

With thanks,
Linda

Dear Mr. Emmanuel,

When we think about the things we appreciate, we think of you and our work with you on the Maple Heights project. The project was a challenge and a phenomenal success for us—thanks to your vision and commitment. We will always treasure that experience.

We saw the enclosed new book on landscaping by [Author], and we immediately thought of you. Please enjoy it with our thanks.

Happy Thanksgiving!
Carl and Vincent

These two messages thank employees for their work. Both are suitable to send to all employees from a manager or management team, with the greeting personalized to individuals.

Dear Qasid,

During this month of Thanksgiving, I have been reflecting on the things I am most grateful for. Primary among them is our talented group of employees.

Thank you for the work you do to make our agency great. You help us provide award-winning services to our clients. Without your commitment, creativity, and high standards, we would not be the thriving company we are. I am very grateful for your efforts.

I wish you a Thanksgiving filled with abundance and bright moments.

Warm wishes,
Rhonda

Dear Raimondo,

This year has been challenging for us, but we turned challenges into successes—thanks to you and your fellow employees. You have focused on the future rather than getting stuck in day-to-day difficulties. You have worked hard to help our business thrive.

On behalf of the management team, I thank you for your accomplishments this year. We are all grateful.

Please enjoy the enclosed gift certificate as a token of our thanks.

Happy Thanksgiving!
David

Thank-You Notes for Condolences

One type of thank-you note can be upsetting to write: the thank-you you send in response to condolences and acts of kindness you receive when a friend or family member has died. This message is difficult because in such situations, feelings of deep sadness and loss can sap your energy and spoil your concentration. Your words can seem feeble compared to the huge support and kindness you have received from coworkers and associates. You may be unable to remember the many kindnesses extended to you, and you may worry that you have forgotten something of major importance. All those feelings are maddening when you want so much to express your gratitude!

The people in your personal and professional lives will not expect you to write detailed messages. Just knowing that you received their note, flowers, or other gift is enough. Use the short templates that follow to craft your own thank-you messages. Each one can begin with "Dear" and the individual's name. They may be expressed in thank-you notes, cards, emails, or other electronic messages. The examples with indented paragraphs would be handwritten or typed notes—not emails.

> Dear Keith,
> Thank you for your kindness and sympathy during our time of loss. It gives us much comfort to know that you are thinking of us.
> Warm regards,
> Nate and Judy

It was very nice of you to think of me in this time of sadness. I appreciate your thoughts and prayers.
Barbara

Thank you for your touching letter. I really enjoyed hearing from you. The story you shared about my mother made me smile.

My mother lived a long, full life. Although her passing is a sad milestone for me, I am grateful for having her with me for so many years.

With many thanks,
Carli

Please accept my sincere thanks for the beautiful flowers you sent for my sister's memorial service. She would have loved them.

I appreciate your thoughtfulness and caring more than I can say.

Sachin

I can hardly express how grateful I am for your attendance at my brother's funeral. It was so good of you to take the time to be with me and my family.

Your kindness and compassion mean a great deal to us.

Sincerely,
Dermott

Dear Friends and Colleagues,

It is difficult to find the words to express our gratitude for the many kindnesses you have shown us during this sad time.

We are so grateful for all you have done for us. The cards, letters, phone and email messages, prayers, and visits meant the world to us as we struggled with our heartbreaking loss. Along with the emotional support you gave us, the meals, chores, and other gifts of your time and energy helped sustain us day to day.

We are unable to write individual thank-yous to each one of you, given the great outpouring of support. Please know that your generosity and thoughtfulness have touched us deeply.

Knowing that we were not alone helped us bear our grief and sadness. Thank you for being there for us.

With sincere thanks,
Sharon and Lynette

If you have experienced a loss and received condolences and kindnesses from others, be assured that no one will judge you on your ability to write a thank-you. They will be pleased to hear from you, but they will not expect more than a few sentences of acknowledgment.

A blog reader asked, "Do I have to write thank-yous for sympathy cards?" No, you do not have to write thank-yous for sympathy cards. But write them if doing so will help you feel better and more connected with others.

Thanking People for Thank-Yous

When you are in the happy position of receiving thank-yous, you may find yourself wondering: Do I need to thank people for their thank-yous? The answer: It depends.

For any thank-you that makes you feel good, why not take a moment to return the favor and enhance the relationship? When I received this brief but enthusiastic thank-you by email from Jeff Chamberlain, a reader of my e-newsletter *Better Writing at Work,* I wrote to acknowledge his message.

Lynn:

Thank you for sending out these newsletters. I've enjoyed getting them for the past few months. They are a great reminder/reinforcer of positive behaviors, and I like the interactive proofreading challenge at the end (I got the missing hyphen correct this time).

Jeff Chamberlain

My brief response:

Jeff, thank you for your kind note. I am very pleased that you enjoy the newsletter and the Error Quests. Thanks for letting me know!

Best wishes,
Lynn

Although a thank-you message does not require a thank-you in response, a thank-you gift does. This inquiry I received from Nancy Doerhoff, manager of the Machacek Branch of the St. Louis Public Library, illustrates the question thank-you gifts may raise:

Hello, Lynn,

We are a public library. Some of our regular patrons (customers) brought us candy, cookies, popcorn, etc., during the days leading up to Christmas. Some of us think we should send thank-you notes to them for their kindness. Others think it is unnecessary or even overkill since they believe the gifts were thank-yous to us for the service we have given over the past year.

What is the correct etiquette?

I recommended that the library staff thank their patrons for the gifts, and Nancy and her staff did write thank-yous. Because of their hard work and graciousness, I bet they received more gifts from patrons the following year!

Brief Does Not Mean Brusque

This chapter includes many references to brief thanks. But brief does not mean offhand one-word thanks or abbreviations. Marketing consultant Cornelia Luethi left this blog comment, which captures the issue: "I once had a manager who would often reply with just 'Thx' or 'Thks' . . . now that is stingy! It was hard to believe he really was thankful, seeing as he couldn't be bothered to type the whole word!"

Don't be miserly when it comes to thanking people. Typing just "Thanks" or "Thx" does not come across as genuine appreciation, especially if it appears at the end of every message. If you do need to type a quick email or text as thanks, take a few extra seconds to make it specific, as these examples do:

Thanks so much for the information. You rock!

Thanks for responding so fast.

Thanks! I appreciate your flexibility.

Thank you for keeping me in the loop.

Thanks for understanding.

Often people use "Thanks" in response to an email when they really mean only to acknowledge something. If acknowledgment is your real reason for writing, try these:

Thanks. Got it.

Thanks. Consider it done.

Thanks. I'll pass it on.

When you choose any of the brief remarks above, don't Reply All or cc the company. The recipients will not thank you!

Do It Now

It's time to reflect and take action. Put down this book and pick up a pen to write a thank-you. Or launch your email and send a thoughtful thank-you instantaneously. No excuses: 31 sample messages in this chapter were 100 words or less. You have time to write 50, 75, or 100 sincere words of thanks. Those words may be the best investment in great work relationships you make this year.

Your thank-you will tell someone that she or he is valued and appreciated. Those positive feelings will reflect back to you, strengthening your relationships. Who knows? They may reverberate around the globe.

Personal Reflection

- ▷ Do you take time to thank people who help you be successful? How would your work relationships be different if you added "Write thank-yous" to your weekly tasks—and wrote them?

Next Step

- ▷ Think of one person who has done something special for you lately or who has consistently supported your work. Nurture that relationship by sending a thank-you email, card, or handwritten note acknowledging the special effort or support.
- ▷ Repeat.

CHAPTER 4

Give Positive, Powerful Feedback

When I was in graduate school at Notre Dame, in South Bend, Indiana, I worked as an editorial assistant at a law center. I was new to journalism, and I struggled to get the lead right in stories and to compose clear, useful articles. My editor, whom I will call Ruth, usually applied a red pen heavily to my writing, or at least it seemed that way to me. Often I wondered whether I caused her more work than I contributed.

For various reasons, I decided to move to New York City to take writing classes at City College. When I told Ruth I would be leaving my job at the center, she responded, "Oh, but you were doing so well!" She went on to say that she would really miss me and the good work I was doing on the newsletter.

Miss me? I was stunned. I had no idea I was doing well. Ruth had never indicated that my work was good. She had never said or written anything to balance the strikes of her red pen.

Had I known I was doing well, I might have blossomed on the job rather than worrying about whether I was worth keeping. I might have found a way to stay in South Bend to work happily with Ruth at the center rather than moving to New York City. But I had not received positive feedback, and I did not know Ruth valued me and my work. It was easy to leave.

I learned many lessons on the job with Ruth. The one that stayed with me is this: Give positive feedback—lots of it.

Here's how giving positive feedback leads to great work relationships:

- When you give positive feedback, you help people recognize what they are doing well. They feel good about their performance, and they are likely to appreciate you for pointing it out.
- Your positive feedback shows that you value your coworkers and associates enough to pay attention to their work and take time to comment on it. It is proof to them that their good work is recognized and valued.
- Positive feedback motivates people to continue doing what they are doing well. In turn, you get to enjoy working with high-performing people, who are likely to seek you out as a project partner.
- Giving positive feedback builds others' trust in your positive intent and judgment. When a sticky issue comes up in the future, that trust helps you work through the problem together.

Positive feedback can be wildly powerful in building relationships and strengthening performance. This chapter shows you how to share positive feedback in writing so it does both.

Do You Give Positive Feedback?

I taught a class called The Art of Giving Feedback several times at a well-known high-tech company. After the class participants and I agreed on the importance of positive feedback, I would ask how many of them gave positive feedback to others on the job. Nearly everyone would raise a hand. Then I would ask how many received positive feedback from their supervisors. Almost no hands went up. The two sets of raised hands were strikingly different: At least 90 percent gave positive feedback, but only 10 percent received it.

My experience at that company corresponds with what I found in my survey on business writing and relationships. In it, 60 percent of respondents said they give positive feedback to others frequently; 19 percent said they give it daily or nearly every day. Yet 80 percent said they have wanted to leave a job or an assignment because they were not receiving the positive feedback they felt they deserved. Clearly, lots of people think they are giving positive feedback, but just as many feel they are not getting it. My conclusion: There is a huge opportunity to build relationships and improve performance by giving positive feedback more often and more effectively—so people know it.

Unmistakable Positive Feedback

Consider this straightforward example of positive feedback in an email:

> Subject: I liked "Vacationing at Home"
>
> Tye, nice job on this month's newsletter! I liked your tips on staycations, which covered both simple and elaborate things to do. You gave me several ideas I am going to suggest to Ellen and the kids.
>
> I always enjoy reading the newsletter. I am sure our clients appreciate it too. Thanks for all you do!
>
> Dana

After reading the email, would Tye recognize he had received positive feedback? Yes! Dana's comments convey positive regard with the phrases "I liked," "nice job," "always enjoy," and "appreciate it," among others. The message gives a specific example of something Tye did well (the tips on staycations). It mentions that Dana will pass on the information, giving Tye's work a wider audience. It expresses enthusiastic appreciation.

When Tye reads Dana's feedback, he is likely to smile, then perhaps write a quick thank-you to Dana for taking the time to compliment the newsletter. He may imagine Dana, Ellen, and their kids out on one of the local adventures he suggested. And the next time he writes the newsletter, Dana is likely to be in his mind as one of his attentive, thoughtful readers.

The following emails also convey positive feedback, but they do so much less effectively.

Message 1:

Re: Vacationing at Home

Tye, nice job on this month's newsletter. Thanks.

Rob

Message 2:

Re: Vacationing at Home

Tye, I liked this issue and your tips, but don't you think we need more balance between urban and rural activities? The special offer was catchy, but I thought we were going to extend the deadline to the 30th, no?

Nice job.

Ricardo

Message 3:

Re: Vacationing at Home

Tye, when I received this, I realized I had forgotten to tell you I enjoyed the January issue on how to fight germs while traveling. It was good advice.

Krissy

Could you feel the difference between Dana's example and Messages 1, 2, and 3? Dana's message, while brief, includes the essential elements of motivating, positive feedback:

- Specifics—not just generalities like the "Nice job" of Message 1.
- Complete focus on positives—no *buts* or back-pedaling like the *buts* in Message 2, which wipe out the positive feeling.
- Promptness—not untimely feedback like the reference to an earlier issue in Message 3.
- Significance—a reason why the positive outcome or behavior matters; for example, Dana's "You gave me several ideas" and "I am sure our clients appreciate it too." Significance was missing from Messages 1, 2, and 3.

Notice how the detailed feedback below includes the essential elements.

Subject: Your fine work with Ed Stern

Hi, Aamani. I wanted to share some positive feedback on our sales call this morning. You were brilliant.

First off, you briefly introduced yourself, focusing on the aspects of your background that would interest the client. Ed lit up when you mentioned your supply-chain experience. Then you segued to his situation and asked relevant though not pointed questions, which would have put him on the spot. Your "Tell me about . . ." approach was perfect. It let him focus on the issues important to him without any awkwardness.

The way you wove in our company's capabilities when you responded to questions was very subtle and effective, not to mention completely natural. You came across as a trusted advisor.

I am certain Ed's request for a proposal was prompted by your warm engagement with him.

Just wanted to share that I admired your work today.

Richard

If you were Aamani, how would that positive feedback make you feel? Appreciated? Pleasantly surprised? Confident? Delighted? Grateful? All of the above? Whether Richard was your manager or your peer, his message would almost certainly have a positive impact on you and your relationship with him.

The Best Feedback Is Specific

It is quick and very easy to say "Great job." But the phrase "Great job" packs much less power than it would with specific details. The phrase could come across as insincere or even sarcastic. To recognize and write about what made something a "great job!" or a "good job," think about the difference between what the individual did and what a bad performance would be like. For example, if a new student intern did a good job on his first day, how was his first day different from a bad first day? Is it that he arrived on time rather than late? That you never saw him on a cell phone, whereas other interns have spent most of the day texting? Was he curious rather than uninterested? Did he offer to help rather than surf the Internet when work slowed down?

In this example, a supervisor conveys positive feedback to an intern:

Subject: Feedback on a Good First Day

Luke, I wanted to give you some feedback on your first day in Engineering. I appreciate how you conducted yourself, and I wanted to let you know.

It was great you were willing to come in early for the safety meeting. I know coming in early on a Monday morning can be a drag. People were impressed you took the initiative to introduce yourself.

John told me you asked very good questions as you shadowed him, and your interest made it a pleasure to work with you. He also mentioned that when he was busy talking with Derek, you read industry magazines rather than just texting or doing nothing.

You are off to a good start, Luke. We look forward to working with you.

Linwood

How would Luke feel if he received a message like that one? If the first day had been stressful for him, he would probably feel terrific that his efforts to keep it together had been successful. If he had had a pleasant first day, he would probably be happy to know that others shared his positive feelings. The feedback would tell him that people noticed him and were pleased with his first day's performance. Luke might also feel lucky to have a supervisor who cared enough to pay attention to him and let him know how he did. That feedback could be the start of a great relationship.

Even though positive feedback can be a powerful relationship and performance builder, some perceptions about it can get in the way of sharing it. Here are three views to consider changing:

"I don't do mushy."

Some people—men more often than women—find it uncomfortable to pay compliments. They say positive feedback isn't their thing. In many cases, they worry that they will come across as mushy, inauthentic, or both if they share positive words.

But positive feedback that is specific is not likely to come across as mushy or insincere. The details make it work. Consider these brief examples:

Hey, Larry. You coming in early last night meant we could get the trucks loaded and out before the weather got too bad. As usual, your flexibility helped a lot. Much appreciated.

Kyle, I observed your interactions with members today, and I wanted to give you positive feedback on your upselling. You mentioned our mortgages, investment services, and business lines of credit, in each case choosing the right product for the member. I can see that you are applying your training and are well on your way to meeting expectations.

Bobby—

Tom showed me the hoist you invented. Sweet! Using that, we won't be straining our backs to move each job. Can't wait to try it. Mind over muscle!

Hi, Chrissy. I observed you assisting the customer who is sight impaired. You made helpful suggestions without rushing her. She might have been the only customer in the store, with the focus and patience you showed her. Thanks for representing us so well!

Delia, I read your response to Dr. Wells. Great job! You were firm while polite, and you made it clear to him that he had several options. It was a very effective message, which presented us professionally.

Hi, Pam. My trip went perfectly with the travel arrangements you made. The hotel was comfortable and right across the street from the center, as you said. It was lucky for me that you gave me the client's cell number—she was waiting for me in a conference room, but no one knew where. So I just phoned her cell and located her.

Thanks for your attention to detail! It made the long trip easier.

———

Alex, I just saw the Tanakas' side yard. It's breathtaking! When Mrs. Tanaka said she wanted a rock wall, I could not imagine how it would work in that space, but you pulled it off. Your design made the most of the limited light, and your plant choices should keep maintenance low for a long time.

Just wanted to compliment you on a job well done.

———

Jackie, I just read your email. Your concise notes captured my understanding exactly. Thanks for taking the initiative to write up what we agreed on. It saved me a lot of time.

Reviewing that feedback, you will find these positive expressions:

coming in early	concise notes
much appreciated	flexibility
right product	well on your way
applying your training	Sweet!
meeting expectations	helpful suggestions
Can't wait to try it.	representing us so well
focus and patience	presented us professionally
very effective message	went perfectly
Great job!	attention to detail
lucky for me	It's breathtaking!
made the long trip easier	your design made the most of
you pulled it off	taking the initiative
job well done	saved me a lot of time

The list includes no mush, no obvious insincerity, and only one "Great job!"

"We don't do positive feedback."

If your workplace culture resists positive feedback, your efforts at building relationships one message at a time may seem out of place. But you are reading this book, so you have the desire or a reason to communicate differently on the job. Start small, putting your positive feedback in writing so that no one feels embarrassed by a public display of admiration. Then keep at it, and watch for results in the form of budding relationships and consistent positive performances. Remember: Every important movement starts with a single action.

"I have no time for this!"

The secret to having time for positive feedback is to write it (or to make a note to yourself to write it) as soon as you notice the excellent work. You don't have to go into great detail. For example:

- Walking through the lunchroom, you speak to a new employee, who praises several aspects of the day's orientation program. On your smartphone, you send a text to the training designer: "Marty, I got a huge compliment on your onboarding program from a new employee. He loved the map challenge and pop quizzes. Nice work creating new evangelists!"

- Finishing with one patient, you notice that the receptionist is engaged in conversation with the elderly patient you have kept waiting. You scribble a note to remind yourself. Then when you have a moment, you write a quick text, note, or email: "Kathryn—I was so relieved that you kept Mr. McGowan occupied. Very thoughtful! He was smiling, even though I kept him waiting so long. Thanks!"

- Reviewing the month's sales figures, you notice that one rep has moved from number 25 to number 16 among your reps. You grab your iPad and text her: "Kayla, your ranking increased to 16 last month. Great numbers! Your preparation is getting results!"

- Learning that your grant has been renewed, you send a quick text, update, or email to the grant writer: "Edgar—good news! They extended the grant. Your attention to the details paid off, literally. Many, many thanks!"

Of course, you may not have even a moment to scribble a note to yourself or type a short feedback message. If that is the nature of your day or week, do your best to share your positive words in writing, by phone, or in person when you can.

Moving Feedback From Positive to Positive and Powerful

To take your feedback to the next level, from positive to positive and powerful, apply these suggestions:

Be specific. It is perfectly acceptable to write a general comment such as "Great work!" but add why the work was great. The details make the message stick.

Avoid using the word *but* after a compliment. *But* is guaranteed to erase any positive feeling in the reader's mind.

Compare these statements:

I liked your rapid turnaround, but the mistakes were disappointing.

I liked your rapid turnaround. It was wonderful to get the document back so fast.

When you do need to communicate both positive and constructive feedback, include the constructive part in a separate paragraph, or at least in a separate sentence. The previous two-sentence "rapid turnaround" compliment might be followed with this statement: "A few mistakes need to be corrected."

Use the pronouns *you* and *your* when making positive comments. The pronouns give credit clearly to your reader. Compare these examples:

> The event-planning ideas were very creative and expertly carried out.

> Your event-planning ideas were very creative, and you carried them out expertly.

> This is the best proposal for cleanup services I have read.

> You wrote the best proposal for cleanup services I have read.

When appropriate, share positive feedback with others beyond the recipient. If you communicate positive feedback in an email, for example, copy the person's supervisor on the message. If you write positive feedback for a peer on your team, copy the team on the message.

Normally copying others makes everyone feel good. However, in a potentially sensitive situation, ask yourself whether the copies could cause hard feelings. Imagine, for instance, that Joseph was named project leader, a role that Amy was disappointed not to get. Copying Amy on positive feedback to Joseph might make her feel worse.

Include why the person's performance or traits are valuable. Perhaps the individual's contribution:

- Made your life easier.
- Made the department look good.
- Enhanced the company's reputation.
- Taught you a helpful lesson.
- Built goodwill.

- Increased efficiency.
- Created positive buzz.
- Saved time and money.
- Created beauty for everyone to share.
- Reduced accidents.
- Made everyone feel good.
- Ensured customer satisfaction.

Whether you are a CEO, supervisor, manager, individual contributor, entrepreneur, consultant, or student, share positive feedback every day. Look for opportunities to recognize people's contributions to your success and contentment.

Tell the chef your blackened shrimp was cooked just the way you like it. Send a personal note to the choir director commenting on his fine musical selections. Send a memo to the office manager commending her successful efforts to hire competent staff. Post a notice on the break room bulletin board praising the entire lab for their contributions to an incident-free site visit.

Give positive, powerful feedback—lots of it! It will strengthen your business relationships, making them more supportive, rewarding, and enjoyable. And it will strengthen performance.

Personal Reflection

▸ One survey respondent said, "In my current position, I have never once been told 'Good job' or 'You did a great job' or even 'Thank you.' Yet I am a diligent, honest hard worker." Could the writer of that comment work with you? Think of evidence for your answer.

Next Step

▸ Add "Give positive, powerful feedback" to your planner or calendar as a daily activity.

CHAPTER 5

Send Congratulations to Warm Hearts and Build Relationships

I t was January 1 when I made a happy announcement to my marketing support group in a program called Marketing for More. I wrote on the discussion board that I had broken a new record for daily page views on my blog—23,543 on the last day of the year—and I shared some ideas about blogging. Then I enjoyed the congratulatory messages that appeared on the discussion board from my marketing mentor, Marcia Yudkin, and from Marketing for More members Doris Jeanette, Lesley Peters, Alice Risemberg, and others.

> Lynn,
>
> That is stupendous. If just a small portion of those people "stick," then it can't help but get your business growing fast.
>
> Congratulations for a great start to the new year.
>
> Marcia

Lynn,

You have done an outstanding job on your blog and your niche. Wow! Great. Enjoy, celebrate, and feel good.

Doris

———

Lynn,

Thanks for sharing, and for your great ideas about coming up with blog post topics! Awesome statistics for you! Congratulations!!!

Lesley

———

Lynn, big congratulations!

And a heartfelt thank-you for posting your thoughts on what works for your blog. Even though they seem specific, I can see ways to draw out the general ideas.

Yay for you!

Alice

Congratulations warm my heart. I glow when people say, "You have done an outstanding job" in response to one of my successes. I enjoy congratulations even more when friends and associates add complimentary details about how I reached my goal—about how hard I worked or how creative I was. I feel as though they have seen me at my best—and have really noticed.

I am not alone. According to my survey on business writing and relationships, 91 percent of people appreciate receiving written congratulations when they achieve a goal or they experience success.

A simple, positive way to connect with people and strengthen your business relationships is to congratulate people on their achievements. The four messages I cited from my marketing support group members average just 28 words each, including my name and the writer's. What could be simpler for you than to write a congratulatory sentence or two to a business associate, customer, or coworker? Yet that small investment brings you and the other person together for that moment, as the sender and receiver of good wishes and a smile.

This chapter gives you inspiration, tips, and examples to help you write notes of congratulations.

Many Ways and Many Reasons to Congratulate

Congratulatory messages can take many forms: printed cards, e-cards, emails, LinkedIn inmail, Facebook postings and private messages, tweets, handwritten notes, and brief, typed business letters.

Send congratulations to your colleagues and contacts for many reasons. For example, when they:

- Get accepted to the college of their choice.
- Graduate.
- Pass a demanding professional exam.
- Get a new job or start a new career, especially after looking for a job for a long time.
- Earn a job promotion.
- Start or expand a business.
- Buy a business.
- Sell a business.
- Complete a challenging project.
- Make significant progress on a challenging project.
- Land a new client or contract.
- Reach or surpass a goal.
- Are featured as a presenter at a prestigious conference.

- Finish a work of art (visual, musical, etc.).
- Write a book.
- Publish a book.
- Win a prize.
- Win an award or receive an award nomination.
- Publish an article in a prestigious publication.
- Are recognized as an expert by a respected news outlet.
- Receive recognition for an achievement or a series of achievements.
- Become a citizen.
- Are ordained.
- Get engaged.
- Get married.
- Have or adopt a baby.
- Have or adopt another baby.
- Become an aunt, an uncle, or a grandparent.
- Celebrate a milestone (an anniversary, a number of years of sobriety, etc.).
- Buy a boat, a horse, or another exciting leisure purchase.
- Buy a home.
- Buy a vacation home.
- Buy a retirement home.
- Retire.
- Begin a new career after retirement.

When they start a new job, venture, or phase in life, people appreciate notes of congratulations. These notes can remind them of their own qualifications and their own excitement—reminders that are especially helpful as they face the intimidating aspects of starting something new.

Joanne Masterson, a web designer and Marketing for More member, sent the following affirming congratulatory note to Leslie Guria, who was making great progress on starting a personal chef business,

Fresh From Your Kitchen. Notice how Joanne mentions Leslie's specific strengths.

> Leslie,
>
> Congratulations. I think you are off to such a strong start because of a lot of things you bring to the business: strong web copy, great design, your love of the work, and your knowledge of how to use local media. Congratulations, and keep up the inspiring work!
>
> Joanne

Write Your Best Congratulatory Notes

Like the success for which you are congratulating someone, you want your messages to be positive and motivating. Apply these suggestions to make your notes their best:

Be specific. Use the individual's name, and mention the specific achievement. If possible, share a compliment that ties to the achievement. In the congratulatory email below, I wanted to remind Bill of his strengths, since an extended search can demoralize job seekers and shake their confidence.

> Subject: Congratulations, Copy Editor!
>
> Dear Bill,
>
> Congratulations on your new job as a copy editor! I am so glad you have landed a job that is a good fit for your editorial strengths. Having benefited from your editing skills and excellent proofreading eye, I know you have much to offer.
>
> I wish you a rewarding, enjoyable experience in your new position. Again, congratulations!
>
> Best regards,
> Lynn

Respect individual preferences if you are aware of them. One person responding to my survey wrote, "I am super private and don't like to be the center of attention. A private congratulations, email, or note is appreciated." For such an individual, avoid notes in public places such as their Facebook wall or the lunchroom bulletin board.

Avoid sarcasm, teasing, and anything that might detract from the positive feeling. A comment such as "It is about time you got a real job" may be intended as playful, but it can come across as judgmental, especially for someone who has endured a long job search. Similarly, "Congratulations on passing the bar; I guess three times was the charm" can wound someone who is embarrassed about the early failures. It is difficult for people—even those you know well—to distinguish sarcasm from seriousness. Personal humor can also hurt unless you make a dig at yourself rather than the person you are congratulating.

Do one job in the message: Congratulate. As with all relationship-building messages, congratulations are most powerful when they have one purpose. A sales letter that begins with congratulations is a sales letter—not a sincere congratulatory note. Its congratulations feel hollow, as illustrated in this letter opening:

> Congratulations on your award as PR [public relations] Executive of the Year! As a sponsor of the celebratory luncheon, we are excited to have an individual like you honored for the contribution you make to the business community in our region.
>
> XYZ Printing is also committed to the success of local businesses. As you may remember from the work we did with you, XYZ's printing services . . .

The following message to Pete, which is a note solely of congratulations, does a better job of strengthening a relationship and therefore paving the way for future business opportunities.

Dear Pete,

Congratulations on your award as PR Executive of the Year! It is proper that you be honored for your creativity, leadership, and contribution to our community.

Working with you on your Save the Zoo campaign, I appreciated your leadership and clarity, and I was struck by your far-reaching vision for our community. It is a delight to see you being widely appreciated and recognized with this honor.

With best wishes,
Jerry Klein
Owner, XYZ Printing

Remember Your Online Communities

With online communities, you can easily read about people's life changes and congratulate them. Communications consultant Deb Arnold regularly sends brief congratulatory messages like these to people in her network:

Subject: Congrats on your new position

Hey Kojo,

Saw your new position on my handy LinkedIn update. Congrats!

Also read about your volunteer deployment, and greatly admire your courage and commitment.

Hope you're enjoying SF and your new role. Keep in touch.

Best,
Deb

Ed, congrats! Fantastic news! And a nice bit of press as well.

Life is falling into place for you, my friend. Couldn't be happier for you.

Wishing you much continued success!

Hugs,
D

I sent this brief message to a contact I did not know well, although we had exchanged emails over the years:

Subject: Congratulations on Your New Position

Hi, Kathleen,

I just saw on LinkedIn that you have a new job. Congratulations! I hope it is everything you want it to be.

Best wishes,
Lynn

Here is Kathleen's response to my message:

Many thanks. It's an amazing opportunity with an amazing company! I'll be in touch if we need your wonderful services!

In fact, Kathleen did need my services and contacted me about doing workshops for her new employer. She may have thought of me to teach writing classes without the congratulations, but I am certain my message jogged her memory of me and my work.

It is not required that you have a close relationship with someone in order to congratulate them. All you need is the desire to maintain a connection. Technical writer Randy Averill described the reason he sent congratulations to someone on LinkedIn:

> I saw that a former peer was promoted. We used to be in the same industry (home building) and, as such, we would cross paths often. We've both moved on in our careers, and we live about 1,000 miles apart, but we remain connected on LinkedIn. I thought a brief recognition of his promotion was in order. We're not close enough that I would send him anything personal, so I sent him a message through LinkedIn."

Below is Randy's message. Notice how it rebuilds the relationship with Kevin by recalling specific details.

> Subject: Congratulations!
>
> Kevin,
>
> I saw on LinkedIn that you've been promoted. I'm glad to see that [Company name] has been able to appreciate your work in the relatively short time you've been with them. It's especially comforting to see you move ahead in these difficult economic conditions.
>
> I hope all is well, and I miss the regular get-togethers we used to have in the home building industry. I trust you're still enjoying your cars.
>
> Congratulations again,
> Randy

Should You Congratulate People You Don't Like?

The reason for congratulating others is to build and maintain relationships. So if you don't want a business relationship with someone, you may choose to skip the congratulatory note. But think twice about that decision. If you do not like an individual but respect him or her, having a polite though not friendly relationship may still benefit both of you. You may share contacts, referrals, and opportunities.

These two congratulatory messages are professional without being overly friendly.

> Dear Tabitha,
>
> Congratulations on winning the Rogers case. Your work on the case was brilliant. I am delighted for you and for the entire defense team.
>
> Congratulations on a job very well done.
>
> Everett

> Dear Conrad,
>
> I am pleased to congratulate you on your new position. You have worked diligently, and it is fitting that your hard work has paid off with this new career opportunity.
>
> I wish you continued success.
>
> David

Congratulations for Many Situations

It is easy to spread joy and maintain relationships by recognizing people's successes. These sample messages may get you thinking about people and situations in your work life. Note: As emails, each might have the subject line "Congratulations!" or something a bit more specific.

For an intern who is graduating:

> Hi, Erika. Congratulations on finishing at U of C! What an achievement! That you finished school while working so hard for our team is something to be commended.

I heard about your travel plans to Europe. It is just like you to set a goal and then set things in motion to achieve that goal. I hope that you travel safely and joyfully.

Please stay in touch.

Warm congratulations,
Katie

For an older college graduate:

Chris, congratulations on your graduation! We know how many years you have been waiting for this day and how hard you have worked to get here. We all admire your perseverance and unwavering focus on your goal.

Congratulations, college graduate!

Your friends in Accounting,
Jessica, Albert, Sumonta, and Nicolas

For someone with a new business:

Hi, Cara. I received the SHRM [Society for Human Resource Management] notice about your presentation this week and realized you have a new business. Well done! I hope it's a great triumph for you.

Your presentation sounds brilliant. If I were in Seattle, I would definitely attend.

Much success to you!
Jake

For someone who has reached a level of prestige:

Dear Donna,

I just did a Google search with an etiquette question, and your site was number 1 in the list of sites. Wow! I was delighted to see that your reputation as an expert has spread.

I poked around on your site and learned a lot. The high quality of your content and your willingness to share your knowledge are very impressive.

Congratulations on building such a positive business and level of success.

Roger Smith

For someone who has published a book:

Hi Cindy,

Congratulations on your new book, *Great Webinars*. I just ordered it online. Can't wait to read your advice and wise words.

I have heard how much blood, sweat, and tears go into birthing a book and just wanted to congratulate you on having done it.

Warm regards,
Carol Morgan

For someone who has been promoted:

Hey, Tina. I just had lunch with some of the women in Sales, and they told me about your promotion. Great news! Congratulations!

You are so deserving of it. Your hard work and smarts have always stood out. You are an asset to the company, and it is terrific that you have been recognized this way—the way it counts.

Just wanted to join those who are cheering for you! Hip hip hurray!

William

For someone you do not know who has been promoted:

Dear Joyce,

I just read RoAnn's announcement about your promotion. Congratulations!

Gizelle Olson is a friend of mine, and she often tells me about the creative work you have been doing in Design. Obviously, other people have noticed your great work too.

Congratulations on moving ahead!

Best,
Deanna Jones

For someone who has bought a new home:

Hi, Cormac. Congratulations on your new home! Uptown is a wonderful neighborhood. I hope you and Debra have many years of happiness in your new place.

Warm wishes,
Suzan

For someone who has announced retirement:

Dear Mr. Han,

Congratulations on your upcoming retirement. I hope you and Mrs. Han will be very happy in this new phase of your lives.

You have been a generous mentor and guide for me as I learned the trade. I am very grateful for the lessons you shared.

Best wishes for a fulfilling retirement,
Adam McLaughlin

The best congratulatory notes communicate in a tone and style that match the relationship. When she graduated from high school and was moving away to attend college, my daughter received this exuberant message from our hair stylist, Lisa Dodge-Johnson:

> Congratulations, Eva! Celebrate a job well done!
>
> This is such an EXCITING TIME. Remember all those "butterflies" you may feel are colored by your thoughts, so when you can, choose to think "I AM SO EXCITED!" (instead of "I'm so scared," etc.). New Orleans is so lucky to get to meet you. Your innate Goodness, Talents, Beauty, and Wisdom, along with your passionate efforts, will be a Gift to the world, especially to all of us who get to share moments with you. May You Be Blessed by God's Grace Forever!
>
> Love and hugs,
> Lisa
>
> P.S. Keep the music flowing!

Like Lisa, you can let loose with all-capital letters and exclamations if you choose to. After all, notes of congratulations are to celebrate something special. Let your writing reflect joy and excitement. This chapter contains 43 exclamation marks!

Personal Reflection

▸ Do you take the time to congratulate others? If so, congratulations! If not, what gets in the way of sending congratulatory messages? Do you want to start a new habit?

Next Step

▸ Review the long list of reasons to send a note of congratulations. Then write one. Enjoy celebrating someone's success and sharing in his or her happiness. Then congratulate yourself for taking action to maintain that business relationship.

CHAPTER 6

Convey Condolences to Connect With Others

When Hurricane Katrina struck the southeastern United States in September 2005, I wanted to do something that would make a difference. Watching the images on TV, the people waiting desperately on the roofs for rescue, the drowning of entire neighborhoods, I wanted to help. Beyond making financial contributions, I ended up writing a blog post to help people write condolences to those who had suffered devastating losses.

To my surprise, that small gesture made a big difference. From that day on, the visits to my blog skyrocketed from just dozens of daily page views to over a thousand views each day, and they continued to rise rapidly.

Blog visitors used search strings such as "writing condolences" and "how to write a sympathy message." With the huge increase in blog traffic, I recognized two facts: (1) Everyone needs to write condolence messages at one time or another, and (2) Most people find the task difficult, nearly impossible.

Do those facts hit you? In the face of sorrow, tragedy, and loss, do you feel you can't find the right words and the ways to put them together?

This chapter will help you with the important task of writing to someone whose life has been changed by loss or suffering. The task is important because for those who have experienced a profound loss, hearing from you is a lifeline. Receiving notes, letters, cards, emails, and calls reduces isolation, loneliness, and helplessness. People who have lost someone or something important need to hear from you.

Should You Send Sympathy Messages in Business Relationships?

If you are wondering whether to send this kind of personal message in a business relationship, the answer is yes! Take the risk. Sending a note or card gives you the opportunity to connect with another human being who is suffering. At the very least, it shows that you care enough to communicate in a difficult time. Your reaching out may establish a memorable bond between you and the person in crisis. In what better way can you nurture a business relationship?

When my business contact Margaret Elwood's father died, I sent her a sympathy card with a handwritten message. Margaret is someone I like very much, but I have met her only twice outside work situations. Here is how she responded to my card:

> Dear Lynn and Michael,
>
> Your sympathy card was timely and very, very helpful to me during difficult days last week. And though I received several notes of condolence through email, I found in my distress that a tangible card I could see on my desk was really much more comforting. Thank you so much.
>
> This week is much better, and though I know that grief takes its own time outside of my control, I am feeling grateful for the years I had with my father and for the time I have with friends like you right now.
>
> Margaret

Although our relationship focuses on work, our personal connection deepened through our exchange of messages about Margaret's father's death.

You write condolence messages because of the pain the other person is feeling. But just thinking about that pain can make you feel awkward and stumbling as a writer. In my survey on business writing and relationships, 28 percent of people said they did not know how to write a condolence message or were not sure they knew how. A larger number of men (37 percent) than women (25 percent) put themselves in this category. Two respondents shared these comments:

> I always have a terrible time with this. Anything I write doesn't sound genuine. I've often just given up and sent nothing.

> It has recently happened [the death of a coworker's family member], and I had no clue how to express sympathy.

Helpful Tips for Writing Condolence Messages

If you feel unsure about how to write this important message, consider these tips to handle the task with confidence and care:

Do not be embarrassed if you can't think of the "right" words. Your goal is not to be perfect but to make a sincere connection with another human being. Write what you feel. Express your care, concern, or understanding. Acknowledge the other person's loss. Even the brief sentence "Words do not suffice" expresses empathy and caring.

Remember that the purpose of this message is to connect with the bereaved. Comfort and support are the reasons for the message—not preaching or gaining converts to your beliefs. If you feel it is appropriate in your situation, you may write, "You are in my prayers." But do not express your beliefs on fate, death, dying, or related spiritual matters (for example, "She is undoubtedly with the Lord now") unless you are *certain* they will comfort the reader. Avoid any comments that may cause discomfort, embarrassment, or defensiveness.

If it will slow you down to send a note or card through the post, send an email or another kind of online message expressing sympathy. If possible, send a note or card through regular mail in addition to the online greeting. Remember Margaret's comment, "Though I received several notes of condolence through email, I found in my distress that a tangible card I could see on my desk was really much more comforting."

It is easy for people to reread cards and notes as they sit quietly and reflect on their loss. Also, sending a card can be easier for you. Printed cards typically include words of comfort, to which you can add your own. But do not wait to find the "perfect" card—you may never find it or get around to mailing it.

Avoid bringing up work-related topics. For example, do not write, "We cannot wait to have you back on the project," which may suggest that you are rushing the individual's period of grieving. Do not include your business card, which suggests you are promoting yourself. If you are worried that the recipient of the card will not recognize your name, include your company name under it.

Sign off with a standard close. People sometimes fret about the way to close a sympathy message, especially if they do not know the recipient well. Below are acceptable closes. If a close doesn't feel appropriate, you may simply sign your name.

Sincerely,
In sympathy,
With sympathy,
In deep sympathy,

Warm regards,
Sincere regards,
With sincere condolences,

When you send a message of condolence, add the date to your calendar. That way you can remember the anniversary with your colleague who lost the family member or friend, if you choose to. You might send a brief note like one of these:

Dear Keina,

At this time of year I remember Sam's passing and think of you. I have been thinking about what a generous, funny man he was and how much you must miss him.

Know that I am thinking of you during this time of remembering.

With warm wishes,
April

⌒

Dear Mr. Robson,

With the holidays upon us, I remember that Jeff died over Christmas break last year. I just wanted you to know that I am thinking of you as you remember and grieve the loss of your loving son.

Sincerely,
Julianne

If you are thinking that it is untruthful to add a date to your calendar and then imply that you remembered it, think again. You remembered to add it to your calendar. Then when your calendar reminded you of the anniversary, you remembered the individuals involved.

Some people prefer to remember happy times rather than sad anniversaries. If you happen to know the birthday or wedding anniversary of someone who has died, you can acknowledge that date with the grieving family member or friend. For example, my father died at age 90. On what would have been his 91st birthday, I received a beautiful card from Hiers-Baxley, the funeral home in Ocala, Florida, that handled all the details of his memorial services. The card prominently showed my father's date of birth and included the message, "On your loved one's birthday, may the happy memories of yesterday be a comfort to you." It was signed by three members of the Hiers-Baxley team. The card acknowledged my father's special day, which I had been thinking about, and it reminded me of the caring way the Hiers-Baxley staff had treated us.

When you have a close business relationship with someone who has experienced a serious loss, take time to check in with the individual and remember the loss. One of my friends lost her husband suddenly to a massive heart attack. Because of my friend's shock and grief, she suspended the violin lessons she had been taking. Two years later she told me, "My violin teacher never checked in to see how I was doing or whether I wanted to start lessons again. It made me feel she did not care, so I decided not to go back to her." Perhaps the teacher had felt awkward about following up, but a brief message—for example, "Just checking in to see how you are doing"—would have indicated that she remembered her student's pain and would have maintained their relationship.

Sample Condolence Messages

Don't avoid sending a sympathy message because you don't know what to say. You will have missed an important opportunity to connect with another human being in a moment of sorrow and loss. Use these examples to adapt to your situations. When you can share a warm story about the individual who has died, share it. You will notice that in some messages the paragraphs are indented. It is standard to indent paragraphs in handwritten notes. In emailed messages, do not indent paragraphs.

Upon the death of a spouse:

Dear Matthew,

We are so sorry about Ellen's death. She was a lovely woman who touched so many lives with her joy and generosity. We miss her deeply already, and we can only imagine the heartbreak you feel.

One of our fondest memories of your dear wife is of the kindness she showed to the refugee family from Rwanda. She treated them like her own family. She involved many of us in that kindness, and we were all better people because of it. Ellen lived her life as a model of grace and goodness. We are very lucky to have known her.

Please accept our deepest sympathy.

Kent and Mary

Upon the death of a parent:

Dear Martha,

Please accept my sincere condolences on the passing of your father. I am so sorry about your loss.

Although I never met your father, I know how much he meant to you. Through your stories of his frugality, his love of nature, and his loving support of you, I feel as though I knew him. I know he was a fine man and that his absence will be felt by many people.

When my father died, it gave me a good feeling to talk with people about him. I would enjoy hearing more about your father and his life if you would like to share memories when we get together. In the meantime, I will be thinking of you and your family.

With deep sympathy,
Joanna

My colleague the late Steve Holtzer sent the email below to his business associate Russ Taylor upon the death of Russ's mother.

> Russ and Margaret,
>
> Like you, let me begin by apologizing for the use of email at this time.
>
> I am so sad to hear the news of the passing of Russ's mom on Friday. Although I never met her, I did have the privilege of hearing Russ speak fondly of her whenever he and I met or talked on the phone.
>
> And even without meeting her, I could tell that she had a very kind heart, for it lives on in Russ. No doubt she was very proud of the son she produced, and rightly so.
>
> If there is anything I can do for you during this time of grief, please let me know.
>
> Steve Holtzer

A year later Steve himself died. That is when Russ shared with me the condolence message Steve had sent him. Clearly, it had made a significant impression on Russ.

Upon a death after a long illness:

> Dear Erik,
>
> Please accept my sincere sympathy on the passing of your brother. Although he suffered for a long time and this moment may seem like a blessing, it is still a grave loss for you. Life is never quite the same when a sibling is no longer present, and I am sorry for the hardship you are experiencing.

I will hold you and your family in my thoughts and prayers as you experience grief and sadness. There are many like me who are thinking of you.

With warm regards,
Linda

Upon the death of a difficult person:

Dear Su,

Please accept my sympathy on the death of your mother. I know she was difficult at times, and no doubt you are experiencing a range of emotions. Nevertheless, the death of someone who has been important in your life always creates an absence. I am very sorry for your loss.

I am keeping you in my thoughts as you move through your bereavement.

With sincere condolences,
Scott

Upon the death of a child:

Dear Dr. and Mrs. Clarke,

All of us in the lab are so sorry about the death of your beautiful daughter. We wish we could find words that would relieve your pain, but we cannot. Losing a child is one of the saddest experiences, and words of true comfort are difficult to find.

Please know that we are thinking of you in your sorrow. You have our sincere condolences.

In sympathy,
Devon, Matt, Yuri, Alex,
Jasmine, Ray, and Terry

In rare instances when you have been informed by an individual of her miscarriage, you may wish to communicate your sympathy in writing:

> Dear Deborah,
>
> I am so very sorry about your miscarriage. From our conversations, I know how excited you and Gary were about conceiving this child. I can only imagine your feelings of loss and disappointment.
>
> If there is anything I can do during this painful time, please tell me.
>
> Nan

Upon a death when you know very little about the situation:

> Dear Monique,
>
> All of us are very sorry to learn that you have experienced a death in your family. Although we do not know the details, we want you to know that we are thinking about you in your bereavement.
>
> Please accept our condolences.
>
> Sincerely,
> The Marketing Team

Upon a death by suicide:

> Dear Neal,
>
> Please accept our sincere sympathy on the tragic death of your brother. We are very sorry that he is no longer with you.
>
> No doubt this awful event has been very disturbing for you, your family, and your friends who knew and loved

David. We are thinking of you and them in this time of loss and bereavement.

If we can help in any way, please let us know.

With sympathy,

Jennifer and Lionel

Upon the death of a beloved pet:

If you have experienced the death of a pet, you know that it can be just as sad as the loss of a human being, sometimes more so. The deep sadness comes from the loss of companionship, loyalty, and unconditional love that a pet gives so enthusiastically. When an employee, coworker, client, or friend loses a beloved pet, send a note of condolence—just as you do when a loved one dies.

Our beautiful English cocker spaniel, Chica, died on her 14th birthday. We were surprised and touched by a sympathy card we received a few days after Chica's death, from the veterinarian, Dr. Hanna Ekström of At Home Vet, who had come to our house to put Chica to sleep (that is, to euthanize her). We were surprised because we had not known the vet until she came to our home that sad day. Yet she took the time to express her condolences in the card:

> You have my deepest sympathy over your recent loss of Chica. I could tell how well loved she was and what a wonderful life she had led.
>
> May you find comfort in your many memories of days shared and of her floating away so peacefully with you all by her side.
>
> Hugs,
>
> Dr. Hanna

We cried just reading the thoughtful words. Yet we deeply appreciated Dr. Hanna's message.

I wrote the email below to friends whose elderly dog had died, then followed it with a sympathy card.

> Dear Tim and Patrick,
>
> I just read your message about Victor's passing. I am so sorry for your loss. In my experience, there is no creature like a dog for unconditional love, enthusiasm, zest for playing, and unending expectation of life's next treat. I imagine that his place in your home, your daily routines, and—of course—your hearts will long seem empty.
>
> I will remember Victor's beautiful bows and his wandering sniffs at picnics. I will also remember how dear he was to you.
>
> Please accept my deep sympathy. I will be thinking of you in your sorrow.
>
> Lynn

Because I had met Victor many times, I was able to write something about my experience of him. But even if you have never met a customer's, boss's, or vendor's pet, you can write notes like these:

> Dear Mandi,
>
> Please accept my sympathy on the death of your dear companion, Isis. I know the big role she played in your life, and I am very sorry that she is no longer with you. I will be thinking of you as you grieve the loss of your beloved cat.
>
> Sincerely,
> Robin

> Dear Julie,
>
> We were so sorry to hear that Sunny died in an accident. From the many photos that have decorated your

desktop, we know she was a light in your life, and we realize that you will miss her deeply. Please accept our condolences on your sad and sudden loss. We are thinking of you.

In sympathy,
Shelly and Annie

Dear James,

I was saddened to hear the news that Ernie's life ended last week. Although I didn't know your pooch, I know how much you cared about him, and I know you will miss him deeply after your many years together. Please accept my sincere sympathy on the passing of your dear friend.

Dan

Upon an illness or injury:

A condolence message is a fitting, thoughtful gesture anytime someone experiences a serious blow or setback.

Dear Mr. Graham,

Joan told me today about your hospital stay and that you are now at home recuperating. I was very sorry to learn of your accident and the injury to your back. Please accept my condolences and warm wishes for your healing.

I hope that as each day passes you will continue to feel better. Know that I am thinking of you as you rest and heal.

Sincerely,
Kay Brooks

Dear Nelly,

Thank you for including me in the email you sent in which you let us know about your treatment for cancer. I am sorry to learn of your illness.

Please forget all about work and focus completely on your healing. All of us will be sending you positive, healthy energy and lots of smiles and virtual hugs.

Get well soon!

Tiffany

Upon an illness or impending death of a colleague's relative:

A woman whom I will call Diana works as a consultant. Diana told me about the time in which her mother was dying. Because of all that was involved in her mother's illness and care, Diana had to postpone several meetings with clients. She explained to each client the reason for the postponement, and all of them replied with appropriate expressions of sympathy and understanding—all except one. He wrote back something like this: "Okay, just let me know when you are back in business. We need to finish the project this quarter." Stunned by the man's insensitivity, Diana decided she would never work with him again.

Don't come across like Diana's inconsiderate client. If an associate is dealing with the challenges of ailing relatives, send a message like one of these emails:

Hi Diana,

Thank you for letting me know about your situation. I am so sorry your mother is seriously ill. I hope the next days and weeks go as well as possible for you, your mother, and your entire family.

I understand your need to put our project on hold. Please take the time you need, and let me know when you can resume our work together.

Edward

Hello, Emmett. So sorry to hear about your daughter! I will keep all of you in my thoughts as you deal with this very difficult situation.

Please stay in touch and let me know if I can be of any assistance.

Best regards,
Amanda

If the project simply cannot wait, express sympathy and understanding before jumping into work details:

Dear Ahmad,

I am very sorry to learn that your father has entered hospice care. I can imagine what a strain this situation puts on you and your family. Please accept my sympathy.

Because we are under a short deadline, I hope it is acceptable to you if I speak with Evan about getting someone to jump in to assist in your role. I trust that knowing the project is moving forward will help you focus on your father's needs and your own.

I will be thinking of you and your father.

Best wishes,
Leo

Upon unexpected job loss:

> Re: Bad News About Your Job
>
> Nadia,
>
> I just learned from Aruna what happened at XYZ. I am so sorry about your job! The news is a shock to me. I can't even imagine how you feel.
>
> As soon as you are ready to, please call me and let me know what I can do to help you. I will contact you again soon to see when you want to meet for coffee or a walk.
>
> Yours,
> Fabiana

> Re: News About Your Leaving XYZ
>
> Hello, Wayne
>
> Thanks for letting me know what happened. From what you described, I am guessing you were not surprised by the news. Still, losing a job is a colossal change. You have my sympathy.
>
> If I can help in any way—introductions, resume review, whatever—just let me know.
>
> Stay in touch—and I'll do the same.
>
> Faazaz

When Natural Disasters Upset or Ruin Lives

Natural disasters touch many people, some more deeply than others. People may lose or be separated from loved ones. Their homes or businesses may be destroyed. Their future may be turned upside down in one way or another.

In early 2009 Australians experienced destructive, tragic bushfires. A blog reader named Fionna wrote to me asking for help to write a condolence message to friends:

> I want to send a card to friends who lost their home in the recent bushfires in Victoria. Luckily they were away when the fires hit, but with the loss of their home and its contents and the damage to the community, I would like to commiserate with them. Any ideas on what to write?

I had many ideas for Fionna because of the condolence messages I had started writing when Hurricane Katrina hit the southeastern United States. I created the examples below for victims of the bushfires, of Hurricane Katrina, of the earthquake and tsunami that devastated Japan in 2011, and of Superstorm Sandy, which crippled New York-New Jersey and other coastal areas in 2012. You can adapt them for similar natural disasters.

For Fionna to send to friends who lost their home and community:

> Dear Simon and Samantha,
>
> I am so terribly sorry about the loss of your home and the devastation of your lovely community. You have been in my thoughts since the blaze struck. I was relieved knowing you were away from home, but I share your sorrow in all that you have lost.
>
> Please know that I am thinking of you in your time of sadness and loss.
>
> Fionna

For someone whose family member died in the bushfires:

Dear Stephen,

Please accept my condolences on the death of your brother Nigel. His sudden death in the bushfires is tragic and heartbreaking. We all wish we could undo what happened and bring him back as his funny, wisecracking self. The world is a lesser place without Nigel in it.

I wish I had words that could make your pain less. At least you know my thoughts and prayers are with you and your family as you grieve.

In sympathy,
Carl

For someone who suffered because of a hurricane; easily adaptable to other situations:

Dear Betty,

I am so sorry about the heartbreaking losses you have experienced through the hurricane. Please accept my deepest sympathy.

As you move through the difficult days and weeks ahead, you will be present in my thoughts. If there is anything I can do to ease your loss, please let me know. I would be grateful for the opportunity to help you.

With sincere sympathy,
Rene

For someone whose business and coworkers have suffered:

Dear Mansour,

We are deeply sorry to learn about your losses caused by the hurricane and its terrible aftermath. Please know that we are all thinking about you and your coworkers as you piece together your lives and your work.

You have our sincere condolences.

Adam and Vincent

For someone whose plans have been crushed:

Dear Mitch,

Talking with Estrella, I learned about how the hurricane has upset your plans for retirement. I am very sorry this happened! I know it must be extremely difficult for you.

I simply want you to know I am thinking of you. I wish you the best possible outcome.

Sincerely,
Jim Downs

For victims of a huge storm:

Hello, Warren. I just learned from Brittany that your cottage on the Jersey Shore was wiped out in last week's storm. Please accept my sympathy on your loss.

As someone who was lucky enough to have been your guest, I know how much fun you and your family shared in that bungalow and how many good memories you must have. I am very sad that the cottage is gone.

You are in my thoughts.

Linda

Kathleen,

How sad I am to learn that your lovely Twinkles was lost in the storm! I know how you treasure that dog, and I can imagine that the lack of knowing what happened to her is extremely painful.

I am sincerely sorry for both you and Twinkles.

Warmest wishes,
Lisa

⌒

Dear Rhonda,

Please accept my sympathy on the death of your wonderful husband. I am so very sorry about the terrible accident that took his life. The fact that Frank died in an attempt to save others illustrates the courage and love that filled him.

I am keeping you in my thoughts and prayers as you grieve this deep loss.

With sympathy,
Marie

For anyone who has experienced serious loss:

Dear Quinn,

Words cannot express how sorry we are about the recent tragic events that have touched you so deeply. Your loss is huge. We can only imagine the hurt you feel.

We want you to know that you are in our thoughts and prayers. Please accept our condolences and our hopes for your healing and renewal.

With sympathy,
Thomas and Ashley

For people in Japan who suffered the earthquake and tsunami:

If you need to write across cultures, the examples that follow may be helpful. They primarily use short sentences and literal language to communicate effectively across the language barrier. To match the Japanese focus on the group rather than the individual, the notes mention the community and the country. I intended the messages to be restrained and dignified rather than flamboyant and familiar.

Dear Shinichi,

As I watch my TV and see the snow falling in northern Japan, I think deeply of you and the struggles your country is facing. I am touched by the bravery, collaboration, and patience of the Japanese people of all ages.

It is very sad that the earthquake destroyed your school. I understand how important your school is to the members of your community.

I hope that you and the people in your community will be able to obtain food, water, and all necessities. I also hope that your spirits will remain positive as you work to reconstruct your society.

With all good wishes,
Barbara Allen

Dear Mr. Suzuki,

Thank you for writing to us. We are thinking of you, your coworkers, your families, and your community as you work to recover from the tragedy of the earthquake and tsunami. We are grateful that your office building in Tokyo was not affected. Yet we recognize that everyone in Japan has been affected profoundly by the recent events.

You are in our thoughts as you strive to recover and rebuild your beautiful country. We wish you strength, peace, and safety in the days and months ahead.

Sincerely,
Carl and Suzanne Gray

Build Relationships in Difficult Times

When you are wondering what you can do to help a business associate who is experiencing a sad loss, stop wondering: Send a sympathy message. For those who receive them, cards and messages of sympathy and condolence provide an essential link with other people in a time of loss and need. Provide that link. Be that lifeline. Establish a strong, possibly lasting bond between a client, customer, or coworker and yourself.

Personal Reflection

 ▸ A respondent in my survey wrote, "It is very touching when someone (anyone) takes the time to acknowledge your pain." Do you feel comfortable acknowledging loss and pain in a condolence message to a business associate? What might you do to reduce any discomfort?

Next Step

 ▸ Prepare yourself for occasions that require a message of condolence by purchasing several sympathy cards and keeping them with your letterhead or notepaper. A card with a brief, tasteful message makes your task easier. You can write a sincere sentence or two, then sign and send the card.

CHAPTER 7

Personal Introductions:
Pave the Way to New Relationships

R on Scott estimates that he has introduced more than 14,000 people in the past 20 years. That's a conservative number, he says. Ron, who works as an independent leadership and organizational development consultant in the Seattle area, calculates that he introduces more than 700 business people each year, virtually all through email. Having known Ron and benefited from his business matchmaking for more than 20 years, I find his figures credible.

You can see Ron's process at work in the following email, which he sent to Deb Arnold and me.

Subject: Introduction

Lynn and Deb, I am pleased to introduce you two.

Lynn, Deb Arnold is a Seattle-based communication consultant. Deb guides organizations to create and deliver internal communications that help achieve enterprise and department goals more effectively and efficiently. Thinking there is high potential for mutual benefit in you two meeting, I suggested that she call you to schedule an appointment. Thanks in advance for meeting with Deb.

Deb, Lynn Gaertner-Johnston is Founder, Syntax Training, a business writing training firm. Her office phone number is [number].

Best regards,
Ron

Ronald G. Scott
Scott Associates

Shortly after we received Ron's message, Deb and I exchanged emails to set up a meeting. Since our first meeting, she and I have had lunch many times. We have called and emailed each other for business advice. She has been a guest speaker in my communications classes in the MBA program at University of Washington–Bothell, and I have attended her choir concerts. Although our relationship focuses more on our businesses than our personal lives, we consider each other good, trusted friends.

We have Ron Scott to thank for our rewarding relationship.

Why Take the Time to Introduce Others?

With his 14,000-plus introductions, Ron Scott is a master of paving the way for others to create business relationships. Why does he do it? Ron views introducing people almost as a way of tithing, a way of giving back to the business community. "I like giving back to a business world that has been so good to me," he says, "by introducing people whose lives I believe will be enriched in their meeting."

Although Ron emphasizes giving back and experiencing personal fulfillment, the benefits go beyond good feelings. Twenty-five years after making an introduction that led a woman named Jennifer to a productive career move, Ron got a call from Jennifer. She was planning to retire, and one of her last acts before retiring was to recommend a consultant for an important project at her firm. That consultant was Ron. In the project, he earned $175,000.

Ron emphasizes that only occasionally is there such a direct return to him for connecting people. But I'm betting the less direct returns are huge. Ron has no website, blog, or Facebook page, and he doesn't tweet. He gets all of his consulting and coaching assignments through personal referrals, and his work plate is as full as he wants it to be.

Referrals come not only from doing excellent work, but also from the high regard of one's associates. Ron has earned high regard over the years, in part because of his willingness to help others. He acknowledges that link: "Connecting people demonstrates that I am not just living this life for myself. I am of service to my community. Obviously, I get benefit from that." Ron's planting the seeds of relationships for others is part of building and maintaining his professional network.

The subtitle of this book is "How to Build Great Work Relationships One Message at a Time." As a first step in building relationships, introductions spark interest, enthusiasm, and often generosity. This chapter shows you how to add introductions to your writing repertoire.

Choosing People to Introduce

It is difficult to imagine introducing 14,000 people, so why not start with just two people you know who do not know each other? Think about ones who have, as Ron says, "matching or complementary values, beliefs, and behaviors." Do they have common interests and goals? Are they at a similar place in their personal lives or careers?

Think about how a business relationship might benefit the two people. Could one offer the other advice on starting a business or restarting a career? Is one of them in a place to mentor the other or to make further introductions? Could one of them share insights on how to thrive in a new city or industry? Is one looking to hire an employee or contractor, and the other seems like a possible match?

Ron Scott looks for a match in which both people will leave the meeting thinking, "Wow! I am glad I met that person." As he explains,

"They may be saying *wow* for both personal and professional reasons, or one of the two." Incidentally, Ron has made three networking introductions that led to marriage.

Making the Connection

You can bring people together by email, Facebook, LinkedIn, or other online services that help you share messages and contact information. Jerry Schlagenhauf, a career consultant in the Seattle area, used the email below to introduce two of his career transition clients. Because he has a coaching role with them and knows them both well, he made very specific suggestions about how they could benefit from meeting. (Details have been disguised.)

Subject: You two need to meet each other!

Greetings, Angela and Ben.

There are numerous reasons that you should connect, and soon:

1. You probably will want to explore your experiences in Chicago and at the U of C.

2. You have a passion for serving and contributing to community justice and understanding.

3. You have professional skills and professional connections that will be mutually beneficial.

Angela has exceptional credentials and experience, with 11 years in broad-based anti-bias curriculum models and multiculturalism. She fervently desires to assist decision makers to achieve cultural competencies that translate into improvements in education, training and access to resources for all. She is the Program Manager for the XYZ Association.

Ben has a professional background in senior public affairs & government affairs, public policy, and as an attorney. He is currently the public policy director at ABC Medical

Center. Ben has a formidable networking capacity in the state of Washington.

Contact information:
Angela—[phone & email]
Ben—[phone & email]

Angela, ask Ben about the LMNOP School (and the organizations to which you have already applied).

Ben, discuss LinkedIn with Angela.

Have a great meeting!

Jerry
The Schlagenhauf Group

That detailed message was an introduction of two people in career transition. This email introduces two people who work at the same company:

Subject: Susan, Meet Ralph; Ralph, Meet Susan

I am introducing you two because I think you would enjoy meeting and sharing your know-how.

Susan, Ralph is an archivist in our SF office. He moved there from Seattle four years ago and can share lots of insights about the SF team and the city. He is a foodie and a baseball junkie.

Ralph, Susan moves from Portland to SF next month. She has been with us seven years as a database expert. I bet she can share wisdom to help with your new project. Susan is excited about her move into the big leagues of the company and baseball. Go Giants!

You now have each other's addresses. You can take it from here.

David

Tips for Making Introductions

Apply these tips to make flawless introductions that your contacts will welcome:

Have one or more reasons for making each introduction. Mention the reasons in your email. That information will inspire the individuals to communicate. Your reasons may be as a simple as Ron's "thinking there is high potential for mutual benefit in you two meeting."

Share a few details that will jump-start the connection. Jerry's email included lots of suggestions to get Angela and Ben talking. David's email includes information about hobbies, which can help start a conversation between Susan and Ralph.

Ask permission from each party before making the introduction unless you know that the individuals are open to introductions. Asking shows respect and an awareness of people's privacy needs.

Include phone numbers if you are certain that sharing them is acceptable to the people involved. Otherwise, just use email, which reveals both people's email addresses.

Avoid making introductions to the same person continually unless he or she encourages you to do so. For example, it would not be wise for David to introduce Ralph repeatedly to San Francisco newbies.

Do not introduce someone you are not proud to present. In other words, avoid introducing a jerk. If you find a person arrogant and pushy, assume others will agree. Forego making the introduction, even if the individual requests one.

Responding to Introductions

If you have been introduced by email, you may take the next step by email or phone. When Ron Scott introduced me to Pete Busacca, an expert in sales and sales strategy, Pete promptly sent this email:

> Dear Ron and Lynn,
>
> Ron, thank you for the introduction and for the kind words.
>
> Lynn, I look forward to meeting you. You and Michael have an intriguing website, and I am so curious how you went from "beautiful" Peoria, Illinois, through South Bend, to find yourself here in the drizzly Northwest.
>
> I wonder if we might get together over a cup of coffee in the next week or two. Would you be available to meet this Friday around midmorning?
>
> If not, please suggest some other dates and times that might work for you. Of course, Michael is welcome to join us.
>
> Thanks, and I so look forward to meeting you.
>
> Best regards,
> Pete Busacca

Pete's email is first-rate. In it, he showed that he had done his homework: He had visited our company website and read our bios. He expressed curiosity about me. Also, he took the initiative to suggest a date and time to meet. After reading his email, I was eager to meet Pete, and we scheduled on the Friday morning he suggested. Success! We both widened our professional circles, thanks to Ron Scott.

Introducing an Individual to a Group

Just as 1-to-1 introductions benefit both people, introducing someone to a group or to the entire company has great benefits for everyone. Consider this email example:

Subject: Welcome Pat Nielsen to Sales

I am pleased to announce that Pat Nielsen will join the Sales group as Sales Assistant on Monday, April 11. Her role is to help us produce outstanding proposals, presentations, web demos, and related materials and events. She reports to Stephanie Brown.

Pat's experience is a terrific fit for the job. She comes to us from XYZ Company, where she worked first in retail sales and then as a store event coordinator. Before working full time, she earned her bachelor's degree in business from the University of Washington. She loves to kayak, hike, and take nature photographs. She did all three on a recent trip to Maui.

If you are at headquarters, stop by Pat's desk on the 4th floor and introduce yourself to her. You can also reach her at Ext. 2003 and pat.nielsen@ourcompany.com.

Bill Richards
Director of Sales

Benefit to the Sales group: Everyone who reads the message will learn a lot—who Pat is, what her role in Sales will be, when she starts, whom she reports to, why she was hired, who she is outside work, how she can be reached, and how to welcome her. People will feel they already know her.

Benefit to Pat: When she reads the email from the Director of Sales introducing her to the group, she is likely to learn how important she is to the team and to feel terrific, especially when people stop by to say hello.

Benefit to everyone: The email will probably inspire Pat to feel that she made the correct choice when she accepted the job. In turn, that feeling will inspire her performance.

Introducing new employees is a step that often gets overlooked, except at the highest job levels. But overlooking introductions can leave new employees feeling alone and anonymous, and it can stifle their ability to contribute and grow.

Tips for Making Introductions to a Group

Follow these tips to write introductions that ignite excellent work relationships:

Include basic information: the new person's name, role, reporting relationship, relevant background and education, and contact information. Adding a personal detail, such as Pat's specific interests in the outdoors, will enrich the introduction and help employees relate to the new hire.

Be consistent about introductions. If you introduce the senior manager, introduce the receptionist. You may use fewer details for the receptionist because his or her career may be shorter and responsibilities narrower. Nevertheless, introduce everyone. Even in economic downturns when people are being laid off, new employees should be welcomed with an introduction.

Decide on the appropriate audience for the introduction. You may choose to introduce the new employee to your department, your division, or the people in your building. If your company is small (100 people or fewer), you may write to everyone. Think about who is likely to interact with the new employee. Those people will need and want the introduction.

Choose a communication medium that makes sense for your company. It may be email, a newsletter article, or a posting on your intranet.

Let the individual know that you will publish the introduction, and give him or her a chance to approve the content. For example, in the message introducing Pat to Sales, the writer or his assistant might have asked Pat's permission to mention her hobbies and her recent trip to Maui.

Do not use sarcasm in your introduction, and be very cautious with humor. Avoid any content that could detract from the positive tone.

Introducing Yourself: Reintroductions

You cannot always have an intermediary make introductions for you, and you don't always need one. Often you can introduce or reintroduce yourself. You can take your own steps to launch business relationships.

You may want to reintroduce yourself after meeting at a networking or professional event or after not seeing someone for a long time. Reintroductions are easier than introducing yourself for the first time. The person has already met you in one way or another, and you can build on that meeting.

Alexandra, a reader of my Business Writing blog, asked me what to write in a follow-up email to people she meets at important meetings. She explained that at the meetings, she often talks to potential clients or partners for only a few minutes, and she would like to take those brief contacts to the next level. She asked what she can say to potential clients or partners in a follow-up email that will make a good impression.

Alexandra had a specific business purpose for her desire to make follow-up contact. Even without a specific purpose, though, it is valuable for most business people to nurture the brief professional contacts that seem to have potential. With nurturing, those contacts may develop into business relationships, not just names in a contact list.

Here are things Alexandra and you can do in a follow-up email:

- Mention the meeting and the conversation.
- Refer to something specific that came up in the conversation, especially a mutual interest.
- Suggest a way to continue the conversation.
- If possible, attach an article or include a useful link that will please the other person (not a hard-selling piece).
- Mention a next step you will take, or ask the other person to respond.

The following examples, whose details are all fictional, show how to follow up in an email after making a good in-person connection with someone.

Subject: Oyster Accompaniments and Meeting in DC

Hi Mary,

What fun it was to meet you last week at the conference! Inspired by our indulging our love of oysters, I have attached my special recipe for oyster accompaniments. My secret ingredient may surprise you.

I would enjoy having lunch or coffee with you when I'm in Washington the first week in October. If you will be available, I would like to learn more about your export business and share information about our company.

When my schedule is firm, I will write to invite you.

Best,
Katia Strauss

Subject: Pleasure to Meet You and Discuss Global Health

Dear Professor Schamb,

It was a pleasure talking with you at the Health Initiatives meeting. I enjoyed learning about your work investigating global health programs. Since we talked, I read the research paper you recommended. I found the data disturbing, just as you had predicted.

You expressed an interest in learning more about my work with refugees on the Thai-Burmese border, and it would be my pleasure to tell you about it. I will let you know when I will be in Cambridge again, and perhaps we can schedule a meeting. You may also be interested in my blog, in which I wrote about daily life in the camps. Here is the link: [link].

I will write or call you to request a meeting.

Sincerely,
Mona Lane

Subject: Eating Well and Working in Vancouver

Nicolai, it was great to meet you at the networking social yesterday. Thank you for sharing information about the best Chinese restaurants in the area. I intend to try the Shanghai Restaurant this weekend.

I would appreciate learning more about how you established your business in Vancouver. Would you be willing to meet for lunch or coffee? I will call you next week to invite you.

It was a pleasure meeting you.

Jeffrey Holmes

Subject: Customer Evangelism—Our Favorite Subject

Hi, Waleed. I appreciated talking with you about customer evangelism at the gathering last night. Based on our conversation, I would say we have a lot of the same concerns, and I'd like to stay in touch. Despite our different industries, we face the same challenges. Maybe we can share solutions.

Attached is an article I wrote about the topic. Let me know if you agree with my premise.

If you are going to be in New York, please tell me and we can schedule a meal. I will let you know when I will be in Atlanta.

Best,
Muhammad

Subject: Scheduling Time to Discuss Business in Romania

Hi Renee!

It was terrific to meet you last week at the symposium. Thanks for recommending *Quiet*. I bought it yesterday and can't wait to learn about my introverted colleagues!

You said you would like to find out more about investment opportunities in Romania. I would love to talk with you about the possibilities. Since you will be traveling for the rest of this month, would you like to schedule a conversation early next month?

I look forward to talking with you again. Just let me know a day and time that suit your schedule.

Donna

When You Do Not Get a Response

At times your efforts to reach out won't get a response. When you do not receive a reply, you can take another step. For example, let's say Donna did not receive a reply from Renee to her email about scheduling time to discuss investment opportunities in Romania. Donna might take one of these two steps:

1. Write a brief follow-up email in which she forwards or attaches her original message. That email might simply say: "Hi, Renee. I am betting your heavy travel schedule is winding down now. Do you want to schedule a meeting to discuss investment opportunities in Romania? Please let me know a good day and time." (Better yet, Donna could suggest several dates and times and ask Renee to let her know which is best.)

2. Call Renee and leave a message similar to the one above.

If Donna still does not hear from Renee, she may wait a month and then make a final try. She cannot know whether Renee is uninterested, extremely busy, or not responding for another reason.

On September 14, 2011, I received an email from Ron Scott introducing me to a Seattle-based coach named Rachel Salzberg. On that same day, Rachel emailed me. I scheduled a coffee date with her but had to cancel because of a family situation that required travel. I let Rachel know that I would get in touch with her when my schedule lightened. It was not until the following summer that I contacted her again! Rachel and I met over coffee, exchanged many helpful ideas, and made an excellent connection. Moral of the story: Do not assume that someone's delay in responding or scheduling means a lack of interest in meeting you. Timing can be everything.

Not every effort leads to a blossoming business relationship. I received an email from a young man I will call Thomas, who was disappointed by a lack of response to his request for a meeting. Thomas wrote to me, in part:

> I am about to kick-start my career after graduating in finance, and I've always realized that contacts are very, very important. Hence, I would like to seek a few words of advice on following up on new contacts.
>
> Recently, I met a person who would serve me well as a business mentor, and I wish to get to know him to share ideas and learn from him. After a quick handshake meeting for the first time at a conference, I took the initiative to text him to establish a relationship the next day. However, he did not reply to my offer to meet and have a more serious conversation. May I know what I did wrong and what I should have done in this case? What should I do now to proceed? I would appreciate your insights as to what made him not respond to my approach.

Many busy professionals guard their time carefully. They weigh each request to determine whether the prospective relationship will be rewarding for them and whether they have time for it. Thomas's request may have been unsuccessful for several reasons:

- When he met his potential mentor, they did not make a meaningful connection. Thomas said it was only a "quick handshake meeting," which is too quick an encounter on which to build. It is possible the mentor could not even remember meeting Thomas.
- Thomas texted the mentor to make a connection. His message was probably short and unremarkable. If Thomas put little effort into his message, it would be unusual for it to spark a reply.
- Thomas's wanting the individual to "serve me well as a business mentor" shows the two men at different places in their careers. Only if Thomas clearly communicated a reason for the other man to want to get to know him and mentor him would the other man respond positively. Most successful relationships are complementary, not with one person "serving" the other.

Thomas asked me what he should do now to proceed. One possibility is to find a mutual business contact—someone like Ron Scott—to pave the way with an introduction. The other is to take time himself to write a more complete, polished introduction than a text message.

Introducing Yourself to Strangers

When you introduce yourself to people with whom you have no previous connection, you need to establish one. That happens by sharing information about yourself and making a logical connection to the other person.

I received the following email of introduction (disguised) from a stranger. What was missing from the message?

Subject: Networking Introduction

Hi. I'm a former Sun reporter who was laid off in May when the paper went online-only. I'm looking for the best fit in the occupational arena for my skills and experience. Lizzie Blake of XYZ Company suggested I talk to you.

I'd like to meet with you for 20–30 minutes, at a time and place of your convenience—coffee, drinks, just talk, whatever. No specific agenda—I just want your perspective.

Thanks.

John Black [phone number]

John's clear, concise message included a bit of information about himself and a referral from someone I knew. The piece that was missing was any tie to me. The message was so generic that it could have been sent to anyone—at least anyone who knew our mutual contact. If the email had not mentioned someone I knew, I would have deleted it. Instead, I replied with two words: "Why me?"

John wrote back and explained why:

> To draw on my experience as a writer and editor to teach writing, maybe targeting business people who want to learn to write more effectively in a time when they may be called on to write more (emails, blogs, internal websites, etc.). From a look at your website, it seems like that's your field—so I would hope to learn more about it, and the opportunities it presents, from you.

Once I understood why John wanted to meet *me*—and not just anyone with a job—I was happy to schedule time and share ideas with him.

When you introduce yourself to strangers, especially when writing to request a professional favor, as John was, be sure to include specific information that helps readers understand why the connection makes sense. This step does not have to slow you down. If John had simply greeted me by name and included a complimentary sentence about my work, blog, or website, I would have replied, "Sure!" instead of "Why me?"

Consider this sample email introduction and request:

> Subject: Request Regarding Music Business Internships
>
> Dear Mr. Wilson,
>
> My neighbor Debra Young suggested I write to you. She thought you might be willing to share your advice on finding an internship in the music business. I am graduating from Ballard High School, and I am starting the music business program at California State University in Northridge (CSUN) in the fall. Until then, I am available for a few weeks this summer and would like to get some industry experience.
>
> I have good computer skills, and I am open to lots of experiences. I would prefer a paid internship, but I am open to some volunteering too. I live in Seattle.
>
> Would you be willing to talk with me on the phone or meet with me? My cell number is [number], and you can text or email me. Thank you!
>
> Dwight Bell

Dwight's polite introduction includes these parts:

- A referral from someone Mr. Wilson presumably knows
- A reason for the message
- A self-introduction, including what Dwight is looking for
- A specific request
- Contact information

If Dwight did not know someone who could introduce or refer him to Mr. Wilson, he might have opened this way:

> Dear Mr. Wilson,
>
> In research on the Internet, I learned that you are a local expert in the music business. You have worked on Folklife, Bumbershoot, and other music festivals. I am writing to you as someone who might be willing to share your advice on finding an internship in the music business. . . .

When you email a stranger to introduce yourself, be clear about your reason for writing. Do you want advice from the other person? Would you like an answer to a question? Would you like to have coffee to discuss a business challenge? Know what you want so you can make your request clear.

Too often people introducing themselves to strangers put very little effort into the message. For example, they send this low-effort standard request for a connection on LinkedIn: "I'd like to add you to my professional network on LinkedIn." The recipient of this invitation from a stranger has little or no idea why the stranger wants to make a connection or why the recipient might want one. Currently, the recipient's only choice on the free version of LinkedIn is to accept or ignore the request. Rather than connecting with strangers about whom they know nothing, many people do nothing.

Yes, the stranger's first and last names are included with the request. The recipient could do an Internet search or even a LinkedIn search to try to find out something about him or her. But why do that work without a good reason to connect with someone?

If you want to connect with a stranger professionally, write your request so that the other person will feel positive about connecting with you. Your introduction need not be elaborate. Consider this example, which fits within LinkedIn's length restrictions:

> Hello Leslie.
>
> I need to institute 360 feedback at our hospital. According to your profile, you have plenty of experience with 360 in health care. May I connect with you about best practices? In return, I'd be happy to share info on our innovative onboarding program.
>
> Jeni Smith [Title, Hospital name]

The request makes it clear what the individuals have in common (their human resources roles in health care) and how the individuals may mutually benefit from the connection. Such a specific request usually wins acceptance.

Introducing Yourself in Business Support Groups and Forums

If you participate in online or in-person groups designed to help you professionally, your introduction to the other members can help you kindle valuable business relationships. Typically an effective introduction lets people know who you are, what you seek, and what you have to offer.

In the following message, Caroline Grimm introduced herself online to the Book Authors Circle, a support group to help authors write and publish successfully, run by Susan Daffron.

> My name is Caroline Grimm. I live in the Great State of Maine, where I spend a lot of time shoveling snow. It's a hobby I'm looking forward to giving up soon.
>
> Since I was a kid, I've been writing. I made up stories for my younger brother and sisters to entertain them or comfort them. When I was in junior high school, I spent

my summers researching various topics (composers, poets, etc.) and then wrote research papers on my findings. Did I mention it was summer vacation? Clearly, I needed to get outside more.

I'm the author of two business books: *Stop the Cash Flow Roller Coaster, I Want to Get Off!* and *Strength in Numbers: The Entrepreneur's Field Guide to Small Business Finances.* I've written a number of business-related articles.

I'm working on my third book: *The Small Church Survival Guide,* based on a campaign I spearheaded to keep my childhood church from closing. The goal is to have that done by November of 2009 (how's that going?). [Caroline was writing this introduction in 2011.]

I have an unusual relationship with a church mouse named Perley. He writes stories, and I help him compile them into books. He has two books published: *Dear Church Folks . . . Letters from Perley* and *God's Own Mouse . . . More Letters from Perley.* He is working on his third book, which I think will be published by the end of this year. Susan was kind enough to let Perley join the Book Authors Circle for free.

I'm also working on a novel based on the real-life diary of a young woman who lived in my town. It takes place between the years 1857 and 1862. I call her a cross between Jane Austen and Scarlett O'Hara. Fascinating story of a very difficult time in our history.

Looking forward to meeting everyone and supporting each other's goals and progress!

Caroline

Caroline Grimm, MBA
Author of *Stop the Cash Flow Roller Coaster, I Want to Get Off!*
www.CashFlowRollerCoaster.com

Like every good introduction, Caroline's is tailored to her audience—in her case, other authors. Her introduction would be very different if she were writing to a group of Maine entrepreneurs or to church members wanting to keep their church doors open. She included enough content to give new group members a good sense of who she is and what she has to offer the group. Her introduction sparkles with evidence of her wit and her comical self-deprecation.

Compare the introduction below of Deb Arnold, whom I mentioned earlier in this chapter. Deb posted her introduction on the online discussion forum of Marcia Yudkin's Marketing for More program.

> Hello to all,
>
> I'm an entrepreneur for the second time around (taking a break to go to business school and work in corporate America). With 20+ years of experience in marketing communications, I specialize in internal communications for large companies and have niche specialization in helping companies apply for and win industry awards. It's with this expertise that I hope to build my "information empire," or at least a modest jurisdiction.
>
> Born in the Midwest and raised in upstate New York, I have also lived in New York City, Jerusalem, Tel Aviv, and Madrid. Now in Seattle, I enjoy travel, art, music, and nurturing my inner outdoors person.
>
> Thanks in advance for your insights and wisdom.
>
> Deb

Like Caroline, Deb offers specific information that makes her unique in the reader's mind, for example, her niche specialization. Her 20 years of experience show that she has something to offer the group, yet she welcomes the insights of the other participants in the forum. It's a strong, yet modest introduction.

Tips for Introducing Yourself to a Group in Writing

When you have the opportunity to build relationships in an online support group or forum, apply these tips to your introduction:

Share information about your professional experience. In a professional introduction, that is what people expect from you.

Leave out irrelevant information, or people may focus on it instead of what you really want them to know. For example, if you were introducing yourself as a new member of a professional chefs' group, you would leave out your master's degree in religious studies—unless it tied to your cooking expertise.

Share at least one detail about your personal life that others can relate to, for example, Caroline's shoveling snow in Maine, and Deb's living in Jerusalem and Tel Aviv. Make it specific enough to be memorable or meaningful. For example, rather than "I love sports," say, "You can find me on the tennis court or the golf course every week." Instead of, "My hobby is spending time with my family," say, "My hobby is keeping up with my 5-year-old twin boys."

Don't share too much. Even if you have had a 30-year career, people will normally take just a minute to read your introduction. Limit it to one double-spaced page or a large screen. Much less than that can do the job and be appealing. Remember: If you want to build relationships, you need to come across as a person—not as a resume recitation.

Avoid bragging. To share accomplishments without coming across as haughty, use language such as "I was gratified to" or "I had the good fortune to." Or use Caroline Grimm's approach, interjecting one or two self-effacing comments among your successes.

Responding to the Introductions of Others

To help launch business relationships, take time to respond to other people's introductions. Kathy Goughenour, another entrepreneur participating in the Marketing for More (MfM) program, responded to Deb Arnold's introduction this way:

> Deb,
>
> You are a world traveler! It sounds like you've had an exciting life. As a fellow escapee from the corporate world, I applaud you for taking the plunge and jumping back into the entrepreneurial pool. I look forward to getting to know you better.
>
> Welcome to MfM!
>
> Kathy Goughenour
> Become a VA or Hire a VA
> www.expertVAtraining.com

Even though Kathy's reply is short, it does exactly what it needs to do: acknowledge Deb's introduction and create a connection between them. Kathy makes that connection by mentioning something they have in common, being "escapees from the corporate world."

"I Am Pleased to Introduce . . ."

Whose introduction will you write? Do you want to introduce two individuals who have much in common? Will you announce a new employee to your organization? Perhaps you will introduce yourself to a professional group or to an individual in your community or across the globe. Whether you introduce yourself or other people, you are quite likely to benefit from the good will you create. Why not write an introduction today?

Personal Reflection

> ▶ Have you ever introduced people or yourself in a written message? If so, how did you benefit from the introduction? If not, how might you benefit intangibly or materially from making an introduction?

Next Step

> ▶ Read the final paragraph of this chapter. Decide on one introduction to make, and add the task to your calendar to complete within the next week.

CHAPTER 8

In Your Job Search: Write Messages That Build Relationships and Create Opportunities

If you needed to cross a wide, rushing river on a blustery day, would you cross by one of many available bridges—or would you swim, gasping and flailing, to the other side? You would use a bridge, right? Unless you were training for a triathlon or testing yourself in extreme sports, it would be crazy to try to swim across when you could cross by bridge.

Using your relationships to help you find a job or a client is the same as using a bridge to cross a swirling river. Rather than struggling on your own, exhausting yourself in the process, you can use your personal and professional networks as bridges to your goal. Getting the job or client may still be a huge challenge, but it will be easier and faster to achieve your goal with your contacts helping you.

Many people do use their relationships as such bridges. In my survey on business writing and relationships, 86 percent of respondents indicated that they had used networking at least once or twice to find a job, client, or customer; 34 percent said they had used it many times. One commented, "The last four positions I've been in have come about purely due to relationships/networking."

In this chapter, you will learn to write messages that help you maintain relationships and use them as bridges during the challenging period of looking for a job. By using such bridges rather than floundering on your own, you can more easily reach your career goals. Although the chapter focuses on using networking to get a job rather than to acquire clients, you can use similar messages to get clients and customers.

My longtime business associate Lynn Takaki was celebrating a new job as I worked on this chapter. Lynn agreed to share her relationship-building messages, from leaving her job, through the process of looking for a new position, and finally to landing one. Her messages, along with other models, will help you recognize effective ways to reach out to your network during your job search, at a time when many people feel vulnerable and uncomfortable. The chapter covers Lynn's and other people's messages, including announcements that you are leaving a job, requests for help in your job search, thank-yous for support, updates on your search, and announcements of your new job.

When Your Job Ends: Announcements That You Are Leaving

Maintaining and using your relationships in a job search begins as soon as you realize you will be looking for a new job. Your friends and contacts must be aware that you are in the job market, readying yourself to cross that raging river, to help you negotiate it. The first message you are likely to send is an announcement that you are leaving your job.

I learned from Lynn Takaki that she would be looking for a new job when I received this first-rate email from her:

Subject: A Message From Lynn Takaki

Dear Valued Business Partners and Friends,

After 14 wonderful years at ABC Company, I will be leaving at the end of this year. This is due to the elimination of the VP, Human Resources role and consolidation with the parent company's regional structure.

I am grateful for the opportunity to have served ABC employees, the company, and the community. This would not have been possible without you—my many valued business partners and friends. I am proud of the work we have done to create a culture where ABC has the highest employee engagement levels globally, even exceeding external benchmarks.

Your support and friendship throughout the years have sustained and inspired me. THANK YOU many times over.

If I can ever be of assistance to you, please call upon me. My contact information is below.

With gratitude,
Lynn

Lynn Takaki
[Cell phone number]
[Personal email address]

Vice President, Human Resources
ABC Incorporated
[Work phone number, work fax number]
[Work email]

In this next excellent message, I learned from a client I had worked with for several years that she was leaving her job:

Subject: Update

Lynn,

Just a quick email to let you know that Friday, July 10, will be my last day at XYZ. I'm heading off to new adventures (not even sure what they are yet, but trust me, they will be wonderful). It has been a joy to work with you during my time here. You are such a warm and engaging individual, and I sincerely hope that we can stay in touch and find future opportunities to work together.

Going forward, Debbie [Last name] (debbie@xyz.com) and Liz [Last name] (liz@xyz.com) will be coordinating the logistics for Learning & Development courses. Feel free to contact them with any questions regarding offering "Business Writing Tune-up" courses in the future. I'll be providing them with your contact information as well.

I wish great success for you in your own adventures! Please let me know if I can ever be of service to you.

See you on Facebook and/or LinkedIn.

All the best!

Marie R. Kelly | Human Resources
XYZ Company

Lynn's and Marie's messages do a beautiful job of announcing their departure, Lynn's to a group and Marie's just to me. Notice these strengths in their messages:

A positive tone. Although both women's jobs had been eliminated, they used positive language to communicate. Lynn's message sparkles with words such as *wonderful, grateful, opportunity, valued,* and *proud.* Marie's message glows with *wonderful adventures, joy,* and *opportunities.*

People are naturally drawn to positive energy, and these messages draw their readers to Lynn and Marie.

Absence of negativity. Not one negative word appears in either message. Neither woman blames the company for her situation. Although readers may have wondered how optimistic the women felt, both chose to come across positively rather than focusing on the negative aspects of job loss.

Connection with readers. Both women solidified their relationships with their readers. Lynn focused much of her message on her "business partners and friends," liberally thanking them for their support and friendship and the good work they have done. In Marie's message to me, she honored me with her warm words, including, "It has been a joy to work with you during my time here." As I read them, I smiled, thinking, "How nice of Marie!" and remembering our interactions.

Offer of help. Interestingly, even though both women were losing their jobs, they offered their help. Lynn wrote, "If I can ever be of assistance to you, please call upon me." Marie told me, "Please let me know if I can ever be of service to you." Beyond that, Marie gave me the names and email addresses of people to contact to continue working at her company. Communicating their interest in others at a time when their work world was radically changing came across as confident and generous.

Contact information. Both Lynn and Marie indicated their desire to stay in touch. Lynn shared her personal contact information; Marie invited me to connect on social media.

Thoughtfulness. Rather than leaving their associates in the dark, both women took the time to let people know they were leaving the company. In Marie's case, I felt honored that she had singled me out for a personal message, especially during a time that must have been stressful for her.

Here is another fine example of an announcement of job loss. It is by Charlie Gadzik, a communications manager, who was saying good-bye to his colleagues and a few people outside the firm. The difference in Charlie's message is that he was already negotiating a job at another firm, although he was not ready to name the company.

> Subject: Farewell
>
> Friends:
>
> After 13 years during which I dodged multiple downsizings, my luck has run out. My last day at ABC Company is Friday, Aug. 1.
>
> It's been a great ride. There hasn't been a day when I haven't looked forward to coming to work. ABC has a wonderful story to tell, and I've enjoyed telling it. ABC also has terrific people. I'm thankful for the opportunities I've had to work alongside you and become friends.
>
> The good news is that after a bit of vacation, I expect to transition directly to a job with another company in the Seattle area. That should make it easier for our paths to cross again. I hope they do.
>
> Charlie
>
> My company email box will be active until Sept. 30. I'll check it periodically. You can also reach me at:
> - [Home email]
> - [Home phone]
> - LinkedIn.com

Lynn, Marie, and Charlie were all leaving their jobs because of company restructuring or downsizing. But what if the reason you are leaving is more complicated than that? Perhaps you have not been able to meet performance goals or you and your new boss have not gotten along. Does that information belong in your departure announcement? No! Such negative information should not appear in writing. As in Marie's message, you can simply omit the reason for your leaving. Or you can touch gently on the reason for leaving, as this opening does:

> Subject: In Career Transition
>
> Dear Friends and Associates,
>
> Friday was my last day as public relations manager at XYZ Company. During my five years there, I had many great experiences overseeing strategic media opportunities, managing crisis communications, and publicizing the company's environmental stewardship and community involvement. However, with the new direction Communications is moving in at XYZ, it is a good time for me to make a career move.

The words "the new direction Communications is moving in" communicate neutrality. In contrast, the statements "My new boss and I do not agree on the vision for PR" and "I can't get along with my new boss" would communicate negativity and conflict.

The following negative model shows what NOT to do in a message announcing the end of a job:

> Subject: Gone but Not Forgotten?
>
> Dear Associates and Friends (you know which you are),
>
> Well, (sh)it happened. My new boss decided he wants to bring in a programmer from his former company, someone who understands him. (Good luck with that, Bill!)
>
> Therefore, Friday is my last day—I mean my last day at work. (I hope it's not my VERY LAST DAY.)

Expect me to call you so I can mooch meals and lattes off you until I snag my next position. Speaking of which—if you come across any jobs that suit my abundant talents, let me know please . . . PLEASE!

Until we meet again (as Dale and Roy used to sing),
Bruce

Bruce's message simmers with negativity in words such as *gone, forgotten, (sh)it, mooch,* and *snag.* Although some of his associates and friends might enjoy his snarky message, for others the message may be proof of why Bruce is out of a job.

If you are feeling awkward or timid about letting people know you have lost your job, consider Lynn Takaki's suggestion about seeing yourself as a product. As a vice president of human resources and someone who had hired thousands of people, Lynn told me: "I was not shy about letting people know that I was looking for a new job. An important aspect of any job search is to let people know. Basically, you are marketing yourself. How do you market a product without some form of advertising or communication?"

Step One is to let people know that you, the product, are available.

Tips for Job-Departure Announcements

Apply these tips when you write messages to business associates and friends to let them know you are leaving your job:

Include the basic information that you are leaving or have left your job. Do not go into detail about the reason for your leaving, unless it is for a promotion or an exciting opportunity. Don't share the reason if it presents you or others in a negative light.

Stay positive. Use the positive language included in this chapter to avoid sinking into job-loss negativity. Even if you feel horrible, keep your message upbeat to attract positive things into your life.

Thank your readers for the ways in which they have helped you, if appropriate. Your graciousness is likely to make your readers feel honored and happy to know you.

Offer ways for people to stay in contact with you. Include contact information they can use once you have left your job.

Mention your next steps, if appropriate, and let people know how they can help. For instance, if you are seeking a job in a specific geographical region, make your contacts aware of your goal so they can consider who or what they know that could help you.

Avoid sarcasm unless you know it suits every one of your readers. Sarcasm typically comes across as negative.

Remember that email out-of-office messages are another type of job-departure announcement. Although they are typically short, think of them as a way to connect with others too, as long as that purpose is acceptable to your employer. Here is an example:

> With the sale of the company, my position has been eliminated effective July 25. All questions about property taxes are being handled by Randy Rose at [email address].
>
> I am looking for a position in another corporate real estate department. If you would like to contact me with leads or ideas, please use my cell phone: [number].
>
> Best regards,
> Jesus Morales

Involving Friends and Associates: Requests for Help in Your Job Search

When you are between jobs, you may feel awkward asking for help. You may feel insignificant and powerless without the symbols of your success—things like your office or other work place, company car and phone, state-of-the-art tools, business cards, an expense account or a steady income, and people reporting to you and asking your advice. Such feelings are often the natural consequence of being unemployed when you have not chosen the circumstances.

It's important to recognize that most people find it satisfying to help others in their job search. Rather than watching a friend or an associate struggle across the roiling river, they want to serve as a bridge to a new job or career. And although they would be delighted to help, they may not always know how and may not want to seem intrusive. By reaching out and involving them, you can help them help you and simultaneously nurture your relationships.

These emails will give you the idea of how to reach out.

Requests to Meet for Advice

Lynn Takaki reached out to many people for guidance. Below is her email to a vice president of human resources, a friend of one of her former team members.

> Subject: Networking referral through Peter [Last name]
>
> Hi Michael,
>
> I am contacting you at the suggestion of Peter [Last name]. Pete and I worked together at ABC, before the VP, HR position was eliminated and consolidated into the parent company's HR structure. Pete thought you might give me some insights on the job market and resources that may be useful as I begin my job search.
>
> Would it be possible to meet at your convenience? I am fairly open next week, other than Monday and Tuesday lunch hours and Friday morning through lunch. The following week of April 16–20 is wide open.

Thanks much and best regards,
Lynn Takaki
[Cell number]
[LinkedIn profile address]

Michael agreed to meet with Lynn. Throughout her job search, he referred many job leads to her, along with referrals to key contacts who had been helpful to him in his job search. All that support began with Lynn's email to him.

In the two messages below, job seekers ask professional contacts to meet with them. Of course, the writers could get information and advice from their contacts by phone or email. But in-person meetings, which provide opportunities to connect on a social level, can strengthen relationships.

Subject: Working on My Job-Search Strategy

Dear Professor Davis,

I am writing to request your advice on my job-search strategy. As you know, I left the Army in June, after several tours in the Middle East as a medic. I could really use help in figuring out how to present my work experience in a way that stateside civilians will understand. Because you have made that transition, I thought of you.

Would you meet with me to talk about ways to package my experience and determine possible jobs to target? My schedule is open next week on Wednesday through Friday if you are free then.

I look forward to hearing from you.

Sincerely,
Rita Oakes
[Cell phone number]

Subject: Lunch and your ideas

Hi Laura. Having left XYZ last month, I am starting to think about what I want in my next position. Do you have time for lunch sometime soon to help me sharpen my focus? I am interested in so many things—it would help to hear your candid responses to some of my ideas.

Please let me know a couple of dates that work for you, and we can schedule.

Best,
Dan

Requests for Feedback on a Resume

It's always a good idea to test-run your resume before submitting it for a position. These examples effectively ask for feedback.

Subject: Requesting Feedback on My Resume

Hi, Rick. I hope all is well with you. I am getting ready to send out my resume for some sales and service jobs in our industry, and I would appreciate your feedback.

Of anyone I know, you are most aware of my skills and strengths in sales and service. Would you be willing to review my resume to be sure I have done a good job describing my experience? Also, if there is anything in the resume that could come across stronger, I would appreciate knowing about it.

My resume is attached. If you have feedback to share, I will appreciate it.

Chad

Subject: A Quick Review of My Resume

Dear Karen,

You are the most experienced HR person I know, and I value your opinion. Would you be willing to give my resume a quick look and let me know your first impression?

Is there anything that comes across as less than professional? I want to be sure to make the best impression I can.

Feel free to email or call me, whatever is convenient for you. I welcome your honest opinion.

With thanks and best regards,
Dorette

Both of the previous messages are specific about the kind of feedback the writer wants; neither asks too much of its reader. "Please review my resume and give me detailed feedback" might be too broad a request, suggesting the reader needs to commit significant time and effort. Both messages also come across positively, with words such as *ready, appreciate, skills, strengths, value,* and *convenient.*

Requests for Help to Approach a Specific Company

If you are interested in working at a specific company, you can ask contacts to make introductions to people or to provide information that will make you a more knowledgeable applicant. The emails below make such requests. Notice that they include brief personal content, which acknowledges and helps to maintain the relationship.

Subject: Contacts at XYZ Company

Hi Gary. How is everything? I hope you are enjoying your new lakeside cottage this summer.

I have applied for a job in Consumer Service at XYZ. Knowing that you worked there for many years, I was wondering whether you could suggest someone who could give me background on the customer-service issues people face there. Or is there anyone in Consumer Service you might contact to put in a good word for me?

If you have any suggestions or contacts for me, please let me know. I will call you next week if we haven't connected before then.

Best,
Christopher

⁓

Subject: Ways to approach XYZ Company (& blueberry cheesecake)

Hi, Carolyn. I created a list of the top 10 companies I would like to work for in our region. One of them is XYZ. Since they are a client of yours, I wondered whether you could suggest people I might network with there. Is there anyone at XYZ you could introduce me to?

Also, attached is the recipe you requested, just in time for blueberry season. Enjoy!

Elizabeth

Lynn Takaki responded to an email of mine in which I had sent her some job listings I was not sure she routinely received. In her response, she mentioned a company she was seeking information about:

Hi Lynn,

Yes, I do receive these. Thank you for thinking of me and asking. I need lots of help so I really appreciate hearing from you!

I recently applied for the VP, HR job at ABC. I know you used to do training for them. Do you happen to know anyone there now?

Best to you and thanks again,

Lynn

If you live in a new area and have few local contacts, be sure to ask your contacts from other areas about people they know in your new locale. Career consultant Jerry Schlagenhauf loves to tell this story: A woman from Maryland—let's call her Kari—had moved to Seattle and felt she had no contacts to introduce her to Seattle-area companies. With Jerry's wise prompting, Kari asked her contacts in other places to help her. A friend living in southeast Africa, in Mozambique, ended up introducing Kari by email to several Seattle-area contacts. One of those introductions led to a job. The lesson is this: No limits! Let your mind think boundlessly about the people who might connect you with others.

Requests to People You Do Not Know Yet

One way to expand your network is to reach out to people you don't know yet, which these two messages do effectively:

Subject: Advice on Launching My Career

Dear Ms. Blake,

Last month I graduated with a degree in communications and English from XYZ University. Researching on the web, I learned that you have established a successful writing business in the area.

Would you be willing to share your advice with me on how I might focus my job search? I have heard there are many highly experienced writers and editors searching for jobs, and I would like advice on how a recent graduate can get started.

I will call your office next week to request a meeting. In the meantime, if you want to learn more about me, I have attached my resume.

Best regards,
Jason Crane, [cell phone number]

⌒

Subject: Networking Request

Hello, Pierre. I read your article in *Philanthropy Today* on using social media as development tools. I was very impressed with your combination of traditional approaches and cutting-edge communications.

I noticed that you are based in Austin, where I am moving next month. I am leaving Chicago, where I have worked for three years as development officer for the XYZ Theater Company.

Would you have time by phone or in person to talk about how to get connected in Austin? I would appreciate suggestions or referrals to help me become established in the development community.

I have attached my resume to give you a sense of my background.

I look forward to hearing from you.

Beth Hall, [cell phone number]

Tips for Job Seekers' Requests

Apply these tips, which the previous examples illustrate, to write requests that get positive responses:

Include normal courtesies such as *please, thank you,* and *appreciate*. Courtesy shows that you value the individual and your relationship.

Make reasonable requests. For instance, ask for a review of one resume, not several versions. Ask for a contact at one or two companies, not ten. Limiting your request makes it doable and satisfying rather than burdensome.

Be flexible about timing. Keep in mind that you probably have more unstructured time than the other person does.

Indicate why you are asking the specific individual for help. That way, he or she will recognize how to be helpful. Also, such information establishes or solidifies your relationship. Avoid generic requests, ones that could be sent to anyone.

Use positive language to communicate positively and professionally. Keep your message free of negative thoughts and feelings unless your contact is one who would relate to those feelings. Although you may feel discouraged, disgruntled, or fearful, you don't want such feelings to make someone wary of engaging with you.

Take initiative. If an individual offers to meet you at XYZ Bakery and Coffee Spot, do not automatically reply, asking for the address of XYZ. Take steps to find it yourself rather than create work for the other person.

The Messages That Make Others Feel Good: Thank-Yous for Support

After you have received the advice, feedback, suggestions, referrals, and encouragement from your contacts, thank-yous will sustain your relationships. Thanks-yous remind the people in your network how useful they have been and how much they enjoyed helping you. Your gratefulness may also inspire individuals to do more.

Lynn Takaki shared several thank-yous with me; I chose two to include here. This first example is to an executive search firm recruiter Lynn met through networking. Her last comment refers to the fact that Randy was moving his office.

> Subject: Sincere thanks, Randy!
>
> Randy,
>
> I truly enjoyed meeting you today and appreciate you taking the time to discuss my work history and experience. I hope we can talk again so that I may learn more about you and your practice. From what I experienced of you this morning, it is evident that you take a very personal approach and care about your candidates as much as you care about your client companies. I like that!
>
> As I move forward in this process, I hope we can continue to be in touch. Please let me know if you have any ideas for me to be effective in my search, and if there is anything I can do to assist you, I hope you will call upon me (except I'm not a heavy lifter of moving boxes—good luck with that!).
>
> Best regards,
> Lynn

In Lynn's message below, she follows up on a lunch in which a network contact arranged a meeting with one of his executive contacts. She thanked them both.

> Subject: Sincere thanks
>
> Dave and Greg,
>
> You both made my day yesterday. A lovely lunch "in town" and your great company and conversation gave me a lift.

Dave, thanks for the gracious introduction to Greg and the opportunity to connect and collaborate.

Greg, thanks for your ideas around my transition and search. I highly value your perspective, and I hope that going forward, we will cross paths again. Please also give my best to Jennifer.

As follow-up, I am attaching my resume. I appreciate any leads, contacts, or information that may come to you. I hope that you, too, will contact me if there is any way I may assist you. I feel blessed to have met so many wonderful people on this journey, and having you both in my network of contacts means a lot to me.

I am out of town next week for a family visit with my sisters in Chicago. You helped to close out a good week and start my vacation on a celebratory note. Sincere thanks again to each of you.

Best,
Lynn

Did you notice how specific each thank-you was? Lynn told me about her intentions for the messages: "I tried to be very sincere and authentic and to not do the perfunctory communications that don't show a sincere attitude. Messages like 'Thank you very much. I appreciate your time. Best regards' would never work for me on the receiving end, and I certainly didn't want to be one who delivers messages in that way." She added, "My follow-up messages were very prompt and personalized and reinforced the relationship that I was trying to build with each individual."

Your thank-yous can be specific and sincere without being as detailed as Lynn's admirable messages. Consider the thank-yous that follow. The first two are emails; the last two are handwritten notes.

Subject: Thanks for Your Help!

Dear Shaaz,

Thank you for meeting with me to talk about my job search. Your ideas about working as a virtual assistant have me intrigued and excited. I will sit down this afternoon to review the websites you recommended.

I appreciate your kind offer to stay in touch and continue to share ideas. You will hear from me!

With thanks and best regards,
Jenn

———

Subject: Thank You, Sydney!

It was super of you to give me resume feedback. I have made every change you suggested, and the new version looks and sounds very professional, thanks to your sharp eye and good ideas.

Thank you for investing your time in me and my job search. It is much appreciated!

Go Sounders!

Maryam
[LinkedIn page]
[Cell phone]

———

Dear Mr. Miller,

Thank you for introducing me to Dee Dee Larson and Annie Tram. Dee Dee and I met yesterday, and she was very helpful with advice about how to stand out as an applicant. She even offered to meet me again to practice interviewing.

Annie Tram and I have an appointment to talk on the phone next week. I look forward to getting her perspective on opportunities in advertising.

I really appreciate that you shared your contacts with me.

Sincerely,
Krystal Hammond

—

Dear Carrie,

Thank you so much for treating me to a delicious lunch and sharing your wonderful, supportive thoughts on my search. Both were very nourishing!

I will take to heart all you shared, and I promise to stay positive and focused. I know an excellent job is out there with my name on it, and I will find it.

Thanks for lending me the latest Sandra Brown thriller. I cannot wait to read it!

Yours,
Carmen

Tips for Thank-Yous

Apply these tips to write gracious, professional thank-yous that nurture your relationships:

Write your thank-you promptly, within a few days. Don't feel you need to take action on the individual's advice or information before expressing your thanks. That might take too long and might lead to a combined thank-you/apology.

Be specific. Mention the particular advice, critique, information, or other support you received, along with how it is beneficial to you.

Let "thank you" take center stage in the message. Do not just add a perfunctory thanks to a message in which you have asked for something.

Use email or another electronic means of communication, or send a note by post. A thank-you note or card that comes by mail often gets more attention than a note on a screen, but thank-yous are welcome in any form.

Don't miss the opportunity to say thanks. Your contacts may notice that you have not followed the normal courtesies, and the lapse may reduce their enthusiasm for helping you again.

Avoid trying to sell yourself hard. This message is a thank-you, not a sales pitch. If you find yourself listing your accomplishments or asking for a job interview, you are going too far.

Keeping Your Network Informed: Updates on Your Search

If you want your network to continue to help you cross the swirling river of your job search, you need to keep them informed. It is not enough to let people know you are looking and then talk or meet with them once or twice. After those first contacts, people want to know what is happening: Have you found a job? Are you still looking? Have you changed your goals or priorities?

This message, which Lynn Takaki emailed to about 300 contacts, shows how to update people on your search:

Dear Valued Colleagues and Friends:

I hope this note finds each of you well—and now that fall is finally upon us, I thought it was time for an update. I wanted to let you know I'm continuing to seek an HR leadership or consulting opportunity where I can assist an organization in leveraging their human resources activities for maximum competitive advantage.

Over the past few months of my journey through the career transition process, I've been greatly energized and inspired by your assistance and support, and would appreciate it if you'd continue to think of me for any appropriate networking opportunities or job leads you may come across relative to my expertise.

While I hope it goes without saying, if there is anything I can do to assist you in return or any introductions I can make on your behalf, through my network, please let me know.

All the best and again, my deepest thanks for your ongoing friendship and support!

Lynn
[Cell phone number]
[LinkedIn profile]

Of the approximately 300 people to whom Lynn sent her update, about 100 responded. Of those 100, about 50 offered suggestions or a referral. Two of the referrals led directly to Lynn getting a job offer less than one month later. She explained what happened:

I sent out the update, and I heard back from a number of people in my network about different opportunities, different leads, people I might want to call. And I happened to get an email from a former colleague who was aware of an opportunity, and he let me know about it. He also knew people in the company who were hiring and he gave them my resume. . . . Had I not sent that email out, I don't know whether he would have thought of me.

Lynn believes that being introduced through a professional contact made her a strong applicant for the position. She said, "I think that my candidacy carried much more weight because of that personal relationship and the familiarity with me, my work, and my history."

Interestingly, a second person in Lynn's network, a recruiter, also let Lynn know about the job opening she eventually filled. The recruiter was able to share a lot of information about the company, its leadership, and the position. Having two people give her information about the company (her original contact and the recruiter) helped Lynn decide that the company was right for her. She explained, "These individuals were able to speak very highly of the hiring manager, the CEO, and the company, so there was immediate credibility from my perspective. The personal introduction actually worked both ways."

These positive connections—inspired by Lynn's email update to her network—all led to Lynn's getting the offer and accepting the position. (Note: Lynn thanks her career consultant Matt Youngquist, Career Horizons LLC, for his input on the update.)

Despite Lynn's success story, you may be thinking about the possible embarrassment of writing to people after months of looking for a job, with no tangible success. I asked Lynn whether she had felt awkward or embarrassed writing to people, given that many months had passed since she had begun her search. She explained that her problem was not embarrassment, but rather a worry about bothering people:

> I was not concerned about being embarrassed. I knew when I started the endeavor that it was going to take awhile for me. However, I had thought about sending an update to my network earlier than when I actually did send it. I felt a little bit of reluctance and hesitation because I didn't want to be a bother. Then I thought back to my own personal experience, and I realized that it's not a bother. People wonder: Whatever happened to Lynn? Where is she? I remembered that, in fact, a lot of people had asked to be

kept apprised of my progress. I also realized that my agenda was not always going to be top of mind for everyone else, so it is natural to do reminders and updates. Even though I hesitated and worked through that, I was actually thanked for the update many times.

Lynn and I share a pet peeve. Like me, she becomes annoyed when she spends time offering advice, referrals, or information to new acquaintances who are in a job search—and then never hears from them again. Although such relationships begin with a lot of promise, they end because individuals do not sustain them with occasional contact by email or phone.

Don't let embarrassment or reluctance get in your way of continuing to build relationships as you look for a job. Send updates to keep people involved in your search. Depending on the length (or projected length) of your job search, you may comfortably update your network monthly, every other month, or quarterly—whenever you feel that it is time to check in with people again.

Here is another great email update, written by a recent college graduate named Cameron Deuel to the people in his professional network. Cameron sent it just before Halloween, as you can tell from the message.

Subject: The Great American Job Search

Happy Halloweekend,

I want to thank you again for meeting with me during my job search and for your advantageous guidance. Since we have not spoken for a few weeks, I want to update you on how my job search is going.

Since we last talked, I have continued to meet with four to six professionals per week to gain insight on how to remain a visible job candidate and to learn more about different career paths I might take. I have also put together a digital portfolio of my strongest writing samples, which can be found here [link]. After learning about different possible routes, I have decided to search primarily for an entry-level content writing or editing position because I am capable of producing quality content at a significant pace.

I have been in touch with a few staffing agencies, one of which focuses primarily on hiring contractual workers for ABC Inc. Though I am comforted by the thought of my information in the hands of recruiters, I find informational interviews to be immensely valuable. Every meeting leaves me feeling optimistic about what's to come, and I am constantly learning about new, crucial skills.

Additionally, I have applied to volunteer with 826 Seattle [link], a nonprofit writing and tutoring center that focuses on many aspects of education, including creative writing. I am looking forward to attending their volunteer orientation next weekend to learn more about how I can donate my time.

I hope you are having a relaxing weekend before the holiday season starts up and I thank you again for your generosity. I hope this message finds you well and I look forward to speaking soon.

Sincerely,
Cameron Deuel
[Phone number]
[LinkedIn profile]

As you can see, Cameron's message is different from Lynn's in its level of detail. Lynn's quick update stated that she was still in the job market and would welcome continued referrals for a leadership-level position. In contrast, the young job seeker built the credibility he needed by informing people of the creative things he was doing in his job search and by providing work samples. Both updates suited their audience and purpose well.

Here is another sample update, which shows how to keep people engaged in your job-search process. This email illustrates how to inform your network of a major change in your plan.

> Subject: Starting a Design Business
>
> Dear Friend,
>
> After getting excellent advice from you and the many others who are receiving this email, I have decided to start my own business rather than work for a company. I will still work as a graphic designer, but I will work independently. I feel very excited and pleased about this decision.
>
> As you can imagine, I have many steps ahead: choosing a business name, deciding on a niche or niches, creating a website, and pulling together my portfolio—to name just a few. As I go through these steps, I will almost certainly contact you for suggestions and feedback, but feel free to share ideas now. Eventually, I will ask you to help me spread the word and to consider hiring me for graphic design projects you may choose not to handle yourself.
>
> I wanted to let you know my decision promptly, and the easiest way was a group message. I hope to follow up with you personally as things evolve.
>
> My best wishes,
> Thalia
> [Cell phone number]

You can also send updates to individuals in your network. In these examples, notice that each one shares upbeat information of interest to the reader.

Subject: Checking in

Hey Dan.

Just wanted to check in and tell you I have been applying your good advice. I am focusing on my activity and output, which I CAN control, rather than results, which I can't.

As you suggested, I have been setting weekly goals. I'm keeping track of networking contacts, professional meetings, resumes sent out, etc., and I feel very good about reaching my goals each week. I am certain these efforts will lead to interviews and eventually the right opportunity.

Thanks for such a great suggestion. Keep 'em coming!

Best,
Hank

Subject: A Helpful Read

Hi Caroline. I have read a terrific book I wanted to tell you about. It's called *Brag: The Art of Tooting Your Own Horn Without Blowing It*. Because you and I have talked about the challenges of "bragging" in interviews and meetings, I thought of you while reading it.

The author, Peggy Klaus, has very practical suggestions. You can get an idea of her style at her website: www.bragbetter.com.

I have now begun "bragging" in interviews, and it almost feels natural. I will be sure to do some bragging with you the next time we meet!

Warm regards,
Pia

The next update ties to the Thanksgiving holiday and is written on a greeting card. Think of holidays and special occasions as additional opportunities to update your network. Around Thanksgiving, Chanukah, Christmas, and New Year's Day, you can send a greeting to every person you talked with who offered help in your career search during the year, whether that talk was in person, by phone, or by email. Even though sending printed cards is an expense, think of it as an investment in your professional network. In your message, let people know you are still looking for a job.

> John, thank you for your advice on my job-search this year. I am grateful for your creative suggestions, and I feel confident that I will find the right opportunity as a substance abuse or grief counselor in the coming months. I will keep you posted.
>
> Happy Thanksgiving to you, your colleagues, and your family!
>
> Stacey Brown

Tips for Job-Search Updates

Your job-search updates will be welcome to people in your professional and personal networks. Just apply these tips:

Do keep in touch with your network by sending regular updates. Your updates and check-ins will nurture both your budding relationships and your longstanding professional friendships.

Stay positive. The previous examples use many positive words such as *valuable, energized, inspired, friendship, advantageous, comforted, opti mistic, honored, generosity, excellent, excited, pleased, opportunity, great,* and *terrific.* These words create positive feelings in readers.

Don't express frustration, discomfort, or self-pity, and certainly don't say anything to make your reader feel guilty (for instance, "I thought you were going to send me some leads"). Leave any negative thoughts for your personal journal.

Provide either a specific update or a general one, depending on your readers and your situation. Cameron Deuel provided specific details about his progress. Lynn Takaki gave a general update that she was still looking for a position in human resources.

Feel free to mention any continued help you would appreciate. For example, Lynn used the words "continue to think of me for any appropriate networking opportunities or job leads."

Avoid selling yourself hard. Remember that your goal is to keep in touch with your contacts, your bridges to a new job or opportunity.

Spreading the Good News: Announcements of Your New Job

The happiest message of your job-search adventure is the one in which you announce your new job. This announcement creates the opportunity for you to share your joy and thank the people in your professional and personal networks. Lynn Takaki's message (slightly disguised for privacy's sake) does both.

Subject: Good News from Lynn

Dear Valued Colleagues and Friends,

I am so excited to share that I will join the XYZ Exteriors team as VP, Human Resources. This is an opportunity to join a booming industry and develop the HR strategic direction, build culture, and develop the workforce to drive company growth—all things I love to do! Affiliation with a strong engineering / manufacturing workforce and a tangible product aligns with my experience and is a great fit.

Initially, I'll be doing a weekly commute to the beautiful north coast area. Eventually, my family and I are looking forward to relocation and a new adventure, exploring the natural beauty of this fabulous region. For a city fix, I think we may have a difficult time choosing between Vancouver, BC, and Seattle!

While it is fun to share my good news, it is more important that I express my gratitude to each of you for your support during my career transition process. You provided encouragement, information, job leads, network contacts, and friendship along the way. You gave me the reason to get up and go; motivating, inspiring, and coaching me on the journey to this new beginning. Managing change in job, company, coworkers, location, etc., is part of living a dynamic life. Throughout all these changes, it is my good fortune to have you in my corner. Please know I highly value your presence in my life. Some things never change.

With gratitude,
Lynn

As a recipient of Lynn's message, I learned about her new job, recognized its excellent fit with her experience, and shared her excitement. I enjoyed receiving her eloquent thanks, and I felt inspired by her perceptive comments on change. For me, and probably for the many individuals in her network, Lynn's message served as a solid reminder of why I enjoy having her in my life.

Lynn mentioned "a weekly commute to the beautiful north coast area" and "exploring the natural beauty of this fabulous region." Readers may have wondered how Lynn felt about taking a job far from her home.

Regardless of her possible feelings, Lynn remained positive and professional, which is always the correct choice in a group message.

Here is the announcement young job seeker Cameron Deuel sent out:

> Subject: The End of the Great American Job Search
>
> Good afternoon,
>
> You may be pleased to know that I've officially landed my first job as a college graduate. Several months ago, I applied to a position within ABC Inc. that specializes in Customer Service for Product X and, though I was not selected for that particular position, I was contacted by the Project Manager in hopes that I might be open to an alternate plan.
>
> I've been hired for a contract position that will seamlessly lead into a full-time Content Developer role with Product X Customer Service later this year. During my contract period, I will be trained on how to utilize ABC's programming software, which will be one of my primary duties once I'm brought on full time. I start on Monday.
>
> Again, I want to thank you for your generosity during my job search. I have grown significantly from this experience and I will continue to stay in touch with you in the future.
>
> I hope this message finds you well and that you are experiencing a fantastic new year.
>
> Sincerely,
> Cameron Deuel
> [Phone number]

Cameron was not kidding about staying in touch. A few weeks after his announcement, I was delighted to receive this message from him:

Good morning,

Since we haven't spoken in a little over a month, I want to let you know how things are going with my new job. ABC is a wonderful starting point. I've learned a lot in the past six weeks. The project I'm working on reminds me of publications I've worked on in the past, but with much more coding involved. Though the project seems immense, I am encouraged by the drive of my coworkers and the overall attitude of the company.

Again, thank you for your help during my job search. I've actually started networking with people who are graduating this spring and your feedback will allow me to help them even more. I can't wait to see where they land.

I hope you're doing well and I look forward to staying in touch.

Sincerely,
Cameron Deuel
[Phone number]

In his early 20s, Cameron already exhibits the qualities of a great networker: the desire and ability to communicate, a positive attitude, and a generous spirit.

Here is another example announcing a new job that has already begun:

Subject: Announcing My New Position

Greetings, friends.

I have looked forward to the day when I could share this good news: On October 1, I became a group home manager for XYZ Homecare. My responsibilities include hiring, training, and supervising group home staff to ensure that residents get the best care possible.

This position fits well with my training and goals, and I am very happy about it. The company has a solid reputation for integrity and high-quality care, and I see a good future for me here.

I appreciate your support and guidance as I searched for a job. Thank you for everything.

My best regards,
Dale Smith
[New company phone]
[New company website]

Of course, you can write to individuals rather than groups, as this sample note sent by post illustrates:

Dear Ross,

Your good advice and high expectations for me have paid off! I am pleased to let you know that I have accepted the position of business analyst at XYZ Pharmaceutical Company. I start next Monday right here in the city.

My job involves the things I love: business analytics, project management, meticulous quality control, and training internal customers. I am excited about how my work will directly support product sales.

You have been a tireless coach and teacher for me as I searched for a new job, and I am extremely grateful for all you have done.

With many, many thanks,
Ellen

This next message, which was sent by email, combines a group message with an individual note. The sender added an individual note to the email to people who had been especially helpful in his job search.

Subject: I landed a great role!

Hi everyone,

I want you all to know that I will be starting my new job this week, as IT Director for the XYZ Association.

The organization is a perfect size, the staff and management are good people, and their mission is very compelling.

If not for networking with friends and associates, my search would have been much longer and far less productive. Thank you for your support, efforts, and good thoughts during this transition time.

Sincerely,
Michael Black

[Personalized addition]

Hi Julia,

This may not have happened without you, you know. Searching on LinkedIn, I noticed you were connected with Louise Smith at XYZ, and I made contact with her after your intro.

I can't thank you enough for your support and efforts. If ever I can reciprocate the support, please let me know.

My best always,
Michael

Tips for Job Announcements

Apply these tips to write successful, relationship-sustaining job announcements:

Present your new position enthusiastically. If you were to describe it as a compromise or as settling for less, people would perhaps feel sorry for you, which is not a feeling you want to elicit. Stay positive.

Provide some details about your new job so people understand what you will be doing. Sharing this information solidifies your relationships going forward.

Thank the people in your network for the help and encouragement they have given you. Sometimes saying thanks in a group message is sufficient, especially if people have given you a similar degree of help. For people whose support contributed significantly to your success, an individual thank-you allows you to express your gratitude explicitly and more deeply.

Include your new contact information if it is available. Do not let your contacts lose track of you now. Help your relationships endure.

Don't overlook this message! Use email, Facebook, or another electronic means, or mail it to your contacts by post. People in your network will wonder what happened to you. They deserve to receive your happy news.

Rely on Your Relationships

Being out of a job disturbs everything: your identity, your emotions, your schedule, your habits, your budget. Your relationships are the bridges across that churning, challenging time.

Despite any feelings of fear, awkwardness, or instability that your job search may cause you, rely on the people in your personal and professional lives. Share your job-loss news. Ask for help. Express your thanks. Stay in touch. Then spread the good news of the job you accept. Although you may worry that you will risk your relationships if you use them during this difficult time, the opposite is true. If you engage people in your search, your relationships with them will grow stronger. And new relationships will develop.

As you look for a job, use the examples in this chapter to write messages that will build and sustain your relationships. Doing so might just help you find the perfect job too!

Personal Assessment for Job Seekers

▶ Which people in your personal and professional networks would be happy to help you in your job search? Have you kept them engaged in your search with messages like those covered in this chapter?

Next Step

▶ Depending on where you are in your career transition, compose and send one of these messages this week:
  - An announcement that you are leaving your job
  - A request for help in your job search
  - A thank-you for support
  - An update on your search
  - An announcement of your new job

CHAPTER 9

Send Meaningful Christmas,
Chanukah, and New Year's Greetings

The Christmas, Chanukah, and New Year's holidays provide great opportunities to connect with business associates and reestablish relationships. But with the opportunities comes the challenge of getting things done and making the gesture meaningful. If you are anything like me, your holidays may burst with traveling, entertaining, shopping, visiting, attending religious services, and other activities. So sending business greetings, which are optional rather than required, may fall into the category of your regretfully missed opportunities or stressfully completed tasks.

This chapter gives you plenty of tips, examples, and ideas to help you seize the chance to connect with business associates by sending sincere Christmas, Chanukah, and New Year's greetings. It uses the Christmas date of December 25, celebrated in much of the Western world, and the New Year's date of January 1. If your business associates around the world celebrate these special days on other dates, make the appropriate adjustments.

Which Are Better: Printed or Electronic Cards?

Both printed (tangible) and electronic cards have their supporters, with printed cards more widely accepted. Some people love one and not the other; some appreciate both. When I asked the question "How do you like your holiday cards?" on my blog, responders shared these preferences:

Printed card preference: 57%

E-card preference: 17%

Both/either: 26%

Those who prefer printed cards mention their warmth and personal touch, their uniqueness and special meaning, the ease of displaying them around the office, the ability to touch and savor them, the effort they show, and their eco-friendliness when printed on recycled paper. People who spend much of their day at computers tend to appreciate tangible cards as a welcome change.

Those who like to receive e-cards value their eco-friendliness, immediacy, interactivity, creativity, possible use as screensavers, and the ability to respond to them quickly and easily. Those who send e-cards lament that sometimes their recipients do not even open them.

Of course, if your only communication with your customers, employees, and others is electronic—or if printed greetings mailed through the post are too expensive or difficult to send—then e-greetings will be your choice.

How to Make Your Greetings Meaningful

From the comments I received about holiday greetings on my blog, I can emphatically say this: Everyone appreciates a personalized message. No one likes holiday spam, in printed or electronic form. But any greeting can come across as mass produced and meaningless unless you take certain steps to make it special. Follow these suggestions to add the little details that help you come across as a sincere communicator rather than a spammer:

Send greetings only to people you know: your current or recent customers, clients, coworkers, employees, and business associates; subscribers to your newsletters; and individuals who have asked to be on your mailing list. If someone has not indicated an interest in you, your greeting is spam.

Send only one card—not several—or you may be perceived as obsessed, wasteful, or scatter-brained. Even well-personalized e-cards are spam when people receive more than one from you per holiday.

Choose cards and messages for the recipients—not for yourself. If you believe "Jesus is the reason for the season," express that view in church—not in your cards to business contacts. If you are not sure whether a specific individual celebrates Christmas, use "Happy holidays" rather than "Merry Christmas" as your message. Consider your readers' tastes. For instance, to outdoorsy contacts, send a photo card of a magnificent mountain or a giant redwood. To dog lovers, send a card featuring an irresistible Christmas puppy. You do not need to purchase these cards individually. You can typically buy boxed cards that match the tastes of many of your business associates.

Personalize your tangible greeting cards in one or more of these ways:

- Handwrite the recipient's name and sign your own—this is the least you can do. Never send a card with no recipient's name and only a "factory-printed" signature. Even if the card has gold-embossed lettering, it will not make a meaningful connection. Do not have your assistant fake your signature—it's bad karma, and it will make your assistant cynical.
- Handwrite a personal message that uses the recipient's name. Just one sentence of greeting will personalize your message

and show your thoughtfulness. Several sentences can make your message memorable.

- If your associate is from another country, consider adding a greeting in his or her native language. For example, use "¡Feliz Año Nuevo!" for a Spanish-speaking colleague or "Joyeux Noël et bonne année" for someone who speaks French. You can find translated greetings on the Internet. It's wise to double-check translations on an additional website to make sure they are accurate.
- Handwrite each envelope. Although it takes a lot of work (and is therefore the exception rather than the norm), this gesture shows serious personal commitment. It virtually guarantees that your card will be opened and read.
- For a card from you and your team, include a photo of the team captioned with everyone's name. This gesture is meaningful if the recipient has dealings with at least several team members.
- Have team members sign the card if they know the recipient. When I led classes for a prominent high-tech company, each Christmas I received a holiday card hand-signed by everyone in the human resources department who knew me. It was fun to read each signature and think of the individuals signing.

Personalize your e-cards in these ways so people open, read, and appreciate them:

- Use a specific rather than a generic subject line for the email. "Happy Holidays 20XX" comes across as anonymous. Instead choose something like "Happy Holidays From Ivona at XYZ!" or "Karl Schneider Wishes You a Joyful New Year" to make an instant connection with your reader.
- Add an individualized message.

- Use the recipient's name and your own. A greeting to your reader as "Dear Customer" or "Dear Employee" might as well say "Dear Stranger."
- Add a photo of team members, signed or labeled with everyone's name, with each signature or label near the appropriate person's photo. It's easy to write on photos using Microsoft Office's Paint feature. Many tips and software programs for adding words to photos are also available on the Internet.
- Contribute to a worthwhile nonprofit organization the money you save by not mailing tangible cards, and let your recipients know about your contribution if it matches their mission. Or contribute in the recipient's name and share the information in your holiday message.
- Show extra effort by uploading the card and providing the link to your recipients, rather than sending them an attachment. Your contacts can click the link to open the card in an instant.

If you create a holiday video (whose play button appears in your message or whose link you send by email), you can personalize the email or even the video. In the video, you can tell a story that engages your recipients or includes mention of them. Or you can list individual recipients' names in the video. For several years running, communications consultant Deb Arnold has created a very funny yet professional and even instructional holiday video. Often she lists the names of people she especially wants to thank at the end of the video, like movie credits. She sends it to those people, of course.

Sample Christmas and Chanukah Greetings

Whether you send a printed card, an electronic greeting, a photo card, a video, or something else, the following messages can help you think of what to write. Mix and match the sentiments to create a message that works for you and your recipients. You may choose to indent paragraphs or not. The samples use both formats.

Dear Friends at XYZ Company,

At this joyous time of year, we are grateful for our work with you. We wish you abundance, happiness, and peace in a new year filled with hope. Happy holidays!

> Your friends at ABC Catering:
> Daniel, Lisa, Natasha,
> Marjorie, Satya, and Joe

Karen, I hope you and all your coworkers, family, and friends have a lovely holiday season brimming with joy and kindness.

> Warm wishes,
> Steven Daly

To all our friends at Marcia's Bridals:

As the year ends, we think about all we are grateful for. Our relationship with you is one thing we treasure. Thank you for the opportunity to serve you. We wish you a merry Christmas and much success in the new year!

> Donna and Dale Burke

Dear Professor Reiss,

Thank you for giving me the opportunity to work with you this year. It has been an honor and a valuable experience for me. I wish you a happy Chanukah and a 20XX filled with light and meaning.

> Marcia Schur

My dear wonderful Jake,

As a person who warms my heart, you come quickly to mind this holiday season. I wish you a happy Chanukah and a new year abundant with miracles of every kind.

Kitty

Dear Naomi,

Each night of Chanukah may you be blessed with warmth and peace. Happy Chanukah!

Jodi

Dear Odaiah,

As gifts are given and received this holiday season, I think of the gift of knowing you. Thank you for the pleasure of working with you this year on the implementation. Happy holidays!

Chad

Dear Carolyn,

Merry Christmas to you and your lovely little girls! I hope you have a holiday brimming with joy and happy surprises!

Traci

Sample New Year's Greetings

Here are generic and audience-specific messages to build on for your New Year's greetings.

Generic:

> We wish you a new year in which peace, joy, and meaning abound.

> Happy 20XX! May your new year be filled with prosperity, hope, and wonder.

> Happy 20XX! I wish you a blissful, magical new year!

> On New Year's Day and every day, we wish you joy and fulfillment. Happy new year!

> I hope you are blessed with delight, serenity, and grace in the coming year.

To a customer or client:

> Thank you for your business this year. It has been a pleasure helping you reach your goals. We wish you a prosperous and happy new year and look forward to serving you in 20XX.

> Thank you for the opportunity to work with you in 20XX. It has been an honor to serve you. We wish you a fulfilling, abundant new year. Happy 20XX!

> I wish you a wonderful new year rich in laughter, pure joy, and treasured moments. May 20XX be your best year yet!

> It has been a privilege and a pleasure to work with you this year. We wish you the best of holidays and a prosperous 20XX!

I hope 20XX is a year of great happiness and success for you. Have a marvelous new year!

Thank you for being a customer at our [event or business]. We look forward to meeting your needs again in 20XX. We wish you peace, contentment, and abundant good health in the new year.

Thank you for shopping with us. We wish you a beautiful new year filled with comfort and gladness. We look forward to seeing you again in 20XX. Happy new year!

We are so pleased to have you as a customer, and we look forward to serving you in the new year. Have a terrific 20XX!

To a patron or volunteer:

Happy new year! Thanks to supporters like you, 20XX was a very successful year for us. We were able to exceed our goals and expand our services to the needy because of the generosity and commitment of people like you. Thank you so much!

Thank you for your contribution to our important work. With your help, we had a very successful 20XX. We wish you a blessed, happy new year.

To employees:

Whoo hoo! We survived 20XX! In fact, we thrived because of your amazing hard work, creativity, and dedication. I am personally grateful to you for your tremendous efforts, and I wish you a fabulous new year.

I am grateful to each one of you for your incredible skills and creative thinking, and I wish everyone a rewarding, joyous new year. I can't wait to see what we accomplish together in 20XX!

I appreciate your contribution to our success this year. I wish you joy, fun, and fulfillment in 20XX. Happy new year!

After reading those examples, you may be wondering about how to render references to the new year. *New Year's Day* and *New Year's Eve* have apostrophes and are capitalized. But if you are simply referring to next year, you do not need to capitalize it: "I hope you have a joyful new year." That said, "Happy New Year!" with capital letters has become a standard greeting. I typically use the lower case version: "I wish you a happy new year!"

Ways to Make Your Holidays Easier

Consider these tips to help you ease the pressure of getting things done while keeping the season special:

Send Thanksgiving cards instead of dealing with the Chanukah-Christmas-New Year's rush. Your cards of thanks will stand out because they will not be part of a mail or email onslaught. See the chapter "Write Mighty Thank-Yous" for examples of Thanksgiving messages.

Send New Year's greetings rather than stressing to get your Christmas cards out by December 20. You can work on New Year's cards during the relaxing days after Christmas, when little work may be required of you (unless you work in retail). Then send them out after January 1. Sending the cards anytime during the first week or so of January makes them on time. Also, with New Year's cards, you can avoid worries about whether and how your associates celebrate Christmas and how to choose the right card. But when you select them, avoid cards that emphasize drinking unless you know your specific readers appreciate wine and spirits. Many of your associates may prefer a safe, sober new year and may not relate to an alcohol-themed greeting.

Celebrate your own Christmas in July by ordering your Christmas cards in the summer, then taking the time to write personal notes on them whenever you have time before the busy holiday season. If you will send group cards, give your coworkers plenty of time to sign them. Or have signing parties to get in the holiday spirit.

If you choose to hand-address cards, begin in the summer or early fall. That way, you and your staff will not have hand cramps just before Christmas. Leadership and organizational development consultant Ron Scott starts early and meditates briefly on each person as he addresses and signs individual cards.

If you choose to print envelopes, do so using a merge-mailing list or a sheet of mailing labels rather than individually printing each one.

Update your mailing list whenever you have time during the year. When you make a new business friend, add the individual's contact information to your list. That way, you will not have to scramble for a business card or contact information when you are ready to send cards.

Decide on your preferred spelling of *Chanukah* (that spelling is my preference) and stick to it. That way, you will not eat up time changing your mind. Other common versions are *Hanukkah* and *Hannukah*.

Try sending email greetings or e-cards to eliminate the need to address and sign dozens or hundreds of printed cards. Make sure to individualize your greetings so they come across as special messages rather than spam.

Responding to Holiday Greetings

You may be wondering whether you need to thank people for holiday greetings or respond in kind. Although neither response is required, acknowledging the other person's effort can strengthen your relationship. Thank-yous and reciprocated best wishes can spread smiles and a sense of connection. Why not send them?

Remember: This time of year is a special, once-a-year chance to connect with people. Think widely when you compose your list of people to remember. Even if you are an employee without clients and external customers, think of the people who contribute to your success: your manager, coworkers, colleagues in other departments, peers in other companies and professional organizations, consultants, and allies in human resources. Remember them! Reconnect! Nurture your work relationships.

Personal Reflection

▸ Connecting with your business associates is a gift to yourself and to them—not an obligation. How can you make the process feel joyous to you? What can you do to reduce stress and enjoy reaching out?

Next Step

▸ Whenever you are reading this sentence—whether it is February, June, or November—what is one thing you can do this week to make progress on sending holiday cards? Do that thing.

PART THREE

The Challenges—Messages That Can Make (or Break) Relationships

CHAPTER 10

Write Apologies to Mend Fences and Support Relationships

Through many years of practice, our teenaged daughter had outgrown her violin, so we went to Olsen Violins, a violin shop in our Seattle neighborhood, to look at new ones. When we walked into the shop, I told the woman who greeted us that we were looking for a violin in the $4,000 range. Soon we were placed in the shop's soundproof room with a variety of violins to try out. They ranged from $3,800 to $8,000, with nearly all of them higher than $4,000.

After we had been in the room awhile, Sten Olsen came into the room, apologizing with words like these: "I am so sorry. I just learned from Nete that you wanted violins in the $4,000 range. I thought she had said $4,000 to $8,000."

I told Sten that although I was shocked at first at the higher price tags, when we heard the beautiful sound of the more expensive violins, we realized we might need to spend more than we had intended.

The next day I received this email from Olsen Violins:

Subject: An Apology

Hi Lynn,

I want to apologize for the price confusion yesterday. I hear stories regularly from people who have gone to other violin shops and get nudged/pushed into a higher price range than they are requesting. I really hate that! I have utmost respect for what people are willing to spend and I never push people higher. I take this seriously. I feel terrible!

I have a lot of really, really nice violins around 3–4K. I hope you give these instruments another look. I also have a couple violins out on trial with someone else that are right in the price category too.

Have a nice weekend and Thanksgiving!

Regards,
Sten Olsen
Olsen Violins, Inc.

Sten Olsen's apology was not necessary because he had apologized the previous day. But his written apology told me that he meant what he had said. It also provided a remedy in the mention of several violins in our price range. It came across as sincere, with the statements "I want to apologize," "I have the utmost respect," and "I feel terrible." Sten's apology was a relationship builder. It showed me that he valued us as customers.

We ended up buying both a violin and a bow from Olsen Violins, spending much more than our original budget. Now we refer other people to the shop. Although it was only one of the factors that encouraged our relationship, Sten Olsen's apology made a big positive difference.

This chapter helps you recognize why and how to write sincere, productive apologies.

The Power of Saying "I'm Sorry"

I don't know about parents around the globe, but where I live parents regularly break up spats between small children, instructing them, "I want you two to both say you're sorry!" After both children complain that it's not their fault, they reluctantly say they are sorry. With the words "I'm sorry" ending the argument, the children move on to their next activity, often playing happily side by side within minutes.

To us as adults at work, saying we are sorry seems more complicated. When we say it (and write it), we worry that we may be accepting blame, admitting liability in our litigious society, and apologizing ourselves into a corner.

But apologies can free us in many ways. As with the *sorries* of children, our apologies let us move on to the next activity. They also free the people to whom we apologize by helping them let go of their bad feelings about the wrong done to them. They help everyone acknowledge that business decisions can negatively affect people's lives, sometimes deeply and lastingly. Apologies communicate the messages "I respect you" and "I recognize that you are a human being with feelings" without actually using those words.

An engineer named Keith Chapman told this story and shared his example of an apology:

> John was the lead engineer assigned to a project, and I was his counterpart at my company. Of necessity, I took a very active role in steering the design, which imposed a level of scrutiny that John was not used to receiving from customers. Because of this, midway through the job the relationship started to sour. Through phone calls, and some intervention from both our superiors, I managed to settle things down and brought us back into a working relationship. As the design work was wrapping up, John asked me how things looked on the job from a budget standpoint. I used the opportunity to try to smooth things over:

John,

I do think we will make budget on the job. [Keith followed with details about the project.]

I would like to say that I think this job has gone really well. We did have a few disagreements early on, but those things happen, especially between people who are both passionate about their work. Despite the disagreements, we worked together well, came to a good design, and were on time to boot.

I would also like to apologize for something that I did earlier in the job. In one of my review remarks I pointed out an error in your calculations. I believe it was a real error, but it was an advance set of calcs from you, not your stamped final submittal. It was wrong of me to point it out in an email that I copied to both of our bosses. I should have brought it to you personally and given you the chance to defend it or correct it. It's a courtesy that should be extended to fellow engineers. When we work together in the future, I will make a point of it.

Keith

In his desire to "smooth things over," Keith apologized sincerely for his unfortunate email choice. His apology validated John in any negative feelings John might have been harboring about the incident, and it allowed John to move on from them. The message also allowed Keith to move on. It helped banish the pangs of guilt Keith may have felt about his behavior.

Dr. Dennis Dennis, an organizational psychologist, shares this important comment on the benefits of apologizing:

An apology benefits the person giving it as much (or often more) than the person receiving it. This thought sometimes helps people get past the difficulty of apologizing sincerely when they really believe the other party contributed in some way to the problem.

The advantage of this approach is that it allows the "apologizer" to maintain their boundary and a sense of personal power because they are in control of the decision to apologize. It is entirely up to the other person whether they will accept the apology. One can sincerely apologize and move on even if the apology is not accepted.

Although our apology may not save a relationship, Dr. Dennis's comment reminds us that our apology can benefit our relationship with ourselves.

The Parts of an Apology

In his excellent book *On Apology*, Dr. Aaron Lazare, retired dean of the University of Massachusetts Medical School, identified four parts of an effective apology:

1. Acknowledging the offense

2. Explaining what happened

3. Communicating feelings such as remorse, shame, humility, and sincerity

4. Making or offering reparations

Dr. Lazare wrote, "The importance of each part—even the necessity of each part—varies from apology to apology depending on the situation."

This sincere apology contains all four parts:

Subject: Apology for My Remark

Dear Sharon,

I am very sorry about referring to you as the "accounting Nazi" in my email to Eduardo. It was a stupid remark, and I am embarrassed that I made it. There is no excuse for that kind of attack, and I appreciate your calling me on it. I understand that it was especially hurtful to you because of your Jewish heritage. I am very sorry and ashamed.

I promise to avoid using that kind of language again in my dealings with you and your colleagues (or anyone else for that matter). Please let me know if there is something else I can do to make up for my ignorant behavior.

Please accept my apology.

David Goode

When she reads that detailed apology, Sharon may be able to forgive David and forget his bad behavior, depending on the history of their relationship. The message seems to communicate everything she needs to hear.

In contrast, this version of the "apology" would do little to mend the relationship:

Subject: Sorry

Sharon, I am sorry you were upset that I called you a Nazi. I was just frustrated about all the bureaucratic hoops you and your coworkers make us go through. You never told me you were Jewish, so I didn't know it would push your buttons so much.

Again, sorry.

David Baad

The Baad version of the message includes a quick "sorry," but it does not come across as sincere. The writer did not acknowledge responsibility. Rather, he hinted that Sharon is at fault for being upset, resorting to bureaucratic hoops, not telling David she is Jewish, and allowing the comment to push her buttons.

This apology, written to a coworker, contains all four of Dr. Lazare's parts:

> Subject: Sorry for missing your presentation
>
> Dear Kim,
>
> I am sorry I missed your presentation this morning. I know it was my job to be there to provide the latest financial data, and I am very sorry that I let you down.
>
> As I mentioned in my phone message, an accident on the floating bridge caused traffic to back up for nearly an hour. Although I left for work in plenty of time to be there for your presentation, the accident caused me to arrive after your time on the agenda.
>
> I emailed the data to you when I arrived. If you would like me to do anything else to make up for my absence, please let me know.
>
> Please accept my apology.
>
> Renee

In Renee's situation, it might be tempting simply to leave Kim a quick phone message of apology. However, the written note makes it clear that Renee regrets what happened and does not take it lightly. She values her relationship with Kim.

The next apology covers a more sensitive situation.

Subject: Apology

Dear Robert,

I wanted to write to you regarding our conversation the other day about the new team member. I apologize for making inappropriate assumptions about your hiring decision. That was very wrong of me. Please accept my sincere apology.

I realize since we talked that I simply liked the candidate from Ghana and was disappointed that I won't have the chance to work with him. I understand now why you chose Santosh and how she will complement our skills and experience.

I regret the comment I made, and I promise to support Santosh 100 percent. If there is anything else you would like me to do, please let me know.

Sincerely,

Roy

Roy's apology communicates several important things to Robert: that Roy regrets the remark he made, understands that his assumptions were inappropriate, and intends to support the new employee completely. Although Roy might have hesitated to "document" his mistake by mentioning it in writing, he has successfully documented his realization and his apology. Beyond that, he has shored up his relationship with Robert and committed to building a relationship with Santosh.

I received the following good apology when I informed a newsletter of misspellings of my name. (I have changed the identifying details.) It acknowledges the error, apologizes for it, and indicates what the magazine will do to reduce confusion for readers of the newsletter.

Lynn,

Our sincere apologies for the misspellings. Our newsletter goes through a rigorous editing cycle with numerous editors, copy editors, and proofers looking at each issue. Unfortunately, the misspellings somehow slipped through.

I have corrected the file, and fortunately, the article was slated to go up on our website on August 15, so it hasn't appeared online yet.

Our subscribers can download a PDF version of the newsletter on our website, which I assume is where your client saw the article. The print version goes in the mail this week.

We will also run a correction in the next issue of the print version of the newsletter.

Again, our apologies for the error.

Sincerely,
Gayle Franson
Senior Editor

Tips for Apologies

Because written apologies last beyond the moment and do not provide an opportunity for immediate two-way communication, you need to follow certain guidelines when writing them. Consider these tips and adapt them to your situations:

Use the words "I apologize," "I regret," and "I am sorry." Use "we" or "on behalf of" when you apologize as a representative of your company or organization. By using the language of apology, you make it completely clear that you are apologizing.

Explain what happened. Your explanation helps the other person understand why the incident took place. Do not rely on your explanation, however, to imply your apology. Use the words in the previous tip.

Name what you will do or hope to do to remedy the situation. For example, in some of the previous examples, Sten Olsen offered lower-priced violins, Keith promised to observe professional courtesies in the future, and the newsletter editor promised me a correction.

Ask the reader to accept your apology. Your request engages the reader and asks for reconciliation.

Avoid bringing up other topics. They will dilute the apology and may make it seem like an afterthought.

Don't criticize the reader or blame others. For example, don't say, "If only you had let me know sooner" or "It was my manager's idea that I . . ." Such remarks reduce the sincerity and power of the apology. They turn it into scapegoating.

Don't offer a "sorry but." For instance, don't say, "I am sorry, but you must also accept responsibility." Such a statement ignites a potential blame war.

A perfect example of criticizing the reader in a "sorry but" appeared in the NetSpeed Learning Solutions blog in a post written by Tim Jones. He described this as an excuse, not an apology, and I agree:

> I am really sorry about missing the budget planning conference call this morning. I would have been on the call, but you never confirmed what I was supposed to present so I figured that the call must not be that important. Why didn't you tell me what I needed to present?

I like Tim Jones's advice: "If you really don't feel you are the cause, then it's okay to push back and defend your position. But if you ultimately know in your heart that an apology is in order, make it a full apology. Make it sincere. And make it count."

If You Cannot Think of What to Write

When you are not sure what to write, think about what the other person needs to know. What would he or she ask you if you were talking? Of course, you won't actually be talking when the other person reads your words, but think of the apology as a conversation.

Let's imagine that you are writing to apologize for missing a business meeting. Your reader might have these questions:

1. What is this note about?

2. Why *did* you miss the meeting?

3. What will you do to make up for missing the meeting?

4. Can we count on you to attend future meetings?

5. Are you sorry for the oversight?

After the introductory Question 1, Questions 2 through 5 are ones the other person is probably wondering about. To write the apology, just answer the questions, as this example does:

Dear Dr. Young,

[What is this note about?]
Please accept my apology for missing the planning meeting on Friday afternoon. I am very sorry about my absence.

[Why *did* you miss the meeting?]

On Friday I had an enjoyable lunch with an old, dear friend, and in the pleasure of the reunion I simply forgot about the planning meeting. I incorrectly thought my calendar was clear.

[What will you do to make up for missing the meeting?]

I have already spoken with Lorraine Clarke about what happened at the meeting. She informed me of the two tasks that have been assigned to me.

[Can we count on you to attend future meetings?]

I assure you that this will not happen again. I have added all the meetings to my phone, with a reminder alarm. I look forward to actively participating in our future sessions.

[Are you sorry for the oversight?]

Once again, I am sorry for missing the meeting. Please accept my apology.

Sincerely,
Samantha

Apologizing for Little Things

Little things can erode good relationships one little thing at a time. In business, take time to apologize in writing for any small mistakes, slights, or oversights. Even though they are brief, such apologies reduce the likelihood that missteps will grow into resentments.

I found these brief apologies in my email inbox. Each was included in a longer message.

- My apologies for the delay. My password reset and locked me out of my system all weekend! I hope this is not too late. Thank you!

- Please accept my apology for dragging my feet on this decision.
- I was hoping to have more time with you. I apologize!
- I apologize for the late request. I have been working from home for the past two months due to my daughter's slow recovery from surgery. Time found a way of slipping by me quickly.
- I apologize that the invoice wasn't paid on time. I am sorry it got lost in the pipeline.
- We apologize for any inconvenience this situation may have caused and appreciate your patience while we work on this.
- I apologize about the phone number confusion.
- We apologize for the inconvenience you experienced in downloading your order.
- I just realized as I was reading your email again that I completely missed your deadline. My apologies!
- Sorry, I just saw your response below. Never mind!

The brief apologies do the important work of acknowledging the delay, the foot dragging, the lack of time, the missed deadline, the late payment, and so on. Of course, repeated missed deadlines and late payments will require much more than a sentence of apology. They will beg for changes in behavior.

Apologizing Does Not Always Mean Accepting Blame

In my survey on business writing and relationships, 69 percent of respondents agreed or strongly agreed that they hate to apologize when they have not done anything wrong. Yet many respondents explained that they apologize despite any aversion to it. Here are sample comments from four individuals:

> I really truly HATE apologizing when I haven't done anything wrong, but I also know that it's my personal perception that I haven't done anything wrong—the person "wronged" obviously feels differently. So I will do it . . .

usually something like, I'm sorry that my [action] made you feel [feeling].

Admitting you were wrong even in just having favored your own perspective without considering another person's goes a long way toward mending fences and finding common ground.

Lately I have accepted the fact that it is the right thing to do for harmony.

I hate doing it but it often works. So I do it fairly often. I work in IT [information technology] though.

Like those individuals, you will sometimes find it helpful to apologize even though you have done nothing wrong. Clearly *something* happened that led to the need for an apology. It's much better to apologize and move on than refuse to do so. Such a refusal saps energy and erects a wall between people.

In awkward situations that seem to require an apology, even when you can't see that you have done anything wrong, tell yourself that you will apologize respectfully because the other person needs it. Then apologize. Do not point a finger at the other person with a sentiment like this: "I am sorry you took it the wrong way." Instead, use statements like these:

- I am sorry for the part I played in this situation.
- I regret that I was not able to respond in a way that was helpful.
- I am sorry that what I said hurt your feelings.

If you are a supervisor or manager, you will find it helpful to apologize when a situation has caused problems or hard feelings—even when you are not responsible for the situation. In these cases, "I am sorry" does not mean "I am responsible." It means "I care about you and your feelings." Examples:

- I am very sorry that the new date for the product launch has affected your vacation plans.
- I am sorry that the construction will require you to park so far from the plant.

Making Official Apologies

HR Magazine featured an excellent article, "A 'Sorry' Strategy," by attorney Jathan Janove. The piece focused on the effectiveness of apologies in avoiding or settling legal claims. These are two important points from the article:

- Although employer apologies have at times contributed to employer liability, those situations nearly always involved apologies that were mishandled.
- Anger plays an important part in employee lawsuits, and anger is often fueled by an employer's failure to apologize. In many situations, lawsuits can be avoided or settled quickly if an employer apologizes and accepts responsibility for its actions.

Tips for Official Apologies

If you must apologize on behalf of your company, apply these tips:

Check company guidelines or get advice from your human resources department before taking action. Although apologies often reduce an individual's desire to take legal action, as Jathan Janove indicated, the apology must be effective to achieve a positive outcome. Get advice to do it right in highly charged situations.

Communicate empathy with an employee's feelings and circumstances. "I am sorry about the frustration this delay has caused you" acknowledges the situation simply and well.

Do not try to justify or excuse the employer's actions if the employer is at fault. Such attempts weaken the apology. If your company's process was faulty even though the outcome was justified, apologize for the process. For example, if an employee was informed of a layoff in a public, embarrassing way, apologize for the way the information was delivered. The apology does not change the layoff, but it can be very helpful in reducing the employee's anger and indignation. It may prevent the situation from going viral on the Internet and damaging countless relationships.

This example apologizes for the hurt and disappointment an employee feels when she does not receive a promotion and for the way the decision was communicated. However, it does not undercut the promotion decision.

> To: Clare Belmont
> From: Andrew Ross
> Date: July 2, 20XX
> Subject: Following Up on Our Conversation Today
>
> Clare, I would like to recap what we talked about today. I want you to know that I understand you feel I made the wrong decision when I promoted Jessica rather than you into the new Level II position. You feel you are the most qualified person for the position and that the decision is unfair.
>
> When making a promotion to Level II, I need to consider a variety of factors. Foremost among them is what is best for the department and our customer-service commitments. Looking at all information, I believe my decision is the right one.

I value your work very much, and I am sorry about the hurt and disappointment this decision has caused. Please accept my apology for the blunders I committed while communicating the decision.

Andrew

Don't Be Sorry About Apologizing

Do you remember the story about Sten Olsen's apology for misunderstanding my violin budget? In the end, I bought a much more expensive violin, along with a bow, and I continue to recommend Sten to others in Seattle who are in the market for an instrument. Here's the moral of the story: Do not be sorry about apologizing. It is one of the best steps you can take to build and maintain good relationships, overcome hard feelings, nurture loyalty, and show respect for other human beings. Beyond that, as Sten's story demonstrates, it can even help you sell products and services.

Personal Reflection

▸ Do you apologize when you have done something that hurts or inconveniences another person at work? Do you see apologizing as a helpful step for both parties, as a necessary annoyance, or as something else?

Next Step

▸ In this chapter, an engineer named Keith apologized to another engineer for something Keith had done awhile back. Think about your work relationships and whether there is something you would like to apologize for. Then write and send the apology.

CHAPTER 11

Share Bad News Without
Fostering Bad Feelings

⁂

For several years I worked as a consultant at an outplacement firm, a company that is hired to help people who have been laid off. We would start by helping them make peace with the circumstances of losing their job. Over time we would coach them to find their next opportunity, whether it be a job, their own business, or retirement.

Perhaps the most challenging assignment at the outplacement firm was to go to a company on the day of layoffs and meet with the employees and managers who had lost their jobs. It was like the role of Ryan Bingham in the book and movie *Up in the Air,* only we didn't actually give the bad news; we cleaned up after it.

Some of us dreaded the assignment because we never knew how the employees and managers would react. Would they weep? Yell? Swear? Sit numbly and not say a word? Run out of the room, calling us names? Or would they thank us for being there and giving them information? Any and all those reactions were possible. The challenge was being able to handle whatever came at us without making the bad news worse.

Like us outplacement consultants, many people dread giving bad news because they do not know how it will go down, and they fear the worst reactions. They also question their own competence. Will they be able to communicate the bad news compassionately and clearly so people will understand and accept it? Will their relationships survive the bad news? Or will the bad news cause bad feelings that end their relationships?

How about you? Which of these words would you choose to describe the act of communicating bad news?

Column 1	Column 2
comfortable	uncomfortable
satisfying	upsetting
rewarding	guilt-ridden
easy	awkward
relaxed	anxiety-filled
risk-free	depressing

If you picked more words from Column 2 than Column 1, here's the good news: You are human! The bad news is that . . . well, this chapter is all about bad news. It shares valuable tips, examples, and encouragement that will make it easier for you to protect your relationships while sharing bad news.

Sharing bad news is no fun. The thought of having to communicate bad news to valued employees, managers, colleagues, applicants, clients, and vendors causes people to lose sleep, eat and drink more than they intend, and try to think of ways to disappear until the bad news blows over.

If just the idea of communicating bad news makes you feel bad, consider using these new words to describe it:

Column 3
kind
considerate

generous

courageous

thoughtful

mature

Yes, communicating bad news thoughtfully and promptly is kind, considerate, generous, courageous, thoughtful, and mature. It is a precious gift you can give to others. Doing it well makes the other person feel respected and can strengthen your relationship. Adopt that positive mindset, and you will instantly feel at least a little better about having to share bad news.

Sharing Bad News in Person and in Writing

Whenever possible, share bad news in person, not in writing. That way, your communication will be two-way. You will see firsthand whether people cry, yell, or take the news in stride, as we outplacement consultants did. You will be able to deal with people's responses appropriately in real time.

Although communicating bad news in person is a first choice, putting bad news in writing makes sense at times:

- When informing a hundred job applicants that they were not chosen for a job
- When informing dozens of customers about the departure of a popular employee
- When letting hundreds or thousands of clients know about an increase in fees
- When informing thousands of students and their parents that tuition is increasing
- When telling all employees about a personnel or policy change that will be unpopular
- When communicating bad news to employees on the other side of the globe

Informing Applicants That They Were Not Chosen

One uncomfortable bad-news message is the letter to applicants who did not get the job. Especially in difficult economic times, the vision of qualified, eager, sometimes desperate job applicants opening your bad-news message can cripple your efforts to write it. Yet the applicants need to hear the outcome.

Of course, you don't want your "rejection" letter to hurt people. You want to avoid alienating potential customers, members, and future applicants. The looming risk is to say too little and seem brusque or say too much and inadvertently wound them.

It is possible to write a clear, thoughtful "rejection" message that leaves no one feeling rejected. It has five components:

1. A warm opening

2. A brief description of the decision-making process that presents it as rigorous rather than haphazard

3. The bad news, sometimes implied rather than directly stated

4. Acknowledgment and appreciation of the effort the individual put into the application

5. Good wishes for the future

Notice in the above list the *absence* of judgment on the applicant's credentials or fit for the position. To avoid making bad news worse, the message does not include any negative comments about the applicant's suitability. Nor does it include positive comments. Positive statements about qualifications could make the applicant more disheartened about not getting a job for which he or she was apparently well qualified.

This advice also applies to other situations such as rejecting a manuscript submitted for publication. Although it may be tempting to encourage the writer, encouragement can backfire into an argument about why the piece will not be published or a time-consuming written exchange about how to revise the writing. If your goal is to share bad news without fostering bad feelings in yourself or others, limiting your message to the five components works best. If your goal is to mentor young writers or others, you may find another way to achieve it, outside the bad-news message.

Below is a model bad-news message, sent from University Baptist Church in Seattle, Washington, to the many people who had applied for the position of pastor.

> Thank you for expressing interest in the position of pastor at University Baptist Church. We have carefully studied the profiles we received, and we have decided to interview four candidates. The skills and experience of the four individuals are a unique match for the needs of our congregation.
>
> We appreciate the time you spent preparing materials for us, and we ask for God's blessing on you as you seek another position.
>
> Cordially,

The message is brief, yet it communicates good will and caring. The mention of God's blessing is perfect in a letter from a church. A similar message from a business could close this way:

> We appreciate the time you spent preparing materials for us, and we wish you success obtaining a position.

The church representative who shared the letter with me made sure I understood this point: The three people who eventually interviewed for the job but did not get it received a phone call, not a letter. A phone call made sense because of the small number of people involved and because those who interviewed now had a personal connection with the church. They deserved a more personal, individual message.

The bad handling of such a message leads to bad feelings, as this true story illustrates: A job candidate who had been searching for a position for quite a while had four interviews on four different days with a prestigious firm. Naturally, he was getting excited. And he should have been—his fourth interview was with a senior executive. Then he got a message from the company, a letter saying he did not get the job.

You might wonder—what's wrong with that? We cannot each be the chosen one when it comes to a position. But the letter he received was canned—an impersonal rejection letter, the kind that is sent to any faceless applicant who was not even interviewed.

Here's why that letter damaged a budding, positive relationship: A job applicant who endured four interviews with the same firm, dressed meticulously on four different days, prepared carefully for several conversation/cross-examinations, graciously met a variety of strangers—such an applicant deserved a thoughtful personal letter or phone call.

A friend of the dejected applicant related this story to me with anger. It would be no surprise if word spread about how the prestigious firm treated the candidate. People who heard the story might retell it at business meetings and lunches, and those in job searches might avoid that company's recruiters if they could. The original job candidate would be slow to consider a job with that company or to do business with it again—all because someone did not take the time to write a personal letter or make a phone call to treat him with care and dignity.

Never underestimate the power of your communication to create or destroy relationships!

Informing Customers of the Departure of a Popular Employee

Customers want to know when changes take place with the people who serve them. These messages can be delicate because we don't want to lose the customer along with the employee.

What follows is an example of how *not* to tell customers about an employee's departure. The paragraph is excerpted from a landscaping company's letter to all customers, updating them on spring landscaping services. All names are fictitious.

> David, Gloria, and Juan will all be back. You are very familiar with these three since they have been at your house for many years now. Michael, who was an invaluable employee for 21 years, forced me to make a very difficult decision last fall. When the evidence of his transgressions became so great and so blatant, I had no choice but to dismiss him. His work was exemplary, as was the value he offered all our customers; however, his actions were eroding the morale of his coworkers and affecting my ability to conduct a sustainable business. I mention this because so many people came to expect Michael every week, and he was so well liked. Also during the lifetime of our company we have had very low turnover, and events like this are rare. Replacing Michael this season is Simon. I have known Simon for over 10 years. He has worked with two other local landscapers. He knows this business, and I am confident that his demeanor and work ethic will be a nice fit for our team.

"The evidence of Michael's transgressions"—yikes! The phrase creates nothing but trouble: anxious curiosity in customers; relief (or doubt) that they were not injured by Michael's behavior, whatever it was; and potential legal repercussions if a customer talks to Michael about the letter.

The paragraph contains all the right information. It just needs editing so the bad news is brief and neutral rather than detailed and destructive. Here is a suitable version that shares brief news of the well-liked employee's departure and lets customers know they will be in good hands with Michael's replacement:

David, Gloria, and Juan will all be back, as they have been for many years. Michael, who was an invaluable employee for 21 years, has moved on. Replacing Michael this season is Simon, whom I have known for over 10 years. Simon has worked with two other landscapers and knows this business. I am confident that his demeanor and work ethic will be a nice fit for our team.

For a communication that goes to all customers, the short version is just right to keep relationships intact. If individual customers ask for more information, it may be shared discreetly in person.

Tips for Communicating Bad News

These valuable tips will help you do a good job of sharing bad news without damaging relationships:

Reveal it—don't conceal it. Don't try to protect others from bad news or yourself from sharing it. If bad news leaks out, individuals may be hurt and angry that they did not learn it from you or through other appropriate channels. Remember: Sharing bad news well is kind, considerate, generous, courageous, thoughtful, and mature.

Communicate bad news promptly. A typical response to bad news is "How long have you known?" If you have known for a long time but have not shared the news, people may feel that they have been cheated or that you do not trust them. Recognize that there is no perfect time for bad news. Share it as soon as you can share it clearly and completely.

Apologize. Saying you are sorry about a situation does not mean you are guilty or liable for it. It means you care. Tell employees, customers, clients, and patrons when you are sorry that the news is not better. And if the bad news *is* your fault—for example, if you missed a proposal submission deadline because of your own mistake or delay—accept responsibility and apologize so that you and everyone else can move on.

In this announcement, the writer uses "Please accept my apology" to avert negative reactions to a change in a longstanding employee perk:

> Subject: Change in Policy on Refreshments
>
> Dear Staff,
>
> Due to serious budget constraints facing our organization, as of September 1, food will no longer be provided at meetings and workshops. However, you may bring your own food to meetings and workshops if you would like to do so.
>
> Please accept my apology for the change. Management will reevaluate this decision during the next budgeting session.
>
> Please contact me if you have any questions about the policy change. Thank you for your patience and understanding.

As a rule, be serious when delivering bad news, or your audience will be confused about the seriousness of the message. In the example about the change in the refreshment policy, it would be clumsy—and for certain readers insensitive—to include a quip such as "Good time to go on a diet!"

Empathize. Recognize that your readers will have feelings about the bad news. Netflix experienced a huge backlash when it sent out a matter-of-fact email from "The Netflix Team" informing customers that their monthly rental fee for unlimited streaming and DVDs would increase from $9.99 to $15.98 (a 59 percent jump!). After two months of customer complaints and cancellations, an email to customers from Netflix Co-Founder and CEO Reed Hastings began this way:

I messed up. I owe you an explanation.

It is clear from the feedback over the past two months that many members felt we lacked respect and humility in the way we announced the separation of DVD and streaming and the price changes. That was certainly not our intent, and I offer my sincere apology.

There is always the risk that a price increase and other changes will anger and turn away customers. But a more thoughtful bad-news message than Netflix's original regrettable communication would likely have reduced customer dissatisfaction and animosity toward the company.

Be compassionate with yourself and others. When you deliver bad news, both you and the recipients will probably feel bad. Do not be surprised or offended if individuals shoot back sarcastic, critical emails. After all, your readers will have just learned the information you have known for a while. Do your best to remain professional, and know that the bad feelings will pass.

If you can legitimately do so, include the good-news aspects of the bad news. (But see the next tip.) For example, downsizing offices may seem like bad news, but it is a good idea if it saves people's jobs.

Do not sugarcoat, minimize, or disguise the message with cheerful, positive language. Bad news is not more palatable with a sweet coating, and a deceptive sweet coating threatens trust and loyalty. For example, companies come across as deceitful when they centralize operations and try to promote the idea that customers will be better served without their local representative. Reducing service while applauding the reduction does not fool anyone.

Avoid making bad news worse by focusing on the negative aspects. Instead of "We have no idea how we will handle the situation," say, "We are working on a procedure for handling the situation." Replace "I can't discuss that with you" with "I will share as much information as I can." When appropriate, replace "I apologize for the inconvenience" with "I appreciate your flexibility."

Use a variety of media, not just email. Often the most effective communication choice is email combined with other methods, but email alone may come across as unfeeling and distant. When RadioShack laid off 403 employees by email, *The Dallas Morning News* ran an online poll asking, "Is it OK to lay off workers via e-mail?" Over 90 percent of poll respondents answered "No, it should be done face to face," and many criticized the company and pledged to boycott it. Less than 10 percent voted "Yes, it doesn't really matter how you get the news."

When you can, supplement written communication with telephone calls, in-person meetings, live online meetings, videoconferences, and other choices. Consider expanding written communication to include memos, letters to clients' offices or employees' homes, and intranet and blog posts.

Communicate first with the people who are most affected by the bad news. For example, if some employees will be transferred, tell them directly before you tell others about the situation. If some customers may suffer because of a policy change, tell them about it before announcing the change broadly. Never blog or tweet about bad news before sharing it completely, clearly, and compassionately with those involved.

Communicate more than once, providing additional details and updates in follow-up communications. Especially if the news is serious, people take in bad news only gradually. After they have grasped the main message, they will want details.

The following example is the first announcement of a company's move to another location, which will be bad news for some employees.

The email does not contain every detail about the move. Rather, it indicates that further information will follow. Note that the news is fresh—negotiations were just completed today.

> Subject: Announcing Our Company Move to Beaverton Scheduled for February
>
> I am pleased to announce that negotiations were completed today for our corporate offices to move to [street address] in Beaverton. The attached sheet shows a map of the location and a photo of the building. Our current plan is that the move will be complete by February 20.
>
> **Benefits of the move:** We have all felt the squeeze of our overcrowded space. Our new offices will provide us with the benefits below, all at a cost similar to that of our current downtown space:
>
> - An additional 7,000 square feet of office space
> - Several additional conference rooms
> - A conference room large enough to accommodate all-company meetings
> - Free parking
> - Other amenities now in the planning stages
>
> **Adjustments required:** This move will require adjustments from all of us, some more than others. For staff who live in or near Beaverton, the commute will be easier; however, for staff who live near our current office, commuting to Beaverton is likely to be an undesirable change. We will make every reasonable effort to ensure that the move is smooth and workable for everyone in the company.
>
> **Tasks of the Move Committee:** Our HR manager, Kamala King, will head our Move Committee. The committee will work on the timing of the move, green commuting strategies,

office space allocation, and a variety of other concerns. If you are interested in being part of the committee, please talk with Kamala [phone, email] about your interest and any expertise.

Opportunities to give input into the design and amenities: We will work with The Design Company on office amenities, décor, and related issues. Design Company president David Washington and his staff will hold meetings to get your input on the features you want to see in the new space. You can learn more about The Design Company and the awards they have won on their website [link].

Answers to your questions and concerns: As details become available, I will share them with you by email. Kamala will hold meetings soon to listen to your concerns and suggestions. If you have pressing questions now, send them to Kamala or me, and we will answer them or forward them to someone who can.

Although change is always challenging, I hope you will join me in looking forward to our new, larger offices and imagining the opportunities the space will offer all of us.

Jacob

Answer essential questions. Your audience is likely to want to learn what, why, who, when, where, how, how much, and what if. Include all the information that is important to them. If you don't have all the details, be honest but have a plan to get the information. (Note the "As details become available" wording in the previous example.) A lack of information often creates a lack of confidence and commitment.

Individualize the message. Your clients need different information from your coworkers; employees have different questions from managers.

Invest the time to write a tailored message for each audience, and it will pay off in communication that is more successful.

Use accurate titles or subject lines for bad-news communications. Avoid titles like "An Exciting Change in Benefits" if the change is unwelcome to any of your readers. Instead use the neutral "Change in Benefits Effective September 1." If a title seems misleading, readers will be skeptical about your entire message.

Avoid blaming other individuals. It may be tempting to blame others for the bad news you must share, but blaming individuals or groups can be seen as unseemly and cowardly. However, vague blame—for example, blaming the economy, government regulations, or natural disasters—is acceptable and understandable to your audience, if it is truthful.

Mention anything you are doing to reduce the impact of the bad news. For example, if a well-liked assistant is being laid off because of budget cuts, tell how you will help the employee find a new job. Or if a delay means you cannot ship an order in time for holiday delivery, state what you can ship as a replacement, what type of gift card you can provide until the product is available, etc.

Write your bad-news messages even when you will speak them. Without a script, it is too easy to state incorrect information and make unrealistic commitments—both of which eventually lead to bad feelings and damaged trust. If you will speak at a meeting, be prepared with answers to questions people are likely to ask.

Keep your promises to communicate. If you say you will provide more information on Monday, do it. If the information is not available, say so. Broken promises make bad news worse.

Communicating Tragic News

This email communicating tragic news at a university displays many features of an excellent bad-news communication. It delivers the news promptly. The message is clear and complete without revealing confidential information. It expresses condolences and empathy, and it shares abundant information about resources for all involved. Note: All specific details in the email have been disguised.

> Subject: Sad News on Our Campus
>
> Dear Members of the University Community,
>
> I have very sad news to report. Last evening one of our students living in Baker Apartments died. The Lincoln County Medical Examiner has determined that his death was suicide. This is a heart-rending experience for all of us, and our sincere sympathy goes out to his family and friends. There is little comfort to be had at a difficult time like this. It is a terrible loss, and we know members of our university community have come together to support each other. We hope you will all continue to do so.
>
> Last night, staff from the Student Life Office were on the scene late into the night, providing support to students. These psychologists and counselors will continue to provide assistance for as long as is necessary. During this trying period, we want to remind you of the array of resources available to the university community, including professional counseling services for students, faculty, and staff. These services include:
>
> > **The Counseling Center,** staffed by psychologists and counselors who provide counseling, assessment, and crisis intervention services to currently enrolled

students. For more information call [phone] or visit [website].

The Craig Mental Health Center offers a variety of services to students, faculty, staff, and alumni, providing high-quality mental health services. For more information call [phone] or visit [website].

Wellness and Health provides consultation, assessment, and intervention services to students in times of need. Wellness and Health works with students, faculty, and staff to provide a safe and supportive response when coordinated services are necessary. For more information call [phone] or visit [website].

Please take advantage of these services if you need support, and please take good care of yourself and one another.

Sincerely yours,
Clayton Washburn
Vice President, Student Life

Recognize Bad News

Anytime information is not welcome to your audience, it is bad news, even if it seems positive or neutral to you. For example, changing health plans is bad news to an employee who likes the current plan, even if the new plan is better. Being enrolled in a training program is bad news to busy managers who don't know why they are there—as this story of mine illustrates:

The group of managers walked into a Better Business Writing class I was set to teach, talking to each other but not to me. They responded to my greeting but did not seem especially glad to meet me.

Despite the chill in the classroom, I led the session as I usually do. By the end of the 1.5-day writing class, people were pleased about what they had learned and enthusiastic about applying it on the job. Only as they were leaving did I find out why they had been cool at the beginning of the class. One manager happened to tell me this: "No one told us why we were signed up for this class. We just found it on our calendars, no explanation. We're busy managers—a 1.5-day class meant we had to cancel standing meetings, without any explanation of why we needed to work on our writing."

No one had taken the time to tell the managers the bad news—that they would have to cancel meetings and put aside projects to attend a 1.5-day training. And no one had taken the time to explain why.

Here is the message the managers should have received:

> Subject: Better Business Writing Class
>
> The members of the executive team took a writing class we all found valuable. We want to extend the same opportunity to you and the other managers. The class is scheduled on [dates] at [times] and has been added to your calendar.
>
> We know your schedule is very busy and that attending this training may feel like a hardship. But taking time now to tune up your writing skills will save you significant time later. We have already seen an improvement in our writing. Note: You can work on real work documents in the class, so you can get your job done while you learn.
>
> Please stop by to talk to your director if you have questions about the class or concerns about the timing.

Whenever you worry that someone will feel bad about an action you will take or a decision you have made, decide how you will communicate about the potential bad news. Even a small gesture such as unsubscribing from someone's newsletter or feed can cause hurt feelings. In those situations, consider sending a message like one of the following. The first is an email; the second, a text message.

Subject: Unsubscribing from feeds

Hi Chloe,

Today I spent an hour unsubscribing from newsletters and feeds I can't make time to read. Rather than having them hanging in my inbox and filling my phone, where I feel guilty that I am not reading them, I decided to unsubscribe.

I wanted to let you know I unsubscribed from your feed. You write about cool, fascinating things, but I am going to keep up with you other ways.

I promise to stay in touch!

Sky

⸻

Hey José. What's up? I wanted to tell you I unsubscribed from your feed. Nothing personal—I just need more time to get things done. When I see you, we can talk about soccer, life, and so on. Manny

If you don't feel comfortable sending such a bad-news message, and the relationship matters to you, make time to talk to the individual. That way, you can reduce the chances that your simple gesture will damage your relationship.

Be Courageous: Communicate Bad News

Rather than communicate bad news, some people just don't communicate at all, as though it will simply blow over. But that behavior can lead to others feeling let down, left out, overlooked, deceived, and unvalued. Although not communicating is often an attempt to avoid hard feelings, it regularly leads to them.

The courageous alternative is to communicate bad news promptly and diplomatically. That means informing job candidates when a position has been filled by another qualified applicant. It means letting vendors know that their contracts will not be renewed. It means being honest about higher prices rather than pretending that prices will not go up to avoid losing customers. And it means telling employees when the company has plans to downsize.

Understand This: Delivering Bad News Can Be Good

In my work as an outplacement consultant, I observed that a layoff message delivered in person or in writing is very difficult to receive, especially when it is unexpected. But even when the bad news is very bad, there is a personal payoff for delivering the message well.

Despite the message—or perhaps because of it—delivering bad news clearly rather than confusingly, carefully rather than thoughtlessly, and straightforwardly rather than cagily can lead to a deepening of respect and understanding between people. People I "laid off" sometimes became friends of mine, even though we were strangers at the time of the layoff. I was there for them at a difficult time, communicating the bad news and helping them understand it.

You can help people the same way, deepening your business relationships, by communicating bad news with courage and compassion. Although the title of this chapter is "Share Bad News Without Fostering Bad Feelings," it helps to recognize that bad news communicated well can lead to good feelings and stronger relationships.

Personal Reflection

> ▶ Remember a time when you had to communicate bad news. How well did you communicate it? Now think of a time when you received bad news. Was it communicated effectively? What do you wish the person who shared it had done differently?

Next Step

> ► For any project plans you are working on, add "Communicate bad news" to the task list. If you plan to implement changes, list the people whose work lives may be negatively affected, at least from their perspective, and be sure to communicate with them about the changes.

CHAPTER 12

Say No Clearly and Courageously

If you have ever had to say no in writing, you realize it can be a difficult message to write. It is not necessarily the wording that challenges you. It's the idea of saying no to other people whose goodwill you value. You worry about how they will react to the no, whether it is with disappointment, anger, disbelief, belligerence, or embarrassment. You may worry that they will complain to others, say negative things about you, or publish harsh comments about you or your company online.

If you have decided to do nothing rather than say no, you are not alone. According to my survey, rather than tell someone no, 22 percent of people occasionally avoid responding; 3 percent frequently avoid responding in such a situation.

Below is the story of Melanie, who could not say no either in person or in writing in a situation that began at work. The story is essentially true, although details have been changed. As you read Melanie's story, notice whether any part of her feelings or the developing situation is familiar to you.

Melanie was 23 years old and worked in a government agency. She had a coworker, Aleea, age 20. They frequently ate lunch together and went shopping occasionally. People often commented on how strikingly alike they looked.

One day Aleea approached Melanie with a strange request: Aleea was going on vacation to Hawaii with a friend and her family. Because the legal drinking age in Hawaii is 21, Aleea wanted Melanie to help her acquire an ID she could take to Hawaii to show she was 21 and old enough to drink.

Melanie was astonished as she realized Aleea had worked out all the details. Melanie was to report her driver's license as lost and order a new one online, which Aleea would pay for. When the new license arrived, Melanie was to lend her old driver's license to Aleea, who would take the ID to Hawaii, pretend to be Melanie, and be able to drink Mai Tais in bars and restaurants with her friend. When Aleea came back to work after the vacation, she would return the ID to Melanie, who could then destroy it.

Melanie thought the idea was nutty, but she could see Aleea's point of view. She herself had enjoyed the bar scene in Honolulu. And the crazy plan would probably work, since the two looked so much alike. At the same time, Melanie wanted nothing to do with requesting a new license on false pretenses, and she knew she would never agree to do it.

Yet Melanie could not say no. She didn't want to let Aleea down, and she didn't want to appear to be unwilling to help. She also did not want to come across as a goody-goody or suggest that Aleea was less than ethical. And she feared a big blowup that would damage their friendship.

Not knowing how to say no, Melanie half-heartedly said she would think about it. She avoided Aleea for a few days and hoped Aleea would forget about it.

Aleea did not forget. When she tracked down Melanie at lunch one day, Aleea let Melanie know that she had gone online, pretended to be Melanie, and ordered the replacement license. The new license would be mailed to Melanie within two weeks, easily in time for Aleea's trip to Hawaii. All Melanie had to do was give Aleea her old license when the new one arrived.

Melanie was flabbergasted. She could not believe Aleea had ordered the license. But then Melanie blamed herself for not saying no right away when Aleea had suggested it. She worried that now she owed the license to Aleea, who had paid $25 for it. She knew she would not turn the license over to Aleea, but still she could not say no.

Melanie received the new license in the mail within a week. When it came, she decided firmly that she would pretend it had never arrived.

Soon Aleea was asking Melanie every day if the license had come, and every day Melanie lied and said that it had not. The night before she was to fly to Hawaii, Aleea phoned Melanie, anxiously asking Melanie to give her the old license, since the new one would surely arrive the next day. That time Melanie did say no. She said she could not give Aleea her license because then she would not have one herself and would not be able to drive.

Melanie dreaded Aleea's return from her vacation. When Aleea returned and eventually asked if the license had ever arrived in the mail, Melanie said it had not. The two women endured a strained work relationship.

A Typical Downward Spiral When You Cannot Say No

Did any parts of Melanie's story seem familiar? Here is what typically happens in situations when it is difficult to say no:

- Someone—a business associate, applicant, vendor, solicitor, employee, coworker, or potential customer, let's say—makes a request that you cannot (or don't want to) agree to. Maybe the request is impractical, not profitable for you, or against your company policy. Maybe it doesn't appeal to you or would require too much effort. Maybe it is illegal (as in Melanie's situation), unethical, or unprofessional.
- You find it difficult to say no for one reason or many. The reasons generally involve fear: fear of a hurtful response from the other person, of retaliation, of letting someone down, of

a negative change in your relationship, of making the wrong decision, of saying it badly, and so on.

- You avoid responding directly to the person, hoping the need to say no will go away. Unfortunately, it rarely does.
- You end up avoiding the person who has made the request. You do not reply to the person's email or voicemail messages, and you avoid places at work where the person might see you.
- You become frustrated with yourself and irritated with the other person for making the request, which has become either a huge presence in your mind or a tiny ongoing irritant.
- The situation may take an unpleasant turn, as Melanie's did, with the other person taking action despite your lack of a response. Or you may end up telling a string of lies.
- If you never communicate the no, the other person will eventually give up trying to get a response from you. But he or she will have less confidence and trust in you as a reliable businessperson.
- If you do eventually communicate the no, your message may be marked by untruths or apologies that make you feel bad.

It does not have to be that way! After reading this chapter, you will look at saying no in a new way that will help you do it quickly and effectively.

Saying No: Think of It as a Gift

Do this: Recognize that what the person making the request really wants is an answer. Of course, the individual would prefer a yes. But a no is normally far better than no answer at all.

If Melanie had said no to Aleea promptly, Aleea might have exploded in anger, or she might have sulked for a while. She certainly would not have spent time and money ordering the license. She would not have wasted time and effort repeatedly asking Melanie whether it had arrived. She would not have waited in anticipation for the license and would not have made the last-minute phone call pleading with Melanie to lend Aleea her license.

Compared with the way things evolved, a no would have been a gift to Aleea.

As the reader of this book, you probably don't care about Aleea. After all, her request was ridiculous and her behavior unethical. But think of Melanie. Saying no would have ended all her worry and wondering about how Aleea would respond. It would have allowed Melanie to move on. Sure, she might have felt awkward around Aleea for a few days, but that discomfort would have been nothing compared to what actually happened.

Think of saying no as courageously giving a gift to the other person and to yourself. It is the gift of being able to move on. Had Melanie thought of saying no as a gift to herself and Aleea, she might have sent this email shortly after Aleea made the request:

Subject: Your Idea for Hawaii

Hi Aleea.

I thought about what you asked me at lunch, about Mai Tais in Hawaii. I have to say no. It's just not okay with me. Sorry!

I hope you have a great time anyway.

Mel

Aleea would not have been pleased. She might have gotten angry and retaliated somehow. She might have ended their friendship, which would have hurt Melanie despite their apparent difference in values. Yet the friendship ended anyway when Melanie could not say no.

It is also possible that Aleea would have responded mildly. She might have gone up to Melanie in the cafeteria the next day and asked, "Are you sure? It's not a big deal, just a driver's license." Melanie might then have said simply, "I'm sure. Sorry." And Aleea might have dropped the subject.

The Parts of a No Message

A written no message typically requires only these three parts:

- A neutral or positive opening
- A clearly stated or strongly implied no
- A positive or professional close

My daughter Eva received this email from her piano accompanist, Valerie Shields, replying to Eva's request for accompaniment at a fundraiser:

> Hi Eva [neutral or positive opening],
>
> I regret that I won't be able to accompany you on April 11 [clearly stated no].
>
> Hope all is well with you and that you are enjoying your senior year [a positive close].
>
> Best wishes,
> Valerie

The message says no clearly and concisely, yet it supports the relationship between the two musicians.

Depending on the situation, you may want to expand the message by adding one or more of these additional parts:

- An explanation for the no
- An offer of an alternative
- A brief apology

Imagine the situation of an entrepreneur named Seth, who was asked by someone in his professional circle to write a review of her book. Seth skimmed the book and hated it. Rather than writing a negative review, which his colleague would not have wanted—or a dishonest one, which he was not willing to do—he decided to send a no message.

Seth felt the message required an explanation for the no. He considered saying he did not have time to read and review the book, but he feared that his colleague would then just ask him to write the review when he did have time.

Here is the no message he sent:

> Dear Ellen,
>
> Thanks for inviting me to review your new book [positive opening]. I have scanned it, and I do not feel in tune with the book's approach enough to endorse it [brief explanation for the no]. Therefore, I am going to decline the opportunity this time [clearly stated no].
>
> Cheers [positive close],
> Seth

Seth's no message is brief and clear without criticizing Ellen's book. Although she would undoubtedly be disappointed, she could not fault him for anything but being "not in tune." On the positive side, Seth gave her the gift of a clear, quick response.

In the email below, I responded to a colleague in my professional network, someone I do not know well. She had written to express interest in referring training opportunities to me, for a 10 percent referral fee. She asked whether I would be open to such an arrangement. This no message includes an offer of an alternative.

> Dear Faith,
>
> Thank you for thinking of me for possible training opportunities. I appreciate your vote of confidence [positive opening].

Paying a referral fee is not something I am interested in doing [strongly implied no]. I prefer to refer work to other people and accept referrals from them without fees involved [brief explanation for the no]. I would be happy to have that kind of relationship with you [offer of an alternative]. Please let me know if you are interested in working that way.

I wish you much success in your business [positive close].

Lynn

"Faith" responded agreeably to the no message I sent. Our professional relationship is intact despite my having said no to her invitation.

Saying No in Many Situations

Here are examples of other situations in which you may wish to say no. Notice that all the messages have a positive opening (sometimes just a simple greeting), a clearly stated or strongly implied no, and a positive or professional close—some close both positively and professionally. Some include additional parts: an explanation for the no, an offer of an alternative, or a brief apology.

When an employee emails to ask for a week of vacation:

Brad,

Thanks for asking me about taking the week before Christmas as a vacation week. Unfortunately, in our retail environment I can't approve your request.

The week before Christmas is the busiest week of the year for us. That's why our policy requires nearly every employee to work that week.

We do have a rotation that permits employees to take vacation time that week or the week after Christmas every four years if they wish to. You will be eligible for either of those weeks in your fourth year with us.

You will have Christmas Day and New Year's Day off as paid holidays because the store is closed. Also, because you are working Christmas Eve, you will have New Year's Eve off. I hope those days off will make up for having to work the week before Christmas.

Let me know if you have questions.

Julian

Before writing the message above, Julian may have been thinking, *Vacation the week before Christmas? Is this guy insane or from outer space? This is retail!* However, his purpose was not to ridicule the employee. It was to say no and maintain a good work relationship. So he kept those thoughts to himself.

When an employee makes a written request for approval to attend a training program:

Lester, thanks for asking permission to attend the conference in Ontario. I believe the program would be excellent, and I wish I could say yes. However, I cannot.

There is a company-wide push toward cost-effective training and education. We are asking all managers and staff to use our own training department, which offers a variety of very good programs. We are also encouraging everyone to consider programs at local colleges and universities. These are often an excellent value.

Please talk with Nathan Griffin in the training department about the courses we offer. Nathan also maintains a database of programs offered locally, with particular emphasis on those serving our industry.

Thanks for taking the initiative on your professional development. Please let me know if you want to discuss this.

Larry

When a potential client asks for a discount:

Dear Mr. Gomez:

Thank you very much for following up on our proposal so promptly. We are pleased that you are enthusiastic about our ideas, and we are all looking forward to the start of the project.

In your message, you asked about the possibility of a discount because of your organization's nonprofit status. We would like you to know that we reviewed a wide range of factors when we computed the proposed fees, and we have offered you our very best pricing. We hope that when you consider the anticipated results of the project, you will agree that the investment is sound.

We look forward to your approval of the proposal. When we hear from you, we will draw up a letter of agreement.

Sincerely,
Maura
Maura Howe
Director of Business Development

When a potential customer asks for a free sample:

Dear Ms. Powell:

Thank you for writing to us and requesting a sample from our catalog. We were happy to hear from you.

We do not provide free samples. However, if you order a sample product and are not satisfied with it, we will refund the cost of the item, along with the shipping costs you paid. You will not pay anything unless you choose to keep the item.

Please phone or email us if you have any questions. We look forward to receiving your order by phone, by email, or online.

Best wishes,
Todd Thrush, Customer Service Representative
[Contact information]

When a peer emails to ask for your participation in a panel or a project:

Dear Jillian,

Thanks for thinking of me. Unfortunately, my schedule and workload for the foreseeable future preclude me from participating in this interesting effort.

Best regards,
Elijah

When a stranger asks for the opportunity to write a guest blog post:

Thanks for asking about a guest post. We are not using guest writers at this time.

Good luck with your business!

Crista Turner
LMNOP Company

When a coworker asks for a conference room he needs for his team training:

Hi Zach. About Columbia—sorry I can't give it up. I want to impress the interns with the view and the free food next door. It's their first day.

Hope you find another spot.

Peter

Consider how Zach might feel if he had received this brief response instead:

No can do.

Peter

If Zach and Peter have a good work connection, the three-word response might be enough. But if their relationship is not solid, the lack of investment Peter made in the message could negatively affect their work relationship.

When a coworker asks for your password to get a discount on a website:

Hey Casey,

I am not comfortable sharing my password for the site. It just doesn't work for me.

To get the discount, you can register yourself and get a password of your own. I believe the membership fee is just $25/year. It's really worth it if you are going to make many purchases.

Ciao,

Sara

Notice that Sara's message does not criticize Casey for asking for her password. The purpose of the message is to say no—not to teach Casey about ethics.

**When a coworker asks for your security card to enter
a building after hours:**

> Hi, Long. I got your message about my key card. Sorry, I
> can't lend it out.
>
> If you need to get into Preston on the weekend, ask Eleanor
> for advice. I know she has arranged with Security for other
> people to enter on weekends.
>
> Best,
> Dell

When an employee asks for an advance on a paycheck:

> Hi Gretchen,
>
> I am sorry I cannot approve an advance on your check. I
> have a longstanding policy of not providing advances, for
> many reasons.
>
> Dorothy in Employee Assistance might have some helpful
> ideas. Also, during the last week of this month, we will
> conduct our annual inventory, when you can choose to
> work overtime. I hope making extra money that week will
> be helpful to you.
>
> Garlin

When You Need to Say No Repeatedly

Messages communicating a no are not always successful. Sometimes you
need to say no repeatedly. For instance, imagine yourself in the shoes of
Susan, a web designer, whose client has asked her to update his website.
However, he is more than a month late in paying Susan's most recent
invoice. Susan is angry about not being paid, and she is not willing to
complete more work before he pays the overdue amount. Her prompt
reply to her client includes all six parts of the no message:

Hi, Dave. I'm glad you are getting web traffic and conversions on your site. That's great [positive opening]!

I am sorry I cannot do updates on your site until I receive payment for the work I have done so far [clearly stated no with a brief apology]. Our contract stipulates payment within 30 days, yet my invoice for $390 is more than one month past due [brief explanation for the no].

As soon as I receive your check or credit-card number for the payment, I will be glad to implement the updates you requested [offer of an alternative].

Best [professional close],
Susan

Within minutes, Susan received Dave's reply:

Susan, this isn't fair. I had no idea you wouldn't do work until you got paid. You never told me that.

I need these changes. I have a gig coming up and I'm up against the wall. We have to get it on the site or I will lose money and you will never get paid. You've got to help me.

Don't let me down PLEASE.

Dave

Now Susan had to decide how she felt about the situation. She stayed firm in her decision that she would not do additional work for Dave until he paid what he owed her. They did not have a long-term business relationship that would make her ignore the terms of their contract in this one instance. It was important to her that he abide by their written agreement.

Notice where her response again includes all six parts of the no message:

> Hi, Dave. Thanks for letting me know how you feel. You are correct that I never told you I would not do additional work until I received payment.
>
> You and I have a signed agreement that states that payment is due within 30 days. It is now over 60 days since I emailed the invoice for $390 to you. Because I have not received payment according to the terms of our agreement, I am not willing to do additional work. I am sorry about this situation.
>
> Please provide me with a check or credit-card number to process for $390. Once I receive your payment, I will perform the updates quickly.
>
> Best,
> Susan

In her message, Susan repeated her offer to get to work on the updates as soon as she received a check or credit-card number. Her messages were consistent and clear.

Dave responded this way:

> I don't have the money or I would pay you. I need to make money with this gig to pay.
>
> Can you make an exception this time PLEASE?

Susan could again decide to perform the work for Dave or say no. Here is the professional email she sent in which she continued to incorporate all the parts of the no message:

Dave, I understand your situation and am sorry about it. My answer is still no. I do not wish to make an exception.

If you can find a way to pay for the work I completed, I will make your updates an immediate priority.

Please let me know if anything changes about your ability to pay. I really hope things work out for you.

Susan

Of course, Susan's messages did not seem like a gift to Dave. He needed additional work done on his website now, and Susan refused to complete the work without prior payment of his unpaid invoice.

But Susan did give Dave a gift whether he recognized it or not. The gift was clarity. Susan made her policy completely clear to him. She did not cause him to waste time or resources waiting for delayed responses, second-guessing her intent, or trying to find holes in poorly stated messages.

Saying No Respectfully and Professionally

Beyond her clarity and quick responses, Susan treated Dave with respect. She did not criticize his money management skills or complain about his delayed payments. She used *I* statements to communicate her no messages:

I am sorry I cannot do updates on your site until I receive payment for the work I have done so far.

Because I have not received payment according to the terms of our agreement, I am not willing to do additional work.

My answer is still no. I do not wish to make an exception.

Those statements work well because her purpose was to say no to Dave and do so professionally. Her purpose was not to label him, teach him, or shame him, as these statements would have done:

Your treatment of me is completely unfair and uncalled for [labeling].

As a businessperson, you need to be able to manage your accounts payable [teaching].

How can you ever expect to be a successful businessman if you treat me in such an unbusinesslike way [shaming]?

Certainly, Susan may be tempted to point out that Dave's request is unfair and his behavior disrespectful. But if her purpose is to say no clearly and professionally, steering clear of language that "puts Dave in his place" is her best approach. Her goal is not to reform Dave. It is to run her business well.

You may have wondered about the use of the word *sorry* in Susan's messages. Susan is not the person who has ignored the terms of their contract. Why should she apologize?

I am sorry I cannot do updates on your site until I receive payment for the work I have done so far.

I am sorry about this situation.

Dave, I understand your situation and am sorry about it.

The word *sorry* is appropriate because Susan *is* sorry. She is sorry about the whole situation. Her *sorry* is not actually an apology (although I have called it that). It is an expression of regret and disappointment that things are not going better. *Sorry* also indicates that Susan has feelings. She is not a machine.

Susan's messages do not refer to her anger, even though she is angry that Dave has not paid her and is frustrated that he is wasting her time in this no-win email exchange. Talking about her anger and frustration would take the focus off the purpose of her message, which is to say no. Focusing on negative emotions could push the exchange into an unproductive angerfest that would threaten their work relationship just as much as Dave's nonpayment threatens it.

Only if Susan is unwilling to work for Dave in the future, even when he does pay, and only if she wants to fire him as a client, should she even consider bringing up her anger and frustration in her messages. If she wants to express her anger and frustration, doing so in a confidential, professional support group is a safer, more satisfying approach for the long term.

Clearly Stated and Strongly Implied Nos

All of the no messages you have read so far in this chapter include either a clearly stated no or a strongly implied one.

Examples of a clearly stated no:

I regret that I won't be able to accompany you on April 11.

Therefore, I am going to decline the opportunity this time.

Unfortunately, in our retail environment I can't approve your request.

Strongly implied no:

Paying a referral fee is not something I am interested in doing.

We are not using guest writers at this time.

We would like you to know that we reviewed a wide range of factors when we computed the proposed fees, and we have offered you our very best pricing.

When you write to U.S. business readers and other people who communicate in a direct style, it is essential that your no be clearly stated or strongly implied. Without an unmistakable no, the other person will wonder whether you said no and may even think you said yes.

The implied no in this message is not strong enough to remove all doubts:

> Hi, Cheri.
>
> I received your message about taking PTO [paid time off] on Friday. Cassy and Fleur are scheduled to take that day off.
>
> Tyler

This version removes the doubt with a clearly stated no, and it includes an apology:

> Hi, Cheri.
>
> I received your message about taking PTO on Friday. Because Cassy and Fleur are scheduled to take that day off, I cannot approve your request. I am sorry it did not work out this time.
>
> Tyler

The ambiguous no message below is a response to a therapy patient's request to change a next-day appointment from 4 p.m. to 6 p.m.

> Hi Christian,
>
> My policy, as you know, is 48 hours' notice except in emergencies, and I must stick to it. Changing an appointment in less than 48 hours counts as a cancellation and is the patient's financial responsibility.
>
> Lyle

This version includes a clearly stated no:

> Hi Christian,
>
> I am sorry I cannot change your appointment from 4 to 6 p.m. tomorrow.
>
> My policy is 48 hours' notice except in emergencies, and I must stick to it. If you are unable to make your appointment tomorrow, I will regard it as a cancellation and expect payment for the appointment.
>
> Please let me know if things do work out for you to come at 4.
>
> Lyle

This story of Professor Bermudez and a student, Ms. Levitt, serves as an example of where indirect no messages can lead.

Professor Bermudez received a request for a recommendation from Ms. Levitt. He did not want to recommend her because of her lackluster performance and limited participation in his course. Writing in a style that is comfortable for him, the professor sent this no message:

> Ms. Levitt,
>
> Regarding your message requesting a recommendation letter, I have had limited opportunities to become acquainted with your strengths and accomplishments. For that reason, a recommendation from me would not be helpful to you.
>
> I wish you success in finding a suitable program.
>
> H. Bermudez

The professor's implied no was not strong enough for his reader. He received this response:

> Hi Professor,
>
> I would be glad to meet at your convenience to discuss my strengths and accomplishments. Once you have this information, I hope you will be able to write a recommendation for me.
>
> My schedule is flexible. Please let me know a good time to meet with you, and I will bring my CV ["curriculum vitae," the name for a resume in the academic world] and supporting documents.
>
> Best,
> Kat

In Professor Bermudez's mind, Ms. Levitt's message gave further evidence that she was not a perceptive student. He wrote to her again:

> Ms. Levitt,
>
> My schedule precludes meeting with you in the near future. May I suggest that you request a recommendation from other faculty members?
>
> Sincerely,
> H. Bermudez

A month later he received this reply:

> Hi Professor,
>
> I was wondering whether your schedule had cleared enough for you to meet with me. I would really appreciate it if you could write a letter of recommendation for me.

Can we schedule 15 minutes to go over my strengths and accomplishments? I am available at your convenience.

Best,

Kat

Here is the final message in the exchange between Professor Bermudez and Ms. Levitt:

Ms. Levitt,

I am afraid I cannot write a wholly positive recommendation for you. I strongly suggest that you request recommendations from faculty members who admire your work.

H. Bermudez

That message from Professor Bermudez finally includes a very strongly implied no: "I cannot write a wholly positive recommendation for you." If the professor had included that statement in his first message, Ms. Levitt would not have continued to ask for his help. However, in some cultures, a direct no is considered rude or highly inappropriate. Perhaps Professor Bermudez finally became direct because he feared Ms. Levitt would never stop pestering him!

Give the Gift of No

The purpose of this book is to build and sustain relationships through effective, heart-filled business writing. In many cases—except when you want to end a business relationship intentionally—the purpose of saying no is the same: to say no while preserving the business relationship. You can achieve that purpose by taking the courageous, difficult step of writing the message. If you do not take that step—if you leave the other person wondering and waiting—you will jeopardize the relationship and possibly destroy it, perhaps before it has even begun.

When you have decided to say no, say it clearly and courageously. Think of your no message as a gift to the other person—and to yourself.

Personal Reflection

> ▸ In my survey, one person commented on saying no this way: "I've learned to say no. I love it!" Have you learned to say no? What do you need to do or to tell yourself in order to say no and love it—or at least tolerate it?

Next Step

> ▸ Think of a situation in which you may need to say no to someone. Use the sample messages in this chapter to draft a response.

CHAPTER 13

Disagree With Discretion, Not Destruction

P avel was a flamer, someone who sends hostile electronic messages. His boss had sent him to my Better Business Writing class because when Pavel disagreed with people in writing, he destroyed relationships. Pavel (not his real name) had been told he was brutal in his writing, and he wanted to find out what he needed to change. He felt clueless.

It was easy to recognize what Pavel was doing wrong. He described a situation in which he had responded to someone whose work, to Pavel, was obviously below standard. He had written to his colleague, "I would rather have my teeth extracted than do what you suggested." When I asked Pavel whether that statement might have been a bit harsh, he told me the harshness was warranted because his colleague's idea was terrible.

Pavel could not disagree without destruction.

His background was the key to Pavel's communication problem. Just a few years earlier, he had come to the United States from an Eastern European country that values directness. Besides the bluntness that was second nature to him, he did not recognize tone differences. For example, he saw little or no difference between the sentences in these pairs:

I have no idea what you are talking about!

I do not understand your point yet.

What in the world do you mean?

What do you mean?

Pavel had the tone deafness of Dr. Sheldon Cooper, a brilliant but emotionally insensitive character in the TV sitcom *The Big Bang Theory*. Considering the sentences above, Pavel (and Sheldon) would argue, "But I *don't* have any idea what they are talking about. Why can't I say that?" And they might both shake their head in frustrated puzzlement, trying to understand why the phrase "in the world" in "What in the world do you mean?" would incense their coworkers.

Although you may not have Pavel's challenge of moving to a different culture and missing linguistic subtleties (or Sheldon Cooper's emotional denseness), you too may feel challenged when you need to disagree. You may struggle to think of ways to communicate your disagreement without offending. You may labor to find the appropriate words. You may wrestle with how much detail to include to make your point without making an enemy. This chapter offers many examples of phrasing and several sample messages to help you.

Or you may agree with Pavel. You may be wondering what is wrong with exclaiming, "I have no idea what you are talking about!" Like Pavel, you may prefer bluntness and forceful delivery of a brilliant argument. This chapter shows you how you can preserve your relationships while communicating your valuable ideas.

The Argument for Disagreeing With Discretion

From what Pavel shared in class, I sensed that his situation was becoming grave. It sounded as though his colleagues avoided him because of his harsh communication. They discounted Pavel's comments, regardless of how brilliant he was, because the comments came wrapped in insults. They did not seek his opinion unless they had to.

Would you want to be in Pavel's situation?

Disagreeing with discretion means disagreeing with care and diplomacy. If Pavel could change his communication style and disagree with discretion, he could:

- Influence decision makers, coworkers, and peers in other departments to design better software.
- Become the expert whose opinion is sought and valued.
- Maintain work relationships rather than trashing them.
- Be promoted.

Happily, Pavel can learn to disagree with discretion, and so can you.

Differences: Destruction vs. Discretion

Consider the story of Kelly and Donald, two recruiters at a rapidly growing high-tech company. In this message, Kelly disagrees with a part of Donald's proposal:

> To: Donald
> From: Kelly
> Re: Problem With Your Recruiting Proposal
>
> I read your proposal for on-campus recruiting. I think you are making a big mistake to invite employees directly. You ought to go through their supervisors. You don't want to have supervisors upset at Recruiting, as they were with the job-shadowing program you instituted without their involvement.
>
> Otherwise, it's okay.
>
> Kelly

Is Donald likely to accept Kelly's suggestion? If he sees the wisdom of her point of view, he might do so grudgingly. However, it is just as likely that he will put up his defensive shield as soon as he reads the subject Kelly wrote on the email: "Problem With Your Recruiting Proposal." The words *problem* and *your* together come across like a dog's growl, signaling a possible attack.

The body of the email does nothing to package Kelly's disagreement pleasantly. "I read your proposal" contains no hint of praise. "You are making a big mistake" implies "You are an idiot." "You ought to" says "I know better." Bringing up the problem in the job-shadowing program says "Here you go again upsetting people." The closing, "Otherwise, it's okay," does nothing to help Donald rebound from Kelly's ego-destroying force.

Contrast this version of the message, which disagrees with discretion:

> To: Donald
> From: Kelly
> Re: Your New Recruiting Initiative
>
> Hi, Donald.
>
> Nice job on your new proposal for on-campus recruitment! I like it. You always have creative ideas about how to introduce our company to students.
>
> I have one important suggestion: I believe supervisors will be most supportive of your plan to take employees on recruitment trips if you issue the invitations through them. If you invite employees directly, I worry that supervisors may feel undermined, which could work against your plan.
>
> To get supervisors to say yes to the invitations, maybe you could offer an incentive such as a first crack at highly qualified candidates.
>
> Again, nice work!
>
> Kelly

Donald will take Kelly's suggestion seriously in this second version for many reasons:

- The words *new* and *initiative* give the subject line a positive feeling.
- The greeting prepares him for a collegial message, not an attack.
- The praise in the first paragraph communicates that Kelly admires his work.
- The phrases "important suggestion," "I believe," and "I worry" communicate Kelly's disagreement without putting her in an opposing camp.
- She offered a suggestion to help Donald encourage supervisors to say yes to the invitations.
- She repeated her praise of Donald's work.

Of course, the 100-word second version requires more thought and effort than the 50-word first one. But the probable payoff from the second version makes the investment worth it. Donald is much more likely to seriously consider and implement Kelly's ideas rather than attack them. The second version also solidifies a good work relationship between coworkers.

But what if Kelly disagreed with *many* aspects of Donald's plan? She could still disagree with discretion:

To: Donald
From: Kelly
Re: New Recruiting Proposal

Hi, Donald.

I read your proposal for on-campus recruitment. I want it to be very successful, as you do, but I have concerns about parts of it.

Can we meet to talk about the parts I believe could benefit from rethinking?

I am free this afternoon or early tomorrow morning. Please let me know what works for you.

I look forward to our conversation.

Kelly

That message includes no criticism of Donald or his proposal, only a mention of Kelly's "concerns." It sets a positive, professional tone with the phrases "very successful," "benefit from rethinking," and "look forward to our conversation."

You noticed that the message did not give details of what is wrong with Donald's proposal. Whenever you can, share details in person or on the phone rather than in writing. A written message does not allow you to gauge how the other person is reacting or to take in information about why the individual approached the subject the way he or she did. What if the weird idea is the CEO's?

Nevertheless, if your business associates work on the other side of the globe while you are asleep, you may have to express disagreement in detailed emails and written reports rather than in real time. And there are other work situations that require you to flesh out your comments in writing.

If Kelly must put the details in writing, here is how she can write the email or memo:

To: Donald
From: Kelly
Re: New Recruiting Proposal

Hi, Donald.

I read your new proposal very carefully. You have put a lot of effort into recommending ways we can improve on-campus recruiting.

Like you, I want this proposal to be very successful, so I am sharing these concerns about it. Please follow up with me if any of these ideas need clarification.

1. Inviting employees to participate in on-campus job fairs: This is an excellent idea. I believe supervisors will be most supportive of the idea if you issue the invitations through them. If you invite employees directly, I worry that supervisors may feel undermined, which could work against your plan.

2. Training for employees participating in recruitment: It is terrific that you thought of this. Too often people overlook training. We will need to sell this idea to managers, and I am almost certain they would balk at four hours of training. I recommend that we consider a one-hour or a 90-minute training program. We can add just-in-time training at the colleges as we set up.

3. Recruiting budget: You have estimated the costs as $25,000. Based on my recent experiences in budgeting, I believe $100,000 is closer to what we will need. I have attached a past budget to give you an idea of unexpected expenses to factor in. I strongly encourage you to reconsider this budget number, since we will all have to live with it. I suggest a minimum of $90,000; $100,000 will give us a cushion in case we want to add campuses or trips.

4. Division of recruiting responsibilities: When I reviewed the geographic breakdown, it appeared that neither of us has an equal mix of colleges in rural areas and in large metropolitan areas, something that is important so that we have similar travel challenges. A trip to Ellensburg, Washington, in December is much more challenging and time consuming than a trip to Seattle. As someone

who grew up on this coast, I would be happy to redraw the territory in a way that equalizes the travel challenges. Otherwise, I look forward to a revised plan from you.

[Kelly can cover more points in a similar way.]

Donald, I hope this input will help you finalize a strong, successful proposal that will enhance our college recruiting.

Kelly

In the detailed message, Kelly disagrees with four aspects of Donald's plan. Yet she never uses the word *disagree*. Avoiding that word helps her avoid a confrontational tone. Reading Kelly's message, you would never guess that her first unpolished reactions to Donald's plan were:

- Invite employees directly? That's doomed to fail.
- Four hours of training? Is he insane?
- $25,000 budget—in his dreams!
- He gets territories like Seattle, Portland, Sacramento—and I get cow towns! Not without a fight!
- I should have written this proposal myself! It's just as much work when he writes it!

Despite Kelly's first thoughts, this message, like the earlier ones that disagree with discretion:

- Uses positive language such as *improve, successful, excellent, supportive,* and *terrific.*
- Avoids using the pronouns *you* and *your* with any negative words. Phrases such as "your error" and "you falsely assume" do not appear.
- Offers an alternative method for each area of disagreement, rather than just being critical.
- Avoids making any assumptions about Donald's motives.

When You Disagree Completely

At times, you may disagree completely with someone's ideas. If you can discuss the issues with the individual, such an exchange of information is a productive approach. However, if you cannot or do not choose to meet in person or talk on the phone (perhaps because you want to go on record as disagreeing), you can still disagree with discretion rather than destruction.

Imagine that Malick, webmaster for a small consulting firm, disagrees with Ahmed, the VP of marketing, who is pushing to use customers' survey comments without their permission. Malick is the person who would be uploading the comments to the company website. The marketing assistant, Alicia, has just sent Ahmed three such comments to add to the site as testimonials.

Here is Malick's memo to Ahmed:

> To: Ahmed Atwal
> From: Malick Badami
> Re: Testimonials for Website—Recommendation
>
> Ahmed, I received three excellent customer-satisfaction survey comments from Alicia. To avoid doing something we might regret, I recommend that we contact these customers and get their permission before publishing their comments as testimonials. Here is why:
>
> 1. We have a signed nondisclosure agreement with one of the companies, ABC Inc., stating that we won't use any of their comments or company information without their permission. Posting their comments online would be a violation of the agreement.
>
> 2. In Ed White's comment (XYZ Associates), he mentions his company in less than flattering terms. If his unedited remarks were made public, he and his colleagues could be embarrassed.

3. Because these quotes will become part of each customer's searchable Internet profile, posting them without approval could lead to mistrust and dissatisfaction.

Yes, requesting and getting permission takes time, and we run the risk of customer denials. However, handling our customers discreetly will help us continue our excellent relationships with them. An "act first, apologize later" policy could alienate our best customers.

I know you feel a sense of urgency about adding testimonials to our site. I am happy to help with that effort. I can work with Alicia to contact these customers, and others, to get permission and help them edit their comments, if necessary.

To ensure we get permission to publish future comments, we can add a permission box to our surveys. Customers can check the box, giving us permission to use their comments in our marketing materials.

Let me know how I can help.

Malick

Although Malick is surprised and annoyed that the VP of marketing would publish testimonials without permission, those feelings do not come out in the message. Saying "I am surprised you would do this" would almost certainly cause Ahmed to defend himself or attack Malick. Describing his annoyance would not promote Malick's point of view, so there is no point in mentioning it.

A strength of Malick's message is that he addresses Ahmed's concerns. He acknowledges that requesting permission takes time and that Ahmed feels pressure to do this quickly. He offers help to speed up the process, and he suggests a way to obtain permission in the future. Malick's message includes three reasons for his "recommendation." (He does not use the word *disagreement*.) None of his reasons belittle Ahmed.

Negative language has an appropriate place in the memo. The words *regret, violation, embarrassed, mistrust, dissatisfaction,* and *alienate* point out the possible negative consequences of publishing the comments without permission. Still, not one of the negative words is coupled with the pronoun *you.* Malick refrains from writing "You will alienate" or "You will embarrass." By avoiding such accusatory sentence structures, Malick allows Ahmed to save face.

Transforming Destruction Into Discretion

This table compares written statements that disagree destructively with those that disagree discreetly.

Disagreeing With Destruction	Why It's Destructive	Disagreeing With Discretion	Why It's Discreet
"I disagree."	Sets up an adversarial situation rather than a collaborative or supportive one.	"I have an alternative to consider."	Avoids adversarial tone. Offers support.
"I disagree with you completely."	Emphasizes *I* vs. *you.*	"I have a different perspective."	Suggests sharing information rather than clashing.
"It's stupid for you to . . ."	Hits the person with a negative label.	"It might also be smart to . . ."	Sounds like support rather than an assault. Is respectful.
"Your plan will not work."	Suggests the person is incompetent. *Your* personalizes the criticism.	"I have strong reservations about parts of the plan."	Uses an *I* statement, which focuses more on the writer's concerns than the plan's deficits.
"Your solution is completely unworkable."	Suggests the person is incompetent. Personalizes the criticism with *your.*	"The proposed solution may have some drawbacks."	Suggests rather than states unequivocally. Depersonalizes.

Disagreeing With Destruction	Why It's Destructive	Disagreeing With Discretion	Why It's Discreet
"Your approach is unethical, if not illegal."	Implies the person is unethical, perhaps even a lawbreaker.	"I worry that this approach might be considered unethical, if not illegal."	Expresses concern rather than criticism.
"You are making a big mistake to . . ."	Suggests the person is foolish.	"There may be unexpected consequences if we . . ."	Comes across as a caution rather than a criticism.
"Your problem is that you focus exclusively on . . ."	Accuses the person of having a problem. Focuses negatively on *you* and *your*.	"One potential obstacle is the exclusive focus on . . ."	Comes across as good advice rather than an attack. Depersonalizes.
"You falsely assume that . . ."	Uses *you* in an attack. Makes an assumption.	"Does the plan assume that . . ."	Asks rather than assumes. Depersonalizes.
"You ought to . . ." "You should . . ."	Comes across as bossy and superior.	"Have you considered . . ." "I suggest . . ." [or] "One suggestion is . . ."	Asks rather than arrogantly announces. Suggests rather than dictates.
"Whose brilliant idea was this?"	Bites with sarcasm.	"I'd like to hear how this plan came together."	Comes across as a sincere inquiry.

Attitude: Destructive vs. Discreet

When you disagree in writing, your most important tool is your attitude. If your attitude is respectful and caring, your message is likely to be supportive rather than destructive. The statements in the "Disagreeing With Discretion" column of the table all communicate support and respect. They convey a positive regard for the reader.

It will be a challenge to write a diplomatic message if your attitude is hostile, disparaging, or unsympathetic—or all three. If you have strong negative feelings toward the person, try hard to imagine the individual as your best friend, your favorite coworker, or your most admired public figure. This visualization may help you adjust your attitude and make it easier for you to see the person in a positive light. Then it will be easier to disagree with discretion.

You and Pavel Can Disagree Without Destruction

Pavel, the man whose story opened this chapter, disagreed with destruction, primarily because of his background. He had grown up communicating bluntly in Eastern Europe, and he did not recognize the differences between tact and tactlessness in English. Perhaps you too have been less than successful because of coming across as insensitive or undiplomatic. Both Pavel and you can disagree without destroying relationships if you apply these tips:

Talk rather than write, when possible, so you can adjust your message based on the other person's reactions and input.

Avoid the word *disagree,* which puts you and the other person on opposing sides. Instead, simply state your views. Or describe them as suggestions or recommendations.

Avoid the use of the pronouns *you* **and** *your* **with blaming language.** For example, avoid "you failed" and "your illogical plan."

Use *I* **statements to express concerns,** for instance, "I worry that . . ." and "I have reservations about . . ."

Turn criticisms into suggestions. Rather than writing, "Your proposal lacks depth," write, "The proposal would benefit from more discussion of . . ." Offer ideas and alternatives.

Communicate carefully rather than cavalierly, sincerely rather than sarcastically. Omit exaggerations such as "I would rather jump off the George Washington Bridge than do as you suggested." Avoid superlatives such as "This is the worst report I have ever read."

Appreciate the possibility that you are wrong. Your ideas may be out of fashion or too cutting edge for the situation. Use tentative language such as "may be" and "could be" rather than insisting things "are" exactly as you interpret them.

Avoid making negative assumptions about the other person's motives, and never include such assumptions in your message. Assume the best of the other person.

Recognize when your negative feelings will be obstacles to writing a tactful message. Try to see the other person in a positive light.

Relationships are built on honest, tactful communication. Disagreeing with discretion will help you create and maintain strong business relationships.

Personal Reflection

> ▸ Are you able to disagree without being disagreeable or destructive? Which techniques and attitudes help you—or could help you—disagree discreetly?

Next Step

> ▸ From the table that compares destructive and discreet language, choose several discreet phrases you could apply in conversations and written messages. Memorize your phrases and start using them this week.

CHAPTER 14

Remind People Without Nagging or Whining

If you are like most professionals, you have to write an occasional reminder. People do not always act as quickly as you want or need. Maybe a client has not paid your invoice promptly or has not replied to your request for a meeting. Perhaps a peer hasn't given you essential data or hasn't finished a report you are waiting for. Maybe your boss or a client keeps you waiting when you need approval to move ahead on a project.

Those situations can be so frustrating! They can also be uncomfortable. Reminding the other person can feel like nagging, grumbling, or begging—none of which promotes good will and satisfying work relationships. Despite those feelings, you must occasionally remind someone of something to get what you need to do your job.

This chapter will help you avoid turning frustration into embarrassment and associates into adversaries. It will help you write diplomatic, efficient reminders—and even eliminate the need to write some of them.

How to Eliminate the Need for a Reminder

Let's start by identifying with the individuals who have not yet done what you want them to do. *Why* have they not paid, replied, approved, or accomplished the task you requested of them? Each case is different, but it is likely that they are reluctant, ambivalent, unaware, unable, or too busy to do what you want. If you can imagine your readers feeling one or more of those ways, you can reduce the need for many reminders by providing what they need from the start—that is, when you make your original request.

When you request an action or assign a task, you can take these steps to increase the likelihood that the person will do it, thereby eliminating the need to send a reminder:

To reduce ambivalence, personalize a message so that every individual who receives it knows it is from you to him or her—not from a department to a mass audience. When a request goes to a group, everyone assumes that someone else will respond, volunteer, or contribute. Use an individual's name, and let the person know why you are making the request of him or her. You will be much more likely to receive a positive response and will not need to send out pleading reminders.

To reduce reluctance and ambivalence, state why something is important. If people understand the importance of your request or assignment, they will prioritize it with their other important activities.

In my role as an instructor at the University of Washington–Bothell, I received a request that I submit grades for summer students. The request provided these details about the importance of submitting grades on time:

> Please make every effort to submit grades on time. Students depend on grades for their academic survival. They need them to:

- Prove satisfactory academic progress.
- Fulfill prerequisite requirements for registration.
- Remain eligible for athletic programs.
- Receive appropriate honors.
- Remain eligible for scholarships.
- Remain eligible for financial aid and other government-sponsored programs like veterans' benefits.
- Graduate.

How could I not submit grades on time when all of the above could depend on my action? I took action promptly.

Another way to reduce reluctance and ambivalence is to show how taking an action benefits the reader. Whenever there is a clear reader benefit, include it. Examples:

- I will start designing your website as soon as I receive the signed letter of agreement.
- When we meet, we can discuss next steps to get the project back on schedule.
- Reserving your booth this week guarantees a space in the main exhibit hall.
- Pay only $485 if you send payment within 10 days. Enjoy a 3 percent discount for prompt payment!

To lessen the likelihood that someone is unable or too busy to complete a task, do as much as you can to help the other person comply. Sometimes the smallest missing details can lead to the biggest delays. Be sure to include all the information he or she may need, taking the following steps:

- Include your phone number, fax number, and mailing address so the person does not need to take time to search for them.
- Provide a payment link for easy credit-card payments.
- Send an Outlook meeting request, or list the dates and times you are available for a meeting.
- Include a map or a link to a map so the person can find your office easily, if something requires delivery.
- Attach a template for the document you need or a sample of what you expect.
- Provide links to resources for more information.

To eliminate lack of awareness, follow up on any requests you make by email. Call, send a follow-up email, or make a personal visit within a few hours or a day of your original request. Make sure the person received your request, understands it, and can comply in a reasonable amount of time.

When Your Best Efforts Don't Lead to a Prompt, Positive Response

Despite doing everything you can to make complying easy, sometimes you will need to send reminders. Communications consultant Deb Arnold helps her clients win prestigious awards for their training programs. She does all the right things to encourage clients to provide timely information for award submissions, but she still has to follow up with reminders at times. Here is an example from Deb:

> Subject: Gentle Reminder FW: Your input requested for award submission
>
> Dear [Name],
>
> As the week comes to a close, I'm getting back in touch to see whether you might have had a chance to review the needed information for the [Award Name].

[Name of an executive] specifically asked for your input, so I wanted to be sure to follow up.

As I mentioned below, I can set up a call or, if you prefer to, please feel free to send written input. Might you be able to let me know by end of day Monday how you would like to provide your insights?

Thank you very kindly in advance for your time and important contributions.

Best,
Deb

Deb communicates well to maintain positive business relationships. She uses the polite "Gentle reminder." She efficiently forwards her original request rather than restating it. She uses the positive phrasing "Your input requested," "getting back in touch," "your insights," "important contributions," and "Thank you very kindly." She hints at the passage of time with "As the week comes to a close." She deftly mentions the executive's desire for input, and she frames the communication as "I wanted to be sure to follow up" rather than "I needed to remind you."

Tips for Gentle Reminders

Consider these tips to help you write "gentle" reminders that support good work relationships:

Use *I* statements—not *you* statements. *I* statements help you communicate facts rather than accusations. Compare these sentences:

> I look forward to receiving the sales data I requested. (*I* statement)

> You have not yet sent me the sales data I requested. (*you* statement)

The *I* statement is true: The writer looks forward to receiving the data. In contrast, the *you* statement is speculation. The writer cannot be certain that the other person has not sent the information. If the other person has sent it, the accusation could damage the relationship.

Notice the difference in feeling in these sentence pairs:

> You have not yet approved my check request.
>
> I would appreciate approval of my check request by tomorrow.

> You haven't responded to my meeting request.
>
> I would like to meet with you ASAP.

The *I* statements state the writer's needs, whereas the *you* statements blame the reader. The *you* statements are much more likely to elicit a defensive or an argumentative response.

Communicate consequences, which help people prioritize. People typically take action on things that have positive consequences if they do them and negative consequences if they don't do them.

These examples communicate positive consequences:

> If I receive your input by tomorrow, I will be able to include your team's activities in my report to the board.

> If I receive your approval by Friday, I will be able to meet the registration deadline.

These sentences communicate negative consequences:

> If I do not receive your input by tomorrow, I will not be able to include your team's activities in my report to the board.

Unless I receive your approval by Friday, I will not meet the registration deadline.

Although I prefer communicating positive consequences, both positive and negative consequences can move the other person to action. If negative consequences are stated with a matter-of-fact tone rather than a threatening one, they can be effective without threatening relationships.

Describe the next step you will take. This description may be similar to the statements of consequences. Its purpose is to show the other person tactfully that you intend to take action or stop action. Consider these next steps, which are all *I* statements:

I will phone your assistant to request an appointment with you.

I will stop by your office on Thursday to pick up the work you have completed.

I will suspend work on the survey until I hear from you.

Include your original request, invoice, or excerpt from a statement of work, if appropriate, rather than restating it. Including the original communication frees you from having to describe what you need and reduces the odds of using any blaming language. You may say something like this:

I have not yet received the [whatever it is you are waiting for], which was due by [date]. I have attached the original [invoice, request for approval, etc.] as a reminder. I look forward to hearing from you by [date].

Frame your reminder as a helpful tool to encourage a positive, prompt response. For example, depending on the circumstances, you might:

- Include your latest contact information.
- Update your availability—list the dates and times you are still available for a meeting.
- Provide new information that makes action easy.

Some businesses take this concept of helpful reminders to a high level of customer service. For example, I was taking a cross-country plane trip one night. On the morning of the upcoming trip, I woke up to reminder emails that helped me travel more easily from two companies: Alaska Airlines and National Car Rental. Both of them had sent reminder messages whose helpful details made my life easier.

Alaska wrote with lots of good information:

> Welcome Aboard. For your convenience, here is your flight information for your upcoming trip to Orlando on Alaska Airlines or Horizon Air starting 9/25/20XX. We've also listed useful information and services to help make your trip easy.

Along with the weather in Orlando, Florida, Alaska informed me of my check-in time, reservation number, flight number, seat number, and tips on carry-on luggage. I appreciated all of these. More than that, I appreciated the fact that I did not have to sort through my email to find information about my flight, whose reservation I had made a couple of weeks earlier. This reminder came at exactly the right time.

National Car Rental provided the same good service. Their email began this way:

Subject: Friendly Email Reminder from NationalCar.com.

Thank you for using National to make your reservation. Below is your confirmation number. You will need it when you get to the rental facility.

Along with my confirmation number, National gave me a link to my reservation. As with Alaska, I appreciated having this information available at the exact moment I wanted it.

The reminders worked for me. Both companies made it easy for me to take the action they wanted. When I got to the airport for my flight and later to the car rental area, I did not drive the agents crazy because of missing information. I had all the details I needed.

Think of Alaska Airlines and National Car Rental when you remind a customer or colleague about an assignment they still must complete, a webinar that requires their registration, or a lunch meeting they have not yet confirmed. How can you add value in your reminder, just at the moment the person needs it?

Never use accusing language such as "You are avoiding me" or "You don't seem to care about the success of this program"—even if you feel those statements are true. They will only elicit defensiveness and escalate tension. At all times, stay professional.

Here is a sample reminder emailed to a client on August 24 involving the touchy subject of a late payment:

Subject: Payment of July Invoice

Hi, Colin. As of today's mail delivery, I have not received payment for my July invoice. According to our contract, it was due on August 20.

If you have mailed a check, please let me know. If you have not mailed it, please send it today. I have attached the original invoice for you.

If you prefer to pay by credit card, please phone with your credit-card details. You can reach me or my assistant, Lydia Smith, from 9 a.m. to 5 p.m. Central Time.

I look forward to hearing from you about the status of the payment.

Best wishes,
Darla

Darla Woods
[Office phone], [Cell phone]
[Mailing address]

Here is a second reminder emailed on September 1:

Subject: Overdue Payment of July Invoice

Hi, Colin. I have not received the overdue payment of $2550. If you have not mailed it, please do so today, or phone me as soon as possible with your credit-card information. If you have mailed the payment, please let me know by phone or email.

I have attached the original invoice for you.

If I do not receive payment by September 8, I will need to suspend work on the new video. As you can imagine, I would hate to have to take that step.

I look forward to hearing from you.

Best wishes,
Darla

Darla Woods
[Office phone], [Cell phone]
[Mailing address]

Neither of Darla's messages criticizes Colin or makes any assumptions about his behavior. When he pays the invoice, their relationship and the project can move forward free of rancor.

Tim Jones, vice president and general manager at NetSpeed Learning Solutions, read those sample emails and sent me information about his approach. He wrote:

> I sometimes have to reach out to delinquent customers for payment. In those situations, I may also include an either-or option to give customers a friendly choice. For example, I might write, "Mary, if you would prefer to have me talk to someone in your accounts payable department, could you let me know the appropriate person for me to talk to and their contact information? Or if you prefer, I can call you later today and take your credit-card information. What works best for you?"

Tim's suggestion of an either-or option gives his customers some control in a situation that may feel out of control for them, especially if they do not have a say about when invoices get paid in their company. He comes across as understanding and supportive.

Should You Remind People Before Something Is Due?

In high-stakes projects, it can be tempting to remind people of deadlines before something is actually due. But that step can backfire. It can make people feel as though you don't trust them to complete the work on time.

I raised this subject on my Business Writing blog with these questions:

> If something is due at 5 p.m., is it okay to email someone at 4 p.m. with a reminder? If you were working toward a 5 p.m. deadline, would you appreciate a 4 p.m. email reminder?

English professor Alfredo Deambrosi shared his view of this situation:

> Emailing reminders to an individual can communicate a lack of trust and can seem like micromanaging. Those problems are drastically reduced, however, if the reminder is sent to a group. If I am part of a group that receives a reminder, then I do not feel singled out as someone who could not get the job done if he did not get a reminder.

Freelance copywriter Neil Wheatley had a different point of view:

> Treat others as you would wish to be treated yourself. I know I certainly wouldn't appreciate receiving an email like that!
>
> I agree that group emails take the sting out a little—but these are not always applicable to the situation. I find it's better to show some trust in the people you're working with, at least until they've proved themselves undeserving of it!

I agree with both Alfredo and Neil. Reminders can come across as micromanaging, and they can suggest a lack of trust, although a group reminder avoids pointing a finger at anyone. You are better off showing trust in people.

One way to eliminate negative reactions to early reminders is to agree on them in advance. For example, when agreeing on project timelines, you can agree that you will send reminders at certain times during the schedule. Sending anticipated reminders, you will not come across as lacking trust. You will simply be doing your job.

For the writing classes I teach, my clients occasionally email attendees reminding them to turn in prework to me shortly before the work is due. Here are two examples:

Just a quick reminder that this is due to the instructor, Lynn Gaertner-Johnston, today.

Thank you.

Have a great weekend!

Jayne

Hi team,

A quick reminder to send a sample to Lynn by EOD [end of day] Monday. This will help her prepare for our workshop on Thursday.

Have a good one.

Donna

Although the reminders are friendly and brief, they may create a kind of dependency. People can get in the habit of waiting for a reminder to take action. That is why I prefer to wait until the deadline passes before sending a quick reminder like this one:

Subject: Quick Prework for Better Business Writing—Please Send It Today

According to my records, I have not received your prework. Can you please respond to the request below today? Thank you!

In a business communications class I taught in an MBA program, one student blamed the lateness of his final assignment (and his corresponding lower grade) on a fellow student. His rationale was that the other student had always reminded him of the assignments that were due—until the final assignment. Although this was somewhat lighthearted blaming, the same situation can occur with serious consequences if people learn to rely on reminders and then do not receive one.

A writing class participant proposed the ideal solution to avoid irritating coworkers or creating dependency with premature reminders: "If you need something by 5 p.m., give a 4 p.m. deadline. That way, if you have not received it by 4, you can comfortably nudge the other person."

I like the approach of creating a deadline that is earlier than your true deadline, especially for important projects. If you need information by, let's say, Monday at noon, why not set a deadline of Friday at noon for getting the work to you? That way, if you do not receive work by the early deadline, you have "wiggle room," and you can send out a reminder like this one:

> Subject: Test Results for Project No. 202031
>
> Omar, I have not yet gotten the test results from your team. I promised a report to the client by Monday, and they are already asking me when it will be ready.
>
> Can you please see that I get the results by the end of the day today so that I have time to incorporate them into the report? We originally agreed on a deadline of noon today, but I can make anytime today work if I know the information is coming.
>
> Can you reply to this email and let me know the status?
>
> Thanks!
>
> Phuong

It is wise not to advertise wiggle room too openly. If people realize you always allow extra time before a true deadline, they may not take your deadline seriously.

When They Don't Tell You They Have Done It!

At times you may be waiting for acknowledgment that a task has been completed, but it does not come. Once again you have to send out something that feels like a reminder. And once again you don't want to nag or whine.

Tim Jones has dealt with such situations and has devised a solution. He shared his approach:

> I have two coworkers who, when they finish a project or task I have asked them to do for me, just move on—without telling me they have completed it. I have a high need for closure and like to know when a project I have requested has been completed (when it's not obvious without my asking). I am left in the awkward situation of not knowing whether they finished the project and not wanting to nag them about it. So I sometimes will email them something like this: "Dee, thanks very much for being willing to help me with the XYZ project. Hey, if you have not yet finished it, can you give me a rough ETA [estimated time of arrival or accomplishment], given the other items on your plate? And if you have already completed it, could you let me know? Thanks a lot."
>
> I find that by acknowledging the very real possibility that they may have already completed the project, my check-in comes across a bit less like nagging.

After sharing his ideas above, Tim followed up with me. He let me know that he had successfully persuaded one of the coworkers to send him a simple email reply with the message "DONE" when he has finished an important task. Now Tim is in the happy situation of not having to send irksome reminder/check-ins to that individual.

How to Follow Up in Email Without Feeling Pushy or Pathetic

In the online class How to Write Email That Gets Results, a participant asked this question: "When I'm following up on an email that I have not received a reply to, what do I start with? I don't like 'Just following up on my last email' type intros."

Such follow-up messages are a kind of reminder. They can be awkward because you don't know why someone has not responded, and you don't want to weaken your relationship by coming across as pushy at one extreme or pitiable at the other.

Try any of these approaches, which I have used successfully when I have not received a reply:

Share something new to get the other person's attention. For example, I might write an opening like this: "Hi, Manu. As you consider ways to improve the executive team's writing, you may find this survey data instructive." I present the data and then ask for an update on the prospective client's process.

Your "something new" might be a report you have written, an article you found in the news, a product review, a speech you heard on YouTube, a case study, or a checklist. The idea is to share something new to make the reader think of you and respond. You might begin with "Since I wrote to you last month," followed by your new helpful information.

Let the person know that a window of opportunity is closing. In my business, I let a client or prospective client know that my schedule is filling up or that seats in a webinar are going fast. For example, I might write, "I know you want to offer the program in July. I have only three days available that month: July 11, 12, and 13. Please let me know if you would like me to hold a day for you." I only use this approach truthfully; that is, I say I have only three days available if it is true. Clients respond well to this approach, either by scheduling or responding that they cannot schedule yet.

Your closing window of opportunity might be a deadline for a pre-season discount, for input into a preliminary design, for a grant application, or for meeting with you before your vacation. Whenever you can show a benefit to replying to you promptly, show it.

"I will call you" often gets people moving too, like this: "Hi, Rahel. I would love to get your reaction to the proposal I sent last week. Have you had a chance to review it? I will call you on Friday unless we have communicated before then."

Try this simple approach: "Hello, John. I am forwarding the message I sent last week to be sure you received it. I look forward to hearing from you." When I use this opening, people frequently respond positively and include a brief apology for not responding earlier.

People are busy. They often cannot respond as quickly as you may hope. Remember that what feels like a long delay to you may be standard turnaround time for them. To preserve the relationship, think creatively and kindly about their schedule and situation.

Below is another example from Deb Arnold, which she uses when she has not yet received client approval for a section of an award submission. Notice that her reminder feels like a good customer-service gesture.

Subject: Gentle Reminder FW: For your review - draft report

Dear [Name],

I wanted to circle back with you about your feedback on the draft report I sent. Your deadline to submit it is fast approaching, and I want to be sure that we have plenty of time to incorporate your comments.

Might you be able to send your feedback tomorrow? If not, what is your sense about the timing?

Thanks so much. Please let me know if there's anything I can do to make it easier for you to provide your thoughts on the draft. I'd be happy to set up a phone call.

Best,
Deb

Remember as you compose a first, a second, or even a third reminder: You cannot control the other person's behavior. You can only control your own. You cannot make the other person pay, respond to your email, send information, agree to a meeting, sign a contract, or anything else. You can only determine what you will do. One thing you can always do is communicate professionally and respectfully to maintain great work relationships.

Personal Reflection

> ▷ When you need to remind someone in writing to do something, do you successfully use *I* statements rather than *you* statements? How do you make your reminders seem helpful rather than hounding?

Next Step

> ▷ Before you write your next request, review the steps under the heading "How to Eliminate the Need for a Reminder." Then try to write the request so that a reminder will not be necessary.

CHAPTER 15

Deal With Anger (Yours and Theirs) to Preserve Relationships—or End Them Well

T rue story, details changed: Jude is a contractor who lost an assignment as an instructional designer for a small, successful training company. He lost not only the challenging assignment he was working on, but also any future assignments with the company. Yet the company loved Jude's work. The owner described Jude as the best instructional designer they had ever hired.

Why was Jude fired?

Because he put his anger and insults in writing. Jude had become frustrated with a stressful training design schedule and unrealistic demands that the training company had agreed to with a client. He felt he was not being adequately paid for revisions the client had requested. He felt mistreated and stretched too far.

So Jude wrote to virtually everyone at the training company, either directly or through a cc'd email, accusing them of stupid project management. He harangued them about their decisions. He called them names. He wrote several of them more than once.

Darlene, the owner of the training company, had no choice but to fire Jude. She had been one of his strongest fans, but he had alienated himself from everyone he needed to work with. She could not support or defend his tirades. Even though Jude was the best instructional designer around, he had handled the stress of the assignment by exploding, hitting everyone around him with a barrage of email shrapnel.

Jude's story is about destroying relationships. It is an example of what *not* to do in response to anger and stress. This chapter gives you language, examples, and tips to help you maintain your relationships even in charged situations—or to end a relationship professionally.

How to Protect Business Relationships When You Are Angry and Under Stress

If you, like Jude, feel pushed to the limit, you can maintain your cool and your relationships by applying these tips unfailingly:

Do not commit your anger to writing. It will live on, long after your feelings of anger have passed. If you are well known, an embarrassing transcript of your angry messages could end up on the evening news.

Talk with the appropriate person, typically the person who can help you change the situation or see it differently. That individual may be a peer, the project coordinator, your supervisor, a mentor, a trusted coworker, or a human resources representative.

If you communicate by email, write only to the person who can make a difference—not to a group. Do not copy others on the message, either by cc or bcc (blind copy). Copying others can make your anger the topic of everyone's online and offline conversations. It can also publicly embarrass the individual or individuals who aroused your negative feelings.

If you communicate in writing or talk with the person with whom you are angry, avoid using *you* statements, in which *you* is the subject. Instead, use *I* statements, in which *I* is the subject and focus. For example, instead of writing, "You are keeping me out of the communication loop," write, "I don't feel that I have all the information I need to do the job." Instead of saying, "You are constantly second-guessing my decisions," say, "I feel I am qualified to make certain decisions, and I would like to be able to make them without your review."

Avoid combining the pronoun *you* with any negative word. These statements only make your audience defensive:

you misled me	you always criticize
you never share	you play favorites
you drag your feet	you lied to the client
you complain	you can't decide
you're impossible	you're never available
you're unprepared	you constantly argue
you expect the impossible	you never see my point of view
you always exaggerate	you won't agree
you manufacture stress	you don't accept responsibility

Even though you may think those remarks are true ("He *does* expect the impossible!"), they come from your point of view, with your understanding of the situation, with the information you have. The other person probably has a different point of view, a different understanding of the situation, and different information. Making such statements almost never builds understanding and better relationships.

If the behavior that upsets you is abusive, get help from your manager, another trusted manager or friend, or someone in human resources. Harassment and other forms of abuse should not be tolerated in your company or agency. An ally may be able to help you deal effectively with the situation.

Do not keep anger and frustration inside until you explode, as Jude did. Do not wait until you feel powerless and out of control. Communicate as soon as you know or sense that things are going wrong.

How to Request a Meeting When You Are Upset

It is often better to talk things out than to conduct a sensitive exchange entirely through email, especially when you are angry. But how do you compose the email requesting an in-person or phone meeting without letting your raging emotions hijack it? The question makes me think of an email I received from my longtime colleague Cynthia Clay.

I used to do a lot of writing for Cynthia. In one situation, I wrote a book review for inclusion in her newsletter. She did not like the review. She felt that my huge praise for the author, a competitor of hers, detracted from Cynthia's own work. (She was right; I had not realized my review was insensitive in that respect.)

Rather than write to tell me angrily what was wrong with the review and my approach to the book, she wrote, "I really have my knickers in a knot over this review, and I'd like to talk with you about it. Please call me when you get a chance."

It was the perfect opening for communication. Instead of telling me what was wrong with my approach to the book, she told me that *she* had a problem we needed to discuss. When I phoned her, I was not the least defensive. She had set me up for a reasonable discussion, and I was able to revise the writing easily.

When something or someone upsets you, do not write a scathing composition and click Send. Just send a short, simple message about your knotted knickers. Own the problem and open the door for a productive conversation.

Follow Cynthia's lead when you request a meeting by applying these tips:

Keep the request short. Don't get bogged down in details that are difficult to communicate tactfully. You have to give enough information so the other person understands the purpose of the meeting, but save details for the conversation.

Avoid *you* statements. Use *I* statements to accept responsibility for your needs. Think of Cynthia's "I really have my knickers in a knot."

Keep the tone light by using neutral rather than negative language. For example, say, "I'd like to talk with you tomorrow about the plans for the retail space." Do not say, "I saw the plans and I am very upset about the square footage for my department." That second comment might put the receiver on the defensive.

Before he reached his breaking point, Jude, whose story opened this chapter, might have requested a meeting with Darlene to discuss what was bothering him. He might have written this message:

> Subject: Concerns About XYZ Project
>
> Hi, Darlene.
>
> I need to talk with you about resolving two important issues in the XYZ project: the schedule and the number of revisions.
>
> Briefly, I have been working 10 hours a day to meet the original deadlines. The new deadlines are going to be very difficult to meet without threatening the quality of the work. I know how important it is to you to deliver an excellent product, and I feel the same way.
>
> Also, my contract stipulates that two revisions of the training design are included in my fee. The client's daily requests for revisions are adding to my time and frustration, yet I don't have a clear way of managing or being compensated for them.
>
> Can we meet by phone today or tomorrow? Please let me know and suggest a time.
>
> Jude

Notice that the message does not attack or blame Darlene or question her judgment for agreeing to a new deadline. It states the facts as Jude sees them and tactfully communicates his frustration. It uses the *I* statements "I need to talk with you about resolving two issues" and "I don't have a clear way of managing or being compensated" rather than *you* statements like "You need to explain to me how these issues are going to be resolved" and "You haven't made it clear how I can manage these or be compensated." It also includes two expressions with a positive tone: "resolving two important issues" and "deliver an excellent product."

In my reimagining of Jude's situation, I saw him requesting a meeting with Darlene to discuss his concerns. But there are times when the last thing you want to do is to talk to the other person—on the phone or in person. That may be because he or she is domineering or manipulative. Or it may be that you feel you cannot win: Perhaps you are reflective and cautious when speaking, and the other person is quick, glib, and persuasive. Or perhaps the situation is simply too filled with emotion to discuss. At other times, real-time communication may be difficult because the other person is too busy or refuses to engage by phone or in person. Or the individual may work on a different schedule, in a different time zone, or on a faraway continent.

Let's imagine that Jude could not meet by phone or in person with Darlene because she did not make time to discuss his issues. Let's say she responded to his request for a meeting this way:

Subject: Re: Concerns About XYZ Project

Hey Jude. Sorry I don't have time to meet in the next few days. Keep on keeping on, and we will resolve the issues as soon as we can.

Thanks.

D.

Rather than exploding in anger and frustration, Jude might have written a message like the one below.

> Subject: Re: Concerns About XYZ Project
>
> Darlene, since we cannot meet about the XYZ project soon, I need to be sure you are aware of several important items.
>
> 1. I will do my best to meet the new deadline; however, it will be very difficult. I urge you to hire a second designer to work on the sixth and seventh modules because of the real possibility that I will not be able to start and complete them on time. I will be glad to orient a new designer to the project.
>
> 2. I talked with Kerry, who agreed to communicate directly with the client so I will not be interrupted continually with requests for revisions. She and I will communicate once a day about any needed changes.
>
> 3. My contract stipulates that two revisions of the training design are included in my fee. However, the design requirements have morphed into something neither of us had planned for or included in the contract. My plan is to track the time it takes to handle additional requests for revisions, and I will present an invoice for the additional changes at the end of the project.
>
> Please let me know if you want to discuss any of the items above.
>
> Jude

Jude cannot control Darlene, the client, or anyone else involved in the project—only himself. So the email does not attempt to control them. Neither does the message attack or blame Darlene or anyone else or make negative assumptions about Darlene's reasons for not agreeing to meet. Instead, it urges Darlene to hire a second designer, presents Jude's plan to have Kerry communicate with the client, and describes how Jude intends to handle payment for additional design changes. It presents Jude's views professionally.

Let's assume that the situation has not improved. Rather than blast Darlene and others, Jude can write this message:

> Subject: Urgent Action Needed: XYZ Project Issues
>
> Darlene, the situation with the XYZ project design has worsened, and I strongly request that changes be made now so I can continue to work on the design.
>
> The newest deadline is impossible to meet given the increasing complexity of the design and the ongoing changes the client has requested. Although Kerry has tried to work as an intermediary between us, the client has continued to phone and email me, literally from dawn until late evening.
>
> I urge you to step in to work with Kerry, the client, and me, so a solution can be reached.
>
> Please call or email me about next steps as soon as you can.
>
> Jude

Now let's assume the worst: With no meaningful intervention from Darlene, the stress has increased exponentially and irrevocably. Jude cannot continue to work on the project without jeopardizing his well-being. Rather than send attack-and-blame emails throughout the company, as he did in the true story, he can exit the project this way:

Subject: Resignation from XYZ Project

Dear Darlene,

I am sorry to have to inform you that I am ending my involvement in the XYZ project. Friday will be my last day of work.

I will schedule a meeting with Kerry before Friday to familiarize her with the work I have completed and to pass the project on to her. If you would like to be included in that meeting, please let Kerry know.

I will submit a final invoice based on the portion of the work I have completed.

Best regards,
Jude

Just as in the true story, Jude is now out of a job—this time by his own choice. But in this message, Jude has not burned his bridges; that is, he has not severed his relationship with the training company. Of course, Darlene will not be pleased about his leaving the project, and she may not rehire him. But because Jude is an excellent instructional designer, she may hire him for a less stressful project, and she will not have to defend that decision to her staff.

Beyond the idea of rehiring Jude, Darlene can give Jude a positive reference regarding his excellent work, although she may indicate that he "deserted" an important project at crunch time. Then it will be Jude's challenge to explain the situation briefly to a future employer. Having to explain his leaving will be much easier than having to explain his attacking everyone with explosive emails.

Why Not Express Anger?

You may be wondering why I did not communicate Jude's understandable anger and frustration in the emails I created from him to Darlene.

After all, Jude might have included an *I* statement like this one: "I am very angry and frustrated with the new design schedule and the client's constant phone calls."

Such a statement communicating anger and frustration is not wrong, but it puts the focus in the wrong place—on Jude's feelings. What needs to change is the situation. Focusing on the situation is more likely to inspire a positive response. An admission of anger and frustration might have moved Darlene to respond this way: "We are all angry and frustrated! Cope!"

Still, Jude's frustration and anger were real, and in the real story, Jude flung his negative emotions at everyone involved in the project. If he had instead found a sounding board for his feelings, such as a friend, therapist, or trusted peer, he could have salvaged his work relationships.

When a Written Message Upsets You

It would be lovely if every email, memo, and letter you received were positive and friendly. But some of them that cross your desk or come up on your screen will be angry, mean-spirited, or hurtful. A supervisor shouts at you in an email—and copies others on the message. A client makes an absurd accusation in email. A colleague sends you a memo filled with preachy, condescending advice.

In my survey on business writing and relationships:

- 64 percent of respondents indicated that they occasionally receive written messages that are angry or insulting; 6 percent receive them frequently.
- 33 percent of respondents indicated that they have been hurt to the point of crying by a written message they have received at work, with huge gender differences: 39 percent of women and 16 percent of men.

One respondent gave details about the hurtful message:

It was the content AND delivery, not just the content. And I would say more lump in my throat/need to take a walk/ head feeling like it's going to explode from instant pressure than crying. I have thick skin, but wow!

How should you respond to such messages? Should you respond at all? In these situations, the usual wisdom is to avoid a written response. The advice is to pick up the telephone to talk with the other person or to schedule an in-person meeting. That is excellent advice. But sometimes a phone conversation or a face-to-face meeting is not workable for the reasons mentioned earlier in this chapter.

Tips for Responding to Upsetting Written Messages

At first, do nothing. Although reacting quickly may relieve some tension, acting without adequate thought and preparation may create more problems and embarrassment. People often regret it later. If the situation allows you to let 24 hours pass, let it. If you can let several days pass, that is even better. As time passes, you are likely to see the situation from a better perspective and feel calmer about it.

Control the damage. If others received copies of the message and you are concerned about controlling the damage, write a brief response in which you reply to all. It will signal that you are handling the situation. Try something like this: "Renaldo, I received your message. I will send you an individual, private response and then follow up with others as needed." After sending a brief message, take time to consider your next response.

Get support from a trusted colleague. It is smart to get support and another person's perspective. Be sure that individual will not share your heated comments with others. Allegiances at work change, so use caution about sharing negative feelings.

Do not broadcast your anger or upset feelings. If you do, it may become impossible to control the spread of private information. Also, you may be perceived as indiscreet or unprofessional because you have publicly disparaged the person with whom you are upset.

Decide whether you need to respond. When you can think of nothing to write in response, it may be because there is simply nothing you can say to make the situation better. You may have heard the expression "I will not dignify that comment with a response." Sometimes the mature response is not to respond.

Consider the possibility that you are overreacting or misinterpreting the message and the intent. Tell yourself, "I am overreacting, and here's how." Then review the possibilities. Is it possible that the message contains unintentional errors? People have been known to send messages addressing the reader as "Stud" rather than the name Stu and to type *incompetent* when they meant *incomplete*. A human resources manager I know wrote "Hell to all!" when she intended "Hello to all!" Giving the writer the benefit of the doubt may lead you to a more positive interpretation.

Try to find any truth in the message. Yes, the message is hurtful. Beyond that, does it communicate any truth? For example, is it possible that you did embarrass the other person at this morning's meeting? Is it true that your incorrect information caused the individual to stay at the wrong hotel in the wrong city? If you can find a bit of truth in the message, you may find ways to forgive the hurtful language and deal constructively with the information.

Write a long, therapeutic message to yourself. In it, say everything you would like to say to the other person. The purpose of the message is to get your own angry feelings out so that you can deal constructively with the other person. Be sure to avoid composing this message in email or in any other format that might be sent by mistake or read by others. If you refer to any people or companies in this message to yourself, give them fictitious names.

Do not accept the other person's statements as facts. Be especially cautious if he or she accuses other people or cites the remarks of others. Discreetly investigate what happened and who said what.

Keep value judgments, emotional language, and unsupported remarks out of any response. State only the facts. Avoid "Everyone agrees" or "It's obvious that . . ." Avoid writing, "Your attack on me is unjustified." Instead state, "I am not sure what prompted some of your statements." Rather than "What the heck are you talking about?" state, "I need more information about what went wrong." If you can avoid putting down the other person, you can avoid becoming embroiled in a conflict. Although making a cutting remark might make you feel momentarily pleased, it will not lead to a resolution.

Keep your response short. Some details may be necessary, but in general, the less you write, the less the other person will be able to misinterpret or try to refute. The more you write, the more time and emotional energy you are likely to expend on the ordeal.

Before you send it, have one or two trusted friends or coworkers review your message. These people should help you edit your reply for emotional language, unsubstantiated remarks, and sarcasm. Instead of saying, "Right on! You told her!" your reviewers should help ensure that your message is professional and mature. Remind them that you are not responsible for the other person's bad behavior, but you are responsible for the professionalism of your reply.

The following offensive email to an administrative assistant came from her manager, who was out of town at a meeting:

Subject: TYPO

Jane, you missed an obvious typo in the brochure. OUR PHONE NUMBER IS WRONG, for God's sake! Every damn one will need to be reprinted. Don't you dare come to me about an end-of-year bonus! This mistake makes me sick. What the hell were you doing when you were supposed to be proofreading?

When Jane read the message for the first time, she focused on the attacking language. She wanted to fire back an email, informing her manager that she would not put up with such treatment. She wanted to take up the issue of the annual bonus and the unfairness of denying her a bonus when she had done excellent work all year.

But Jane let 20 minutes pass during which she acknowledged that it *was* her job to proofread the brochure. She found a copy of the brochure and saw that the phone number was indeed wrong—on a print run of 5000.

After thinking through what she wanted to say, Jane composed this fitting email reply:

Subject: Re: TYPO—I Am Very Sorry

I am very sorry about the mistake. It makes me sick as well. I have no explanation except that I proofread it the day I left early with the flu.

I have left a message for the printer to find out what our options are, and I will let you know as soon as I hear from him.

Jane

In Jane's brief reply, she apologized for her mistake and empathized with the manager's "feeling sick" over the costly error. She responded to the factual part of the message and showed that she was taking action to correct the mistake. Nothing else needed to be done immediately.

How Not to Handle a Situation When You Are Angry

In this next scenario, Martin let his frustration overcome his professionalism in an email to Henry, a peer in another department:

> Subject: THANKS FOR HELPING ME OUT
>
> HENRY:
>
> I EMAILED YOU THREE TIMES ASKING YOU TO GIVE ME LAST MONTH'S FIGURES SO I COULD INCLUDE THEM IN MY PRESENTATION TO THE EXEC. MGMT. GROUP THIS MORNING. WELL, SUFFICE IT TO SAY, I GAVE THE PRESENTATION WITHOUT THE FIGURES. OF COURSE, I WAS ASKED ABOUT THEM AND HAD TO SAY I COULD NOT GET THEM IN TIME.
>
> THANKS FOR MAKING ME LOOK LIKE A FOOL. I LOOK FORWARD TO RETURNING THE FAVOR.
>
> MARTIN

Martin's frustration took over, from his sarcastic "THANKS FOR HELPING ME OUT" to his closing "I LOOK FORWARD TO RETURNING THE FAVOR," all in blaring capital letters.

In his reply, Henry took the high road rather than responding in kind. He took the emotion out of the message:

> Subject: Re: THANKS FOR HELPING ME OUT
>
> Hi, Martin. I am very sorry you didn't have the figures you needed this morning. Unfortunately, I was sent to China on short notice to meet with a manufacturer, and

everything was rush-rush until I left. Then I didn't check email on the plane. When I checked it today, I saw your second and third requests. I wish I had activated my out-of-office message.

I plan to be back in the office on Friday. If there is any information I can get for you after my return, just let me know. Again, sorry for missing your deadline.

Henry

Henry chose not to focus on or match Martin's anger and inappropriate message. Instead, he apologized, explained, and offered to provide information when he returned. Then he apologized again.

When Martin received Henry's reply, his own blaming email embarrassed him. Although he was still annoyed that he had not had the data when he needed it, he understood why Henry had not responded, and he was irritated with himself for not tracking down the data another way.

Martin composed this reply to undo the damage of his first insulting email to Henry:

Subject: Have a good trip!

Hi Henry,

Thanks for letting me know why you didn't get back to me. I apologize for my earlier email. I should have followed up when I didn't hear from you with the data.

At this point there is nothing I need from you. I will talk with you when you are back in town. Enjoy the flight home.

Martin

Martin's second message was simple and sincere. He thanked Henry, apologized, and let Henry know that he did not need any information. Martin's "Have a good trip" opening and close will begin to heal any rift in his relationship with Henry.

Both Jane and Henry took the emotion out of the situation by responding calmly and considerately. They turned a potentially ugly, drawn-out battle into a small skirmish that avoided long-term wounds. Their messages can mend the potential damage to their relationships.

When Effective Writing Doesn't Work

One of the hard facts of life is that some people can make our jobs miserable. Sometimes no amount of effective writing can salvage the situation. If you repeatedly receive hostile, angry, or critical messages from someone whose influence matters—and you cannot change the situation—you may need to find a new job. Certainly, you will not want to maintain a relationship with the offensive individual.

Or like Jude, the training designer whose true story opened this chapter, you may find that the demands of a job are unworkable. Unlike Jude, you can leave on *your* terms, having maintained a professional, positive demeanor and salvaged your business relationships.

Remember: There *are* professional ways to deal with other people's anger and your own to preserve relationships or end them well.

Personal Reflection

> ▶ In my survey on writing and relationships, 30 percent of people admitted having told off someone at work in writing and regretting it. How do you handle your feelings of anger on the job? Do you avoid putting them in writing? Do you have any messages you regret sending?

Next Step

> ▶ Reread this chapter whenever you find yourself in a heated situation.

CHAPTER 16

Share Constructive Feedback to Improve Performance—and Relationships

⁓

It was my second day on the job at the bookstore warehouse on New York City's Union Square, where I was a part-time biller-typist in the days before desktop computers. My first day had been a long, ultimately satisfying one. I had learned how to type invoices to college bookstores that had ordered foreign language books, the bookstore's specialty.

My desk was prominent in a huge open space that all employees walked through to get to their work areas. As I approached my desk that second morning, I saw, propped up tall on a typing stand, a note from my supervisor. The note went something like this:

> Lynn, attached are all the invoices you made mistakes on yesterday. Please be more careful today!
>
> Patty

Why do I remember this short note from my second day in a part-time job a long time ago? Is anything memorable about it to you?

I remember the note because I felt demoralized and publicly embarrassed. The note announced my incompetence to all who walked past my desk before I arrived at 9:30. I felt foolish because I thought I had had a good first day, taking in endless details about foreign language books and publishers and carefully trying to avoid errors. This note showed clearly that my first-day efforts were in vain.

This chapter will help you give constructive feedback the right way—not the way Patty did—to improve performance while building relationships.

What Patty Did Wrong

Here is what my supervisor did wrong:

- She wrote the message at the end of a long day, when she had no energy for thinking about how I, a new employee, might feel.
- She gave me feedback by placing a note on my desk for me to find and read in a vacuum.
- She displayed the note prominently so I would not miss it—but neither would anyone who walked past my desk.
- She provided no information about how I might avoid errors.
- She did not point out anything I had done well on my first day.
- She did not acknowledge that errors might be expected since I was just learning my job.

An Opportunity Missed

Effective constructive feedback is an indispensable part of everyone's professional development, especially for people who are new on the job. Good constructive feedback helps individuals and groups improve, adapt, and achieve their goals. Giving me feedback on my first day on the job could have been an excellent opportunity for Patty to help me succeed and to develop a supportive relationship with me. She might have written a note like this one and placed it in a sealed envelope on my desk:

Good morning, Lynn!

You did a great job yesterday. You completed 60 invoices, which is a terrific achievement for your first day, especially since most of our titles and publishers are in foreign languages.

Some of your invoices had errors. I have kept copies of them so we can go over them. I will show you where the errors occurred, and we can talk about how to catch errors in the future.

I will be in late today because of a midtown meeting. When I get in, we can talk about the invoices and about how it's going. Until then, be sure to check each invoice before going on to the next one.

Thanks for your hard work yesterday!

Patty

The second version has a completely different tone: appreciative, supportive, nonjudgmental, and forward looking. Yet it addresses my errors.

But what if I had done an awful job on my first day? The feedback would still need to be constructive. In the following message, you will notice changes from the previous one, which make it appropriate for someone whose performance needs significant improvement:

Good morning, Lynn!

Congratulations on surviving your first day. The biller-typist's job can be very challenging, especially since most of our titles and publishers are in foreign languages.

Some of your invoices had errors. I have kept copies of them so we can go over them. I will show you where the errors occurred, and we can talk about how to catch errors in the future. Also, I will sit with you as you work on some new invoices, so you can ask questions and I can guide you.

I will be in late today because of a midtown meeting. When I get in, we can spend time together. Until then, take your time with each invoice and be sure to check it before going on to the next one.

Thanks for your hard work yesterday!

Patty

The Secret to Giving Constructive Feedback

In my survey on writing and relationships, 77 percent of respondents said they have felt extremely hurt when receiving written negative feedback on a job. That hurt should not be happening. The secret to giving constructive feedback is to recognize that it must be *constructive*—not destructive. It must build up the other person. Its tone should be positive, helpful, and focused on future success. Otherwise, what is its point?

Imagine a situation in which Karla, a new junior executive, sent an email to her peers. In response, she received the following two emails. Although both messages shared the same information, one message built her up; the other tore her down.

Message 1:

To: Karla
From: Maria
Re: Marketing Tips

Hi, Karla.

Thanks for the excellent marketing tips. I recognized several that I can apply to our new insurance product.

I noticed that your email included the greeting "Ladies." We have had many conversations about that greeting in the past. The consensus is that "Team" or "Greetings, everyone," or even using no greeting is preferable. When I am back in town, we can have a conversation about this, and I will give you the background (dirt). For now, I just wanted to let you know that "Ladies" does not work well as a greeting for our group. By the way, Lee Ralston is a man, which you would not have known.

Again, thank you for the tips. I look forward to seeing you next week.

Maria

Message 2:

To: Karla
From: Priscilla
Subject: We Aren't "Ladies"

Regarding your message with the greeting "Ladies"— besides the fact that some of us have worked too hard to be given that dainty label, Lee Ralston is a heterosexual man—definitely NOT a lady.

"Ladies" may have been the right greeting where you came from, but it is dead wrong here. I suggest you lose it.

In Message 1, Maria communicates appreciation, shares helpful feedback, and begins to build a relationship with Karla. In contrast, Priscilla's destructive, biting feedback in Message 2 has the power to wound, embarrass, and discourage Karla, destroying any relationship with her before it can even begin. In some cases, negative feedback like Priscilla's shuts down and silences people, who then no longer contribute their ideas and energy. Yet if Priscilla had made her goal "Be constructive, not destructive," she would never have written such a message.

Tips on Giving Constructive (Negative) Feedback

At one time or another, you will be required to give constructive written feedback. If you supervise people, you will provide feedback on your employees' work in performance evaluations and other documents, and sometimes you will have more negative than positive comments to share. When your coworkers or peers ask for your comments, you will need to point out things that are not working or not effective, along with the commendable parts of their performance.

The following tips will help you meet the challenges of giving constructive feedback. Use them to write messages that help to enhance performance while building and maintaining solid work relationships.

Establish a positive climate by making at least one sincere, positive comment before constructive comments. Here's a simple example from a message I received from John Cline, a training manager in Vancouver, British Columbia. John was responding to a description of a new seminar I was creating for him. His email began like this:

> Hi, Lynn,
>
> Thanks for your creativity. I like what you have created so far.
>
> May I suggest the following modification?

When John started with a compliment, I became open to his suggestion. If he had started like this, I might have resisted his idea:

> Lynn, I got your email. The title doesn't work. Can we change it to this? [followed by a new title]

This opening would have disappointed me because it doesn't acknowledge anything good:

Lynn, thanks for your work. Don't you think the title is a little too broad? Please come up with something different.

Sometimes opening positively requires just one word. Can you recognize the word in this emailed comment from a reader of my blog?

Hi Lynn,

I just visited your fabulous business writing blog and noticed a minor typo. Because you are a professional writer, I thought you might like to know. Here it is:

The word *fabulous* set the tone of the message. How could I reject a comment when my work was being called *fabulous*?

Notice how the tone changes when that one word is missing:

Hi Lynn,

I just visited your business writing blog and noticed a minor typo. Because you are a professional writer, I thought you might like to know. Here it is:

Remember: It may take only one word to make constructive feedback palatable.

Share positive feedback too. Try to balance the positives and negatives so your reader will be able to accept the constructive feedback. Even if a project, proposal, plan, or customer interaction feels like a disaster to you, some aspects of it must be worthy of praise.

Example A:

In your press conference, you did a good job of handling the difficult questions about compensation. Your use of specific examples built credibility, and the story about your first job was appropriate and persuasive.

One area to work on for the next press conference is keeping responses short and on topic. Detailed responses on subjects such as pension law can lose some listeners. We can work on concise responses in our next coaching session.

Example B:

I appreciate how quickly you got this mockup to us. You and your staff worked fast! The colors and fabric are perfect, and the design is generally correct.

These three details in the mockup need to be changed:

1. The pocket on the left side should have the same placement as the pocket on the right side. In the mockup, the right pocket is correctly placed. The left pocket should be 4 cm lower.

2. The zipper should be full-length. The mockup has only a 25-cm zipper.

3. The ribbing along the bottom should be 5.08 cm. The ribbing on the mockup is only 2.54 cm.

Sometimes you can plan the criteria you will use for your feedback ahead of time, to ensure that some feedback items will be positive or at least acceptable. For example, I often use a 12-point checklist to give people feedback on their writing. Among the 12 areas for feedback, there are always at least 3 or 4 the writer does well. Maybe the tone is professional, the message is complete, contact information is included, and the writer avoids inappropriate passive verbs. By ensuring that every writer gets to recognize and enjoy what he or she is doing well, I can freely share what each person needs to do better.

Avoid the pronouns *you* and *your* in constructive comments, when possible. By avoiding the use of *you* with constructive feedback, you will reduce your reader's defensiveness. Notice the absence of *you* and *your* in the constructive parts of the previous Examples A and B. Here is another example: "The test data do not seem convincing to me. That might be because I had difficulty understanding Table B."

By contrast, in positive comments, *you* and *your* are encouraging: "Your test data are very convincing, and you communicated them clearly in Table B."

Be specific, not vague. If you comment on a speech by saying, "The introduction doesn't work," the presenter will not know why it doesn't work or how it might work better. Without specifics, the remark comes across as a putdown. Instead, write something like this:

> The introduction seems to go on too long. I understood and agreed with your approach within the first minute, but then the explanation continued. Why not explain the approach just once? If the audience wants more information, they can ask you when you invite questions.

Avoid the word *but* after a compliment. *But* is guaranteed to erase any positive comment in the reader's mind, as it would in this example: "Your ideas are excellent, but you are not communicating them clearly." Notice how this revised example lets the compliment shine: "Your ideas are excellent—very creative and exciting. Here are some suggestions for communicating them more clearly."

Provide suggestions or offer to provide them. People often need specific suggestions to be able to improve their work. Example:

> Because there is a lot of text on this screen, the customer may become frustrated and abandon the shopping cart. Some content that can safely be deleted is . . .

Be sure your correction is valid when you correct other people's work. Don't hold too tightly to your view. Recognize that there are many ways of doing things. You may see a graphic design as cluttered, while others see it as intricate. To you, a recommendation may be too direct, but others may find it straightforward and confident. There may be more than one way to attach a widget to a whatsit. It is even possible that your approach is inefficient, outdated, overly conventional, or risky.

Ask yourself: Is his or her way wrong? Or is it just that I do things differently based on my experience? When you realize your correction is actually just another way of handling something, think twice about communicating it at all.

Management guru Marshall Goldsmith, in his book *What Got You Here Won't Get You There*, warns against "adding too much value," that is, contributing your two cents to a colleague's or employee's idea. He based his warning on the contention that such feedback makes the project or idea partially yours rather than completely the pride and joy of the other person. Goldsmith writes, "You may have improved the content of my idea by 5 percent, but you've reduced my commitment to executing it by 50 percent, because you've taken away my ownership of the idea. *My* idea is now *your* idea."

Focus on the future. The past cannot be changed. These two examples each focus on a future opportunity:

> The next time you talk with a patient about treatment options, you may want to refer to the printed brochure that is in the holder in each of the exam rooms. It will help you cover everything, and the patient will be able to take the brochure home with her.

> In the future, empathize with the customer before saying that we cannot replace the item at no charge. Empathy

helps customers feel heard even when they don't get what they want. Try a response such as . . .

Put your feedback in context. If you are making a small point, say so, as this example does:

> This is a small point: If the names were alphabetized rather than listed by rank, it would take the emphasis off corporate hierarchy.

This introductory statement helps the reader take in the feedback:

> I have one major comment and two minor ones.

If you think someone's idea is weird or stupid, ask questions instead of commenting, like this:

> Thanks for sending me your ideas for the new flooring. Not having seen this approach before, I have some questions:
> 1. How will this flooring hold up in a room that gets a lot of traffic?
> 2. Do you see it as a good match or a contrast to the executive suite it leads up to?
> 3. How does the material fit with the overall budget?

Whenever you can give constructive feedback in person, choose that approach—even if you have written your comments. Your task is much easier when you can accompany your comments with smiles, nods of encouragement, and other attentive body language, and you can notice and respond to the other person's feelings. Written feedback alone provides no opportunity for direct two-way communication. The words on the screen or the page must stand alone, communicating your support, fairness, accuracy, professionalism, and even compassion. Your comments must try to anticipate and answer the reader's questions. So whenever you can be there to support your written words, do it.

Tips (Don'ts!) on How to Be Kind and Constructive

When you give feedback, recognize that you are dealing with human beings. Individuals may have a demanding travel schedule, a sick child, an overdue project or credit-card bill, a sore back, or a broken heart. You can make their lives easier by providing feedback that is clear, compassionate, and easy to act on. To write meaningful comments that help rather than harm others, follow these tips. I have worded them as don'ts since they cover behaviors to avoid.

Don't exaggerate. Instead, be careful and courteous. For example, do not write, "On a 10-point scale of confusing, your budget proposal is a 12." If a budget proposal *is* confusing, write, "While reviewing the budget, I got confused several times. I have noted those places below."

Don't be cute or clever. Do not write, "Your film is the solution to my insomnia. I put it in the player and was asleep in seconds." Do not comment, "I would rather have a root canal than try to sell your design to our client." When giving constructive criticism, your job is not to make yourself look good. It is to make the other person feel good while absorbing the criticism.

In the situation of commenting on a boring film, write something like this: "The film did not keep my attention, and I wanted it to. I was trying to be engaged, but I found my mind wandering repeatedly." Then give examples of dull scenes (without calling them dull) and suggestions for editing or cutting them.

Don't equate rudeness with straight talk. Edit your gut reactions. Instead of writing, "I thought you would be smarter than my previous assistant," describe specific behaviors you would like the assistant to improve. Instead of writing, "Your home page is a mess," write, "I couldn't find certain standard information on the home page." Then give specific examples.

Don't act dense. For instance, do not write, "I have no idea what you mean." Unless the person is working from a unique perspective or is communicating horribly, you must have some idea. Try to understand. If you still cannot understand despite trying, write, "I tried, but I don't understand your point yet."

Don't be a hit-and-run critic. Have the courage to sign your constructive comments—with your real name. On the Internet, on evaluation forms, and sometimes even in email, it is easy to slam into someone with a truckload of negativity, then sneak away anonymously. If your comments are legitimate and helpful, you deserve credit and thanks for writing them. If they are unreasonable and destructive, destroy them before they do harm.

Don't copy other people on constructive feedback. Broadcasting constructive criticism is the same as criticizing a person publicly. If a third party asks for a copy of your written feedback, encourage the individual to get it from the person to whom you gave it.

Don't assume someone else has a problem you can help to fix. Recognize that some problems are yours—not the other person's. For example, if you can't stand to look at an associate's long bangs (fringe) hanging into her eyes in meetings, she doesn't have a problem—you do. No amount of "helpful" feedback will make her accept your advice. Similarly, if you cannot bear a coworker's nasally voice or cheerful

outlook, you have a problem. Neither of those features deserves constructive criticism.

**Don't comment if it is not your job to do so and you have not
been asked or paid for an opinion.** It is no one's responsibility to give
constructive feedback to the world. Assume that if people have not asked
for your comments, they do not want them. Even if you feel compelled
to share your expert judgment of another's thought process, eyeglasses,
parenting skills, tattoo, attitude, accent, office décor, or hair color, don't
do it! Your treatment for someone else's problem is likely to be a bitter
pill they will not swallow no matter how expert your views are. If you
are in a critical mood, focus instead on how you can improve your own
skills, traits, appearance, productivity, worldview, etc.

But let's not confuse constructive criticism with helpful information. People want to know if they are walking around, smiling, with
spinach between their front teeth. They want to know if they have hung
a drawing upside down. Writer-editor Anne Boardman took the right
step in this situation:

> I recently pointed out to the digital editor of my local paper
> that their domain name had been dropped from their RSS
> feeds. The consequence was that every click to an article
> resulted in an error message. I just added the domain name
> manually so I could read the articles, but it was annoying
> and I thought if I were in the same situation, I'd want
> to know about it. Most people wouldn't go through the
> trouble to fix the URL and would just stop reading their
> feeds. . . . In fact, no one had pointed it out to them, which
> they wrote back to me with extreme gratitude.

Don't counterattack. If someone has given you harsh criticism, do
not return the fire. Provide fair, courteous, specific criticism that you
would give to any other person.

Don't give feedback when it is too late to incorporate. When someone has printed 500 marketing packets, it is too late to recommend a stronger slogan. If you are not sure whether your feedback might be too late, phone or email the other person to learn the status of a project before writing comments. Feedback is also too late when the other person no longer remembers or cares about the situation you are addressing in your comments. Wait for the next opportunity to give useful feedback rather than sharing stale remarks.

Constructive Feedback Tips for Managers

Common employee complaints about feedback are that it is always negative and often a surprise. You can eliminate such complaints by creating a work environment that is rich in feedback. Here are three proven tips:

Build feedback into every project. If you do, people will anticipate feedback rather than being blindsided by it. At a team meeting, for example, ask what went well on a project. Then, using a blame-free approach, ask what might be done better in the future. In written messages include the same balanced approach.

Give constructive feedback privately. Feedback should never be public shaming. Even if you, as a manager, have a strong ego, assume your staff members are still developing their ability to accept constructive criticism. If appropriate, copy others on complimentary feedback.

To balance constructive feedback, share positive feedback liberally. Add "Give positive feedback" to your daily calendar. Be sure your positive feedback is specific, sincere, and meaningful. To make it meaningful, mention why the behavior or performance is important to the team and the company. See examples in the chapter "Give Positive, Powerful Feedback."

Examples of Feedback That Builds Performance and Relationships

Everyone deserves constructive feedback that will help them work more effectively. When it is your job to give feedback, welcome that responsibility. Use these examples to help you succeed at the task.

In this first example, a maintenance and grounds manager emails feedback to someone in his department who made a serious mistake:

> To: Frank Harris
> From: Gerry Nielson
> Re: Safe Work Practices
>
> I heard from Hector what happened in the warehouse today. I know he talked with you about the risk of carbon monoxide poisoning, Frank, and I want to emphasize the seriousness of the situation. All of us must follow this rule: <u>Never</u> use gasoline-powered equipment in an unventilated area. Example: Do not use the gas-powered pressure washer in any part of the warehouse unless the windows and doors are open and a fan is on.
>
> I believe Hector told you to use an electric pressure washer in any unventilated area, and I am telling you the same thing. Now you know where the extension cords are. Whenever you have any questions, ask.
>
> Hector told me you are learning the job fast and are easy to work with. Glad to hear it! Just remember to use gas-powered equipment in <u>ventilated areas only</u>. We want you healthy and on the job. We don't want you to end up in the emergency room!
>
> Gerry

Gerry's message is constructive, not destructive. It does not criticize Frank for his serious mistake. Because of the seriousness of the issue, Gerry got into the subject right away, without a buffer of positive feedback. However, he included positive comments in the final paragraph.

Feedback is rarely all positive or all constructive. Here is an example of peer-to-peer feedback that includes both kinds:

Subject: Your Request for Feedback

Candice, I'm glad to give comments on your presentation. You did an impressive job, and the clients left smiling and eager to move to the next step. Here is what I observed:

- **Preparation:** You were very well prepared. You exhibited great insights into the client's problems and were able to describe their pain points well. The client appeared very comfortable and impressed that you heard and understood them.

- **Terminology.** For the most part, you used language that was clear to the client. However, several terms were our jargon. When those terms came up, you had to spend time explaining them, and that took you off message. For the next presentation, I suggest that you ask June to do a final review to catch jargon. Then you can choose to replace the jargon or be ready with a quick definition or analogy.

- **Q&A:** The connectivity questions and answers went on a bit too long, and it was unfortunate that they came up in the middle of your presentation. If that happens in the future, I recommend that you briefly answer the initial question and explain that there will be time for more questions at the end of your presentation. You responded well to their questions about the documentation. You were clear and brief, and it was smart to defer the details to a follow-up message.

- **Consistency:** The comments of the sales team were completely consistent with yours, so there were no cracks in your presentation. I mention the sales aspect here because I know you helped them prepare. Your work with them paid off. You were able to present the client with a coherent, realistic solution.

Candice, congratulations on a fine presentation!

Don

In this 90-day performance evaluation, a manager includes positive and constructive feedback for a new receptionist:

To: John Frost
From: Doris Davis
Date: December 1, 20XX
Subject: 90-Day Performance Evaluation

John, your overall performance during your probationary period has been very good. I would like to give you feedback on the five areas we discussed during your first week on the job.

1. Attendance and punctuality. Your performance in this area has been outstanding. You have not missed any days of work, even though we have had bad weather. Also, you were late only one day. Regarding punctuality, I really appreciate that you are at your desk ready to work at 8 a.m., rather than getting coffee or walking around. As you know, we often have visitors as soon as the doors open. Your being at your desk working at 8 o'clock increases our efficiency and presents our unit positively.

2. Professional appearance. Both you and your work area look professional. Since receiving feedback in September,

you have kept your desk and the reception area free of clutter. The area looks tidy whenever anyone visits. Also, you present yourself well, with neat, appropriate clothing.

3. Courtesy. You treat each of our visitors courteously. No one is kept waiting unnecessarily, you greet everyone by name, you request identification diplomatically, and you offer refreshments when appropriate. One change I would like to see is for you to greet visitors you do not know well, especially those who are older, by using a courtesy title or professional title and their last names. Even though the professional staff may call visitors by their first names, that familiarity often comes from long relationships. For example, when Dr. Krikorian visited the other day, it was appropriate for Joanna to address him by his first name because they have known each other for many years. Please ask me if you have any questions about how to greet specific individuals.

4. Communication. Your oral communication with staff and visitors is excellent. You speak clearly and courteously. When I call in, you are always easy to understand, and you have mastered our challenging phone system. Regarding written communication, you have been applying the feedback you received on your emails, and your messages have improved noticeably. The next step is to make your emails more concise. I would like you to find and take an email class during first quarter to help you strengthen your messages. Your IMs [instant messages] are generally clear and effective.

5. Accuracy. Not once have I found any significant errors in your work, and no one has mentioned any problems with the accuracy of your messages, scheduling, or other

tasks. You manage details very well. I really appreciate the care and high standards you bring to your work.

Hats off to you for completing your probationary period successfully! I am delighted to have you as part of our team.

Doris

The two previous messages go a long way in providing helpful information, both positive and constructive. Candice and John learned what they have done well, and they can implement specific suggestions to improve their performance. Beyond that, the messages are likely to solidify the relationships between those who wrote the feedback and those who received it. The positive and constructive comments and rich details help to build trust between the people involved.

You may have noticed that Doris's feedback to John in his 90-day evaluation briefly mentions constructive feedback he received earlier, on his desk clutter and email. Doris did not save that constructive feedback until she wrote this formal evaluation. Prompt feedback helps recipients change their behavior promptly. It also minimizes any embarrassment they might feel about having performed badly over a longer period. And it averts mistrust for the people delivering the feedback. After all, they did not store it up, then dump it on the recipients.

If you take just one idea away from this chapter, make it this: "Negative" feedback should not be negative, but rather *constructive*. It should build up the reader and help him or her correct errors or improve behavior that is less than optimal. Building up the other person in this way will help you build and sustain good work relationships.

Personal Reflection

▸ Whether you are a supervisor, an individual contributor, a teacher, or a consultant, which techniques do you use to make your feedback constructive rather than destructive? Did any ideas in the chapter surprise you?

Next Step

▶ Review the list of feedback don'ts in the chapter. Make a note of any that you need to remember.

CHAPTER 17

Communicate Around the Globe
With Courtesy and Wisdom

Exhausted from two nights and days of traveling from Kenya to Dubai to Delhi, in clothes he had not changed (his luggage was delayed), the American human resources professional arrived in Delhi to facilitate the retreat. His NGO (nongovernmental organization) had sent him to work with their local Indian leadership. The man, Richard Wilkinson, tells the story:

> I walk into the meeting room and, much to my surprise, it's a converted restaurant. The staff are seated in low booths, banquettes, and small tables. There is no wall to stick stuff on—just a stage. We jerry-rig a way to record participant contributions, and off we go.
>
> The first topic of the retreat was to make plans for the coming year. First question: What would you be celebrating as a country office a year from now if you enjoyed an extraordinarily successful year? Dutifully the India staff

discuss this among themselves, then write down their views on small sheets of paper, which are then posted on the jerry-rigged wall-that-is-not-a-wall.

I then asked what challenges may be encountered that could get in the way of realizing the great year they envisioned. This time I wrote their ideas on a scratchy old whiteboard teetering on a wonky easel.

This was my first trip to India, I'm seriously tired, I'm standing in front of my colleagues in two-day old clothes with streaks of black tar across my behind [from the seat of a taxi], and I'm struggling to catch on with Indian-accented English. Finally, let's call him Singh, pipes up from a back booth, "Starved for attention." "Starved for attention?" I ask. "Not quite sure how that might be an obstacle, but . . ." I say as I write "Starved for attention" on the teetering whiteboard.

The room erupts in laughter. I turn to the participants and ask, "Okay, what did Singh really say?" "Staff retention!" came the chorus of replies.

Smiles or Scowls? It's Your Choice

Stories like Richard Wilkinson's take place every workday in interactions between people of different cultures and countries. Global miscommunication happens. In my survey on writing and relationships, 43 percent of women and 64 percent of men indicated that they had had a serious miscommunication at work with someone from another culture or country. Happily, Richard's story is not one of those statistics. It led to smiles and laughter rather than scowls and anger. The retreat succeeded, and Richard succeeded in developing positive work relationships.

But the situation might have been different if Richard had made different choices. He might have opted to postpone the retreat because of the delayed planes and his resulting exhaustion. He might have refused to work in a space without the equipment he needed. He might have frowned at participants when their accents challenged his understanding. Had he made those choices, he might have left India without success for himself or the Indian leaders and without any new blossoming relationships.

Richard, who has been working in global health since 2001, believes that communication across cultures must be intentional. He says:

> I am very conscious of choices we make in the moment about how we are going to relate to one another and how those have implications for the future. I think about the question "What is it we are trying to create here?" and the choices we have in creating it. It matters a lot what we say and how we say it. That lays the foundation for expectation and trust down the road.

Wanting to be successful in his first trip to Kenya in 2001, Richard asked the vice president of administration at his NGO for his advice on interacting effectively across cultures. The answer was "Have patience and smile."

But in our written messages, how do we make the right choices? How do we communicate patience and a smile? This chapter shares stories, tips, and strategies to help you build friendships across cultures and across the globe.

Consider the following approaches, which are inspired by Richard and his experiences:

Communicate first as a person, then as a professional. If you are from a results-focused culture like the United States, communicating first as a person may mean taking the opposite approach of your normal pattern in your emails. In the United States, emails frequently get down to business at the start, then end on a friendly note. But as Richard Wilkinson explains, "Getting to the point in settings where there is more sensitivity about relationships is really discourteous." He adds, "Sometimes I express empathy or appreciation at the beginning before getting into the meat of a message."

Richard shared this example of an opening to a colleague going through a difficult time in India: "Hope you're holding up given all that is going on!" To a colleague in Botswana, he began with "It was great catching up with you today."

You can use or adapt these openings to begin your messages with a focus on the person rather than the action:

How are you? I hope you are healthy and happy.
I hope you are well.
We hope you are enjoying the season.
I trust you and your coworkers are fine.
I trust you are doing splendidly and enjoying the season.
I send you and your esteemed colleagues my warm wishes.
Greetings from our research team!
Greetings to you and your family.
It is a pleasure to be in touch with you again.
It was a delight to see you in São Paulo.
I hope you enjoyed your trip to New York.
Welcome back to work! I hope you had a wonderful holiday.

Think twice about greetings that refer to time of day. When beginning an email to coworkers around the globe, remember that your "Good morning" message may instantly arrive in their late afternoon, or even at midnight.

Use polite language such as *please, thank you,* and *appreciate* throughout your message. Close with a courteous sign-off such as:

All the best
With best wishes
Best regards
Warm regards

Sincerely
Respectfully
With many thanks

Recognize that there is more than one way to get results. If you do not insist that business be done your way, you will be able to feel more patient and therefore communicate more patiently. For example, recognize that people from other cultures may find it uncomfortable and unseemly to give feedback directly, even though you ask for candid feedback and are used to it. Your emails asking for their feedback may not lead to a reply, or not a useful one, and your expectations may put a strain on your relationship. Richard uses Survey Monkey, an online survey tool, to get input from his African colleagues in simple, short surveys. He finds the tool helpful because it forces him to be clear about what he needs, it shows his African colleagues that their opinion matters, and it makes it easy for them to provide input.

Be humble. Recognize that you do not know it all. Richard was humbled by his humorous "starved for attention" misunderstanding. In that situation, clearly the mistake was his. But it makes sense to humbly assume that you may be wrong in other, subtler situations, for example, when dealing with a culture like India's, which is thousands of years old. When dealing with less experienced colleagues in other countries, Richard says, "It would be easy to condescend or to be high-handed and directive," adding, "but instead of being condescending, you accept a situation for what it is, then show respect by asking questions. Not pointed questions, but open ones."

For clarity across cultures, Richard asks just a few questions at a time, and he lists and numbers them rather than including them in paragraphs.

Explore to Learn More

Like Richard Wilkinson, Jerry Schlagenhauf has always loved international travel and working with people from other cultures. He began his travels as an exchange student in Switzerland; studied anthropology in college and graduate school; lived for two years in Kuala Lumpur, Malaysia; and worked for many years in human resources in Saudi Arabia. Now he works as a career consultant in the United States.

In Switzerland, Jerry's Swiss family away from home treated him very well. For instance, they spoke only standard German rather than their Swiss dialect so that he would learn a language he could use. One day Jerry was talking on and on about how special something American was, when his Swiss mother sat him down and told him in German:

> Jerry, I want you to know one thing. I am absolutely certain that America is a wonderful place and that you have many, many things that we probably don't have. But do you understand that this is *my* home, *my* country? This is where *I* was born, and this is where *I* have that feeling, that connection that you are expressing to me.

Jerry described his reaction and where it has taken him:

> I felt grateful some place deep inside me, but I was so embarrassed. I thought, oh my goodness. I really haven't been learning and listening as much as I thought I was.
>
> One of the points I try to keep in front of me all the time regardless of who I am working with is: You don't know it all, Jerry. There are still things to learn. There are still things I should explore, questions I should ask rather than telling so much.

Jerry has developed these specific practices to help him explore and learn more, which you can apply too:

Ask questions. In email across cultures, ask and acknowledge rather than make assumptions and assert your knowledge. Like Richard

Wilkinson, Jerry has adopted asking questions as a primary way of learning about people and developing strong cross-cultural relationships, demonstrating a keen interest. When he begins working with a career-counseling client, especially one from another culture or country, he asks questions to discover unique interests and preferences:

What brings you to me?
Where do you want to be?
What is most important to you?
What are your obstacles?

He asks such questions rather than starting with "Here's what I am going to do for you" or "Here's the information I have for you." Besides expressing curiosity, Jerry shows respect for others by not assuming that he knows their situation or that he will be able to "fix them" by applying a generic solution.

Do your homework. Learn general information about others before you start the relationship. Before Jerry begins working with a client from another culture, he researches the country and culture on the Internet. He also gets information from former clients, colleagues, and networking connections to find out what is going on in the country now. Human information sources often provide the best guidance. "If you want to just ignore it all," he says, "you might get along, but you won't really have learned very much." Jerry has found that many lasting relationships have developed because he has made a special effort to learn about people rather than focus on himself and what he has to present.

Cultivate acceptance. Recognize that people from other cultures are different in many ways, but they are also the same. Over the years, Jerry has listened to people's stories that have shaken and saddened him. But he has focused on understanding people and looking for common bonds. He explained:

> I may disagree with the politics and the handling of domestic affairs in a particular culture. Even though I am trained as an anthropologist, I don't think I can be so valueless that things don't offend me. But to understand where they are coming from means that I have to hold back that judgmental piece. We are all connected regardless of where the political boundaries have been drawn. No matter what the cultural differences are, the basic emotional needs of human beings are very, very similar.

Applying Jerry's approach, you can accept that colleagues from certain cultures will be blunt rather than diplomatic in the messages you receive from them. Viewing their candor as refreshing rather than barbaric will improve your relationship. If "no" is an intolerable answer in the culture of some of your coworkers, you can change your questions rather than force the issue. For example, rather than asking, "Can you do it?" and requiring a response, you can ask, "When can you do it?" or "How does this fit in your work schedule?"

By asking questions and doing your homework, you will learn how others are the same as and different from you. By focusing on acceptance, you can build relationships rather than dissect them.

Simplify for Clear, Welcoming Communication

Deb Arnold is a communications expert who has a degree in international relations, an MBA, and experience working and traveling around the globe. At the time of this story, she was working in the United States at a marketing agency that had approximately 50 offices in 32 countries serving a huge multinational account. Agency staff around the world came together in quarterly online meetings, "global rallies," to share best practices and news about the account. Communicating as a worldwide team, they used English as their language. They would sign in to the virtual meetings by office, with the cities London, Paris, Frankfurt, and so on, popping up on the screen. It was global communication at its best.

At one quarterly meeting, headquarters staff decided to use online polls to illustrate how the offices might use such polls in their own online meetings. They included this poll question:

> Which is your favorite breed of dog?
> a. Chihuahua
> b. German shepherd
> c. Poodle
> d. Dachshund

Deb worked at headquarters and typically planned the quarterly meetings. But she had been out of town for this meeting. Telling me the story, she described people's reaction to the meeting:

> When I came back, I looked at the meeting evaluations, and there were all these comments about dogs: "I didn't understand about the dogs," "It was very frustrating," and "Why did you give us something we couldn't understand?"

At offices around the world, employees and managers alike expressed frustration and anger.

Do you understand what went wrong? Take a moment to think about what caused the problem.

Deb explained:

> I speak Hebrew fairly well. I speak Spanish fairly well. Yet I don't know how to say the name of any breed of dog in either of those languages. We were talking to people in 32 countries, in only three of which is English their first language. The people didn't know what the words meant!

The leadership was caught off guard. The teams were turning to the leaders to ask "What does this poll question mean?" and the leaders didn't know what it meant. So the question just made everyone feel stupid and uncomfortable. And it exacerbated all of the issues that you would imagine between headquarters and satellite offices, with satellite offices thinking, "They don't understand our situation. They don't understand our particular context."

Not a good way to build relationships around the globe!

Deb's "dog story" illustrates how easy it is to damage relationships, even in communication-savvy companies, when people do not simplify their writing and think clearly about their audience.

To write clear, welcoming global messages that build trust rather than wariness, consider these tips:

Use plain English. As the marketing agency learned in Deb's story, it is essential to choose words that are part of your readers' vocabulary if you want them to understand your message. Replace any word your readers are likely not to know. Consider these examples: *pussyfoot, upshot, intrinsic, drive-by, cascading, canny, purview,* and *thumbnail.* If you replace such words, you will communicate more clearly with both native and nonnative English speakers.

Use words and phrases that have few meanings. The word *manufacture* has several meanings, whereas *make* has dozens. If you mean "manufacture," use that word. Likewise, the words *appropriate* and *correct* have few meanings; *right* has over 40.

Avoid words that have opposite or very different meanings. *Oversight* may be a close review or a failure to review. *Transparent* may be plainly visible or invisible. *Sanction* may mean to approve or to penalize. Such is the beauty of English to confuse and alienate your readers!

Use concrete language rather than figurative language or slang. As Deb Arnold says of this advice, "It tests our creativity to actually be creative within these boundaries, but it's important to do." From stories I have heard in classes, on my blog, and in my survey, I would say that the most frequently misunderstood slang expression is "bang for your buck." A writing class participant told about a colleague who used the expression at a business meeting in France. When he uttered the phrase, people in the room visibly shrank from him in apparent disgust, perhaps because the word *bang* is vulgar slang for sexual intercourse. The audience would have understood "return on our investment," which is what the U.S. businessman intended. Other problematic figurative language comes from sports ("This will be his third strike") and the military ("What's the blowback if we take this position?").

Use simple verb forms such as present, past, and future tense (*write, wrote, will write*). Avoid less common, more complicated verb tenses (*will have written, should have been writing*) that your readers may not have mastered despite years of studying English. For example, use "Will you attend the seminar?" rather than "Will you be planning on attending the seminar?" Use "If you have questions" rather than "Should you find you have questions."

Write short, simple sentences rather than complex, convoluted ones. Long sentences are more difficult to follow for all readers. But they present special challenges for people who read English as a second, third, or fourth language. Long sentences make readers work harder to understand the relationships between the pronouns (*it, they, their*), conjunctions (*but, yet, which*), and other sentence parts.

Know your audience. Deb Arnold—whose slogan is "Who do you think you're talking to?"—recommends answering these questions about your readers:

- Who are they?
- What do they care about?
- What are they afraid of?
- What are their hopes and desires?
- What do they know?
- What do they not know?

If the agency meeting planners had thought about Deb's first three questions, they might have recognized that some attendees don't care about dogs and might even be afraid of them. In many places in the Middle East, dogs live as security guards rather than pets. In certain African countries, they are associated with apartheid.

When you think about what readers know and do not know, keep these tips in mind:

Consider geography. Just as *poodle* and *dachshund* meant nothing to agency professionals around the world, Olympia, Calgary, and Espoo may be unknown cities to your readers. Provide necessary details about their locations. Clarify references such as *the Mainland* and *East Texas*, which may not be named that way on a map.

Consider objects that have different names for various English-speaking audiences. You may call that fleshy purple fruit *eggplant*, when your reader knows it as an aubergine. You may recognize these punctuation marks as *parentheses* ( ), but your reader thinks they are brackets. (The "Recommended Resources" chapter includes an online resource on differences between British, Canadian, and U.S. English.)

Avoid contractions, abbreviations, acronyms, and nicknames. Some international readers can easily recognize contractions such as *that's*, *it's,* and *who's.* But others may confuse them with possessive forms such as *Sue's.* Readers near and far may misunderstand abbreviations (*Mass Ave* for Massachusetts Avenue), acronyms (*IRA* may be your individual retirement account but your reader's Irish Republican Army), and nicknames (who is *Ole Miss* anyway?).

Include both metric and U.S. standard (Imperial) measurements, when applicable, to communicate accurately for all your readers.

Spell out dates. Use, for example, September 2, 2014, or 2 September 2014, rather than 9/2/14 or 2/9/14, which may confuse half your readers, depending on the style they are accustomed to. Some companies follow the ISO 8601 (International Organization for Standardization) standard format, 2014-09-02, but your readers may still be confused unless they recognize the standard.

Consider using the 24-hour clock for time, and indicate time zones to reduce confusion. For example, 10 a.m. Pacific Standard Time in Los Angeles would be expressed as 10:00 PT (UTC-8). And 4:30 p.m. Daylight Saving Time in New York City would be 16:30 ET (UTC-4). UTC is a commonly used successor to GMT (Greenwich Mean Time). To convert time easily for your audience, use the website timeanddate.com.

Do research. Like Jerry Schlagenhauf, Deb turns to the Internet to prepare herself for work with people from other cultures. For a brief project with someone from another culture, she searches for best practices for doing business in that culture or country. Depending on the depth and length of the interaction, she recommends investing more time and effort:

Let's say your company has just merged with an overseas competitor, and you are going to be working extensively with these new colleagues. You may want to hire a consultant with expertise in doing business with that country, who can walk you through the steps and make you aware of potential pitfalls and best practices. You will save a lot of headaches and a lot of explanations and apologies if you know in advance the things you should be aware of.

If you write to a group in another country, develop a relationship with a colleague there who may be willing to review your messages before you send them out broadly. That individual could advise you about any sentences or expressions that do not come across the way you intend.

Think twice about your formatting. Like readers everywhere, your global readers will find it difficult to read long paragraphs. However, some international readers cringe at the heavy use of bullet points, finding them too direct and inelegant. Try using short, clear paragraphs for analysis and background, and use bullet points for lists and action items. If your readers can view attachments, use graphs and charts to present details.

This sample email from Richard Wilkinson to his African colleagues in Dar es Salaam includes effective short chunks of text and short sentences (averaging 13 words each). You will notice that rather than getting to the point the way he would have with American colleagues, Richard took a more leisurely, personal approach that acknowledged his relationship and recent visit.

example email

Subject: Next Steps for Our Salary Survey

Greetings from a sunny Seattle! Hope both of you are doing well. We are cherishing the sun here in these final few days of summer. I had a great time in Tanzania and Malawi, but it is great to be home, too.

Now, on to business. It is time for us to work on the custom salary study we want to do. I have attached several documents for you to review.

INSTRUCTIONS

1. Custom Salary Survey: Attached is the draft of the survey. It would be ideal for one of you to complete the survey to see how it works. If there are any problems, we can edit the survey before sending it to others. I will share this draft with my colleague to get her suggestions, too.

2. Positions to Survey: Please carefully review this list of the positions we will survey. Are there one or two other positions we should include? I do not think we need to survey drivers because the original survey is fine for that level of position.

3. Position Descriptions: I included brief descriptions for each position from another survey. The purpose of the brief descriptions is for others to judge whether their job is a match for ours. We will probably want to edit these to be more like what our positions do, but remember that they need to be somewhat generic, too.

4. Invitations: Please contact the organizations next week to invite them to participate in our survey. Tell them we will share a summary of the results with them.

TELEPHONE MEETING?

To keep this project moving along, I suggest that the three of us talk soon. Any day next week is fine with me. As usual, because of our million time-zone differences, it will need to be 16h00 in Dar/6h00 in Seattle. Please let me know which day or days are best for you.

All the best,
Richard

Below is a polite request for action from a writer who does not know the reader. Notice the greeting, brief introduction, short sentences (averaging 14 words each), short paragraphs, use of a graphic illustration, and absence of acronyms and abbreviations.

Subject: Cloud-Computing Webinar—Action Requested

Dear Mr. Khose,

Greetings from XYZ Company. As a member of the Information Technology department in our Washington office, I am organizing the December 11 webinar on cloud computing. This email is to confirm that you will be able to log on to attend the program.

Action Requested: Please click this <u>link</u> to test your ability to log on to the online "classroom." (The attached picture indicates how the classroom should appear on your screen.) If the link does not connect you to the classroom, please send this email to the computer software expert at your company. Your expert can find the problem, which might be a computer firewall.

Please let me know that you are able to log on to the classroom.

I look forward to working with you and your team. Please email or call me if you have any questions or requirements.

With best regards,
Reena Leonard

[Job title]
[Company name]
[Telephone number]
[Website URL]

More Global Communication Tips

These additional tips will help you succeed with global relationships:

Think of your readers as valued partners, and communicate with them that way. This approach is especially important if you work in the international headquarters and your readers are thousands of miles away. Avoid language such as "We expect your group to comply," which emphasizes your rank rather than building a relationship.

Avoid email, if possible, if you have bad news or a controversial topic to discuss. Use a teleconference or web conference in which information can be exchanged and questions can be answered.

Communicate good news, thanks, and congratulations. Avoid only writing when you have bad news or a request. Sending positive messages builds rapport with people far away.

Write different versions for people in different countries if the message affects people differently. For example, if you are moving a project from Indonesia to India, recognize that the people in each location will have different concerns, and write separate messages.

Learn about holidays and holy days that are observed in the various homelands of your readers. Acknowledge those occasions in your messages if appropriate, and do not expect a prompt response when your readers are on holiday. Use the University of Kansas Medical Center Diversity Calendar (www3.kumc.edu/diversity/january.html), which lists ethnic and religious dates, as a helpful starting place.

Recognize the World You Work In

Consider this truth: Communicating around the globe goes beyond email, online postings, and virtual meetings with people who work on the other side of the globe. It also includes communication with people who work at the lab bench or in the cubicle next to yours but happen to be from other cultures or countries. Not only geographical distance, but also cultural differences and simple unfamiliarity, can get in the way of cross-cultural understanding and great work relationships.

Learn from the stories and suggestions from Richard, Jerry, and Deb. Apply the tips in this chapter and throughout this book. Then enjoy your growing relationships with people around the world and right next door.

Personal Application

▸ Do the stories related by Richard, Jerry, and Deb remind you of your own experiences in global communication? Do you think you might have done something differently to enhance relationships in those situations? What did you do well?

Next Step

▸ Consider your relationships, no matter how developed or undeveloped they are, with people from other countries or cultures. Choose one relationship to strengthen by applying the ideas in this chapter.

PART FOUR

Take Action

CHAPTER 18

Create Your Action Plan for Building Relationships One Message at a Time

If you are wondering whether you can incorporate the ideas from this book into your work life, this chapter is for you. You *can* build better work relationships one message at a time. In fact, you can make it happen easily, just by doing what you normally do a little differently, even if your work plate overflows or you think of yourself as antisocial. There are also extra steps you can take whenever you have the time and inclination to focus on relationship building through writing.

Let's begin with a story.

I was talking to a fourth-year medical student named Xavi, who was applying for residency programs. Xavi told me about the programs she was considering and said she was very impressed with Tulane, a medical center affiliated with Tulane University in New Orleans.

When I asked what impressed her about Tulane, I learned that it was a personal note! Xavi said something like this:

The director followed up on my interview by sending me a personal, handwritten note. Usually all the communication is by email. From his personal note, I think he must be very interested in the residents.

No doubt the residency programs at Tulane have other strong points, but Xavi did not mention any of them. She mentioned receiving a personal note.

When I told this story on my blog, marketing expert Marcia Yudkin chimed in with a similar experience. She wrote:

> When I was thinking about where to go for graduate school, I visited Cornell and was introduced to a very distinguished professor whom I was hoping to study with. Within a week, a handwritten note arrived from him saying how pleased he was to have met me and he hoped I would choose their program. I had already decided to attend Cornell, but if I hadn't, this note would undoubtedly have swayed me to choose Cornell over two other schools that had higher reputations.

Xavi's and Marcia's stories illustrate that building relationships one message at a time requires two things: having a positive intent and taking action.

Positive Intent

Since you are reading these words, you probably have already taken the most important step to build relationships one message at a time. You have experienced the desire to enhance your business relationships through writing. Having that desire is a requirement of reaching the goal.

Positive intent is the ticket to communicating with heart and building business relationships. It is the desire to engage with other human beings at work in supportive, mutually rewarding relationships, spreading positive energy rather than negative feelings (also known as "bad vibes").

The professors who met with Xavi and Marcia communicated their interest and positive feelings about the two student applicants through personal notes. Your positive intent is something you can bring to virtually all your business communications.

Consider the following example of a brief but far-from-routine message from a service provider.

My husband and I had been away from our home office all day at a conference. At that time, we were rarely both out all day, but when we were, a pet sitter named Allison would come by during the day to visit and walk our English cocker spaniel, Chica. When we returned in the evening, we found Allison's "report" on her visit. She wrote, "Positively grand seeing Chica again. She always surprises me—remembers me immediately and doesn't miss a beat before she rolls over for belly rubs!" The brief handwritten note from Allison came on her special form, which had as its heading "Walks & Playtime Notes."

Allison might have left just an invoice for us. She might have simply scribbled a note saying she had come by at 11:30 in the morning. She might have left nothing at all. Instead, Allison's simple 24-word message, from "positively grand" to "belly rubs," communicated her positive intent. She communicated to us that in our long day's absence, our Chica was visited, cared for, and loved.

Perhaps the professors' personal notes, along with Allison's delightful report, will move you to think of ways to communicate your positive intent and make people smile. How can you encourage, delight, please, inspire—in general, create a positive experience for another person? In this chapter and throughout this book you will find examples of ways to connect with others and communicate positively.

Let's assume you have the positive intent. Now all you need is to take action. How many ways will you communicate?

Send the Handwritten Note or Card

Email and other electronic communications are easy to send and nearly instantaneous. But one can still make a strong argument for the handwritten note, as demonstrated by Xavi's and Marcia's feelings about the messages they received.

Other people commented on the Business Writing blog post about Xavi's reaction to Tulane, nearly all of them in favor of the handwritten message. Paula Diaco, owner of the SignARama shop in South Burlington, Vermont, put it this way:

> When I receive business correspondence that is packaged in a lovely envelope, or clearly has a greeting card inside, I'm immediately intrigued and open it right away. I agree that a personal handwritten note rises above email and standard business stationery in terms of being interesting.

Freelance writer Ben Curnett left this comment on the blog:

> We've gotten calls and referrals years after sending handwritten letters to people we've met or done business with.
>
> Plus, I like the feeling I get when I write them. I know that the letters will get noticed. I know that I'm showing someone that I'm listening to them. To me, that's very cool.

English professor Alfredo Deambrosi expressed the sole dissenting view on personal messages, but he also acknowledged their effectiveness:

> Traditional mail frustrates me. It clutters my desk (maybe, that's my fault) and takes longer to open and to trash or file. But it does get my attention. Because I carry it with me to read before meetings, I am more likely to discuss it with a colleague, if it's appropriate for me to do so.

Reflecting on her letter from the Cornell professor, Marcia Yudkin pointed out the wisdom of writing personal messages today:

> Any school or workplace that uses this technique has a marketplace advantage that flies under the radar. Competitors won't normally know why they're losing out!

Such comments argue for the handwritten note as intriguing, interesting, compelling, rare, powerful, sincere, attention grabbing, memorable, satisfying, powerful, and competitively advantageous. Who can argue with those characteristics?

Send Electronic Messages

Email, LinkedIn, Facebook, Twitter, e-cards, and other online ways of communicating do win in some situations. For example:

- When your work relationship with the other person is strictly electronic. In some relationships, your only contact information is an email address, Facebook page, or LinkedIn connection.
- When you are communicating with someone on the other side of the world. Airmail letters across the globe can take two weeks or more to reach their recipients, and in some countries delivery is unpredictable.
- When your message requires near-instant delivery. When you learn that today is your client's birthday or anniversary, only an electronic greeting is quick enough—unless you have a message or a gift hand-delivered.
- When your message is informal. Sometimes a quick electronic message is all you need to send to convey your good wishes and positive intent—for example, in a thank-you to someone who just made your day or in "Way to go!" congratulations on one of life's small successes.

- When you will not get around to putting something in regular mail. It is always better to connect virtually than not connect at all.

Take Action: Gather Supplies to Make Relationship Building Easier

If you intend to send handwritten notes and cards, good for you! To turn your intention into reality, have these supplies on hand:

- **Notecards and notepaper with envelopes.** Having both cards and notepaper allows you to choose what feels right for your message. Stores such as Papyrus and Hallmark sell attractive stationery sets and boxed cards in the United States and Canada, as do museum gift shops. Ordering greeting cards from museums, UNICEF, World Wildlife Fund, and other nonprofits gives you the added pleasure of supporting an organization while buying the cards you need. If you are a photographer, you can make your own cards with your photos, pre-scored card stock paper, your laser or inkjet printer, and simple instructions from manufacturers such as Avery.
- **Postage stamps.** In the United States, you can buy "forever" stamps, and in Canada, "permanent" stamps, whose value is sufficient to cover a first-class letter or card even when postal rates increase. Or choose stamps whose graphic or message you like, for example, Breast Cancer Awareness stamps in the United States. Buy at least one booklet or sheet of 20 stamps as a start. If you think you will send oversized or square cards, which may require additional postage, purchase those extra stamps in advance, so you won't be slowed down later because of a lack of postage.
- **Sympathy cards and get-well cards** are useful because they allow you to send a thoughtful message without having to compose it. Add a few of these cards to your collection, and

you will be ready for delicate moments that require a timely message.

Store your supplies so they are at your fingertips. For minimal cost, you can buy a cardboard or plastic storage box at your office-supply store to keep the cards, stationery, and stamps together with a ballpoint, rollerball, or fountain pen. Or simply slip your postage stamps, a pen, and any extra greeting cards into the box or boxes from the greeting cards you purchase. Then slip your supply box onto a handy bookshelf or into a desk drawer with your copy of this book.

My Toolbox

I have taken my "toolbox" a step further by assembling a collection of cards in a decorative box, with cards separated by labeled dividers. (Before the decorative box, a standard letter-size accordion-file folder did the job, one with a top that closes and fastens to protect the contents.)

In front of the first divider are my postage stamps. I include postcard stamps for sending the occasional postcard to a business associate.

The rest of the dividers are labeled *Blank* (for blank cards), *Thank-You, Congratulations, Get Well, Sympathy, Birthday, Postcards,* and *Miscellaneous.* The Miscellaneous category is for any card I buy that simply doesn't fit the other categories. It may be something silly I think will come in handy, a retirement congratulations, or another unique card.

Each category contains a few items. My blank greeting cards are typically one-of-a-kind cards I select at a gallery or specialty store. They may be landscapes, cityscapes, photos of doors or windows (my favorites), or reproductions of the work of artists such as Matisse, Cezanne, and O'Keefe. Anytime I find a card I like, I add it to my collection, then enjoy sending it to just the right person.

Take Action: Gather Your Contact Information

Assemble your contacts' email and mailing addresses in one, or at most two, places. Whether you use a contact management system, an Outlook address book, a day planner, a Rolodex, or something else, having just one or two go-to places for addresses is easier than tracking down slips of paper or loose business cards when you want to send a greeting.

If you have a lot of contact information in various places, you may need to set aside several hours to pull your contacts together. Or consider hiring someone to finish the job for you.

Take Action: Decide on a Calendar System

When you remember their birthdays, anniversaries, and other special occasions, your employees, clients, and other business associates are touched by your thoughtfulness. But it's hard to actually *remember* such occasions, especially when your list of contacts grows. That's why a system that remembers them for you is essential.

Your calendar system may be Outlook, the Mac's iCal, your smartphone's system, a day planner, or another approach. Whatever system you choose, make sure it will sustain you over the years. You don't want to have to copy special dates from one year to the next on New Year's Day. With Outlook, you can program dates to appear annually, with a flag that reminds you of the upcoming event several days in advance. Those several days give you time to put a greeting card in the mail or to send an early electronic greeting.

Don't Contemplate, Communicate!

With your supplies at hand, your contacts organized, and your calendar at your service, you are ready to take action. Here is a range of one-off and ongoing action steps you can take to build and sustain great work relationships. Choose just one or several, and get started!

Choose someone randomly from your contact list or address book. Send the individual a note of hello, appreciation, positive feedback, or if appropriate, congratulations. Librarian Roger Green has used the same random approach with phone calls despite a girlfriend's criticism:

> I had a girlfriend about 20 years ago who chastised me for pulling out my address book and deciding who I might want to call rather than just KNOWING who I wanted to call. I thought it was important to keep up with people I hadn't been in touch with. Her irritation with my methodology baffled me; still does. Those people getting the call were pleased by the call; how I got to calling them "out of the blue" should not have mattered.

If you have Roger's desire to connect with people, then copy his way of making it happen. Just pick someone from your list. Your contact will be pleased, as Roger's were, to hear from you. Your positive words may make their day and lead to unexpected rewards for you.

Take action in the moment—don't put it off. If you receive a thoughtful email, respond immediately with a quick thanks. Thinking *I'll get to it later* has led to millions of unsent messages. This step means reading your email and regular mail at a time when you can respond to it—not just check it for urgent messages.

Strive for completion—not perfection. This point is related to the item above. You do not need to write the perfect thank-you, condolence, or get-well message. You need to send *a* message. Do not let perfectionism get in the way of sending a heartfelt, timely message.

Psychologist Doris Jeanette emailed this simple thank-you to me in response to a holiday card in which I had included a bookmark of the rules of rendering numbers:

Hi Lynn,

I want to thank you for such a thoughtful and beautiful card. I did read the bookmark and it has raised my awareness about numbers. Thank you for thinking of me.

Doris

The entire message, including both our names, is just 34 words. It is perfect in its simplicity. Writing the thank-you removed the task from Doris's to-do list and probably gave her a feeling of satisfaction and connection. I know it made me feel appreciated.

Make a routine communication into a special one. Whenever you can quickly connect with another person in a way that recognizes him or her as a human being, do it. When people unsubscribe from my newsletter, they have the option of sharing their reason for unsubscribing. They often mention that they have been laid off, are retiring from work, or are taking a leave of absence. I respond in email to those messages. Here's an example:

> Unsubscribe comment from Jamie: "I am going out on maternity leave."
>
> My response: "Jamie, have a happy, healthy maternity leave. I wish you a safe delivery and a joyous welcome of your baby into the world."
>
> Jamie's response: "Lynn, thank you very much for your warm wishes."

Writing and emailing the message to Jamie took me about a minute, just one minute for a meaningful connection with a subscriber.

If you write checks to vendors, as I do in my business, you have an opportunity to write a message of thanks. I include my check in a greeting card. When I included my payment in a thank-you card to a sales consultant, she wrote back saying she enjoyed the card and wondered whether I paid my phone and electric bills with a personal note. No, only when someone I know is at the other end of the envelope do I send a personal message.

You can apply this approach when someone forwards a contract or a check request to you, asking for your signature. Add a quick note of appreciation for their handling the paperwork for you. Or if someone asks you to sign off on a graphic design, an annual report, or a program change, add your positive feedback to your approval. If someone asks for your advice, include along with your words of counsel your thanks and praise for approaching the situation so carefully.

You may have daily opportunities to make routine communications into special ones. Why not take advantage of them?

Set aside time each week to send relationship-building messages. Even if you can manage only 15 minutes, that small chunk of time is enough to send four or five emails or two greeting cards or notes. If your Friday afternoons are calm, that might be a perfect time to reflect on the week and the people you would like to communicate with. Some managers set aside a few minutes each day to extend thanks and positive feedback to staff and colleagues.

Add a positive-tone check when proofreading your emails, memos, and letters. Do not send a message unless it includes at least two positive or courteous words: *please, thank you, appreciate, grateful, delighted, happy to, excellent, welcome,* etc. If this step seems odd or awkward to you, ask yourself why you would want to send a message with nothing positive in it. Even in an email in which you request a meeting, one that might be a tense encounter, you can include this positive sentence: "I look forward to working through the issues."

I remember a business writing class in South Carolina in which a communications specialist was stumped about how to state this concern more positively: "Supplies are limited, so any delays in ordering might result in unfulfilled orders." She was referring to a glossy publication the communications department had produced for employees. We transformed her message to "Supplies are limited. Order now to reserve copies for your department." Our revision eliminated the negative and doubtful *delays, might,* and *unfulfilled* and communicated positively without using obviously positive language.

Add a communication review step to your project plans and decisions. This step is a point at which you can ask yourself:

- Could this project or decision be bad news for others? If so, add one or more bad-news messages and apologies to your task list.
- Is this project or decision the result of the work of others? Add one or more messages of congratulations, thanks, and positive feedback to your tasks.
- Did this project or decision necessitate hiring new staff? Add an introduction of new staff to your tasks.
- Will communications about this project or decision involve email? Review the chapter "Protect Your Relationships by Avoiding Bad Email Behaviors" to avoid email pitfalls.
- Will this project or decision involve communications with people around the globe? Review the chapter "Communicate Around the Globe With Courtesy and Wisdom" for reminders about what can go wrong and right in international communication.
- Will this project or decision create additional work or require a special effort from any individuals? Add a reminder to your calendar to send thank-you notes and positive feedback at appropriate times during the implementation.

Add a note to your calendar to check your contact list in May, August, and December for people who may be graduating. Without making a conscious effort, it is too easy to overlook graduations from high school, junior college, undergraduate school, MBA programs, and other degree and certificate programs. Mark such hard-earned milestones with a special card, note, or gift.

Start early if you intend to send Chanukah, Christmas, or New Year's cards—or all three—to various people. Steps include buying, writing, addressing, stamping, and mailing the cards to your contacts. Even with a contact list of 25 people, that effort takes time. Begin in November or earlier, and pay attention to the date of Chanukah, which may start in late November.

Add the birthdays of your coworkers, employees, and other business associates to your calendar. With LinkedIn and Facebook, your connections and friends have the option of posting their birthdays. Pay attention to those days, and add them to your calendar system. Then send a card, note, or electronic congratulations on their special days.

Add clients' birthdays to your calendar, and send a greeting by email or card. If sending birthday cards is too costly because of your volume of clients, consider tasteful postcards. If you are a dentist, resist the temptation to send a card with an open mouth, and if you are a chiropractor, leave the spine illustration to the poster in your office. Your clients know your profession without cheesy reminders of it on their birthday greetings.

Add to your contact list the names and birthdates of the children of your business associates. You don't need to remember the children's birthdays, but you will enjoy being able to talk about them in situations like this one:

Someone in my professional network, a woman I may see once a year, ordered 20 booklets from me. In my emailed thank-you for her order, I said I hoped she and her young daughter were having a beautiful summer. I used her daughter's name. She wrote back, "Thanks! I am so impressed you remembered my daughter's name :-)."

Confession: I did not remember her daughter's name. I had recorded it, along with her date of birth, in the notes in my Outlook contacts. Having recorded it rather than remembering it does not make the gesture any less meaningful. After all, I *want* to remember her daughter. I *want* to have warm relationships with customers and others in my professional network.

You earn an easy win when you keep track of the personal milestones in people's lives and mention them in the natural flow of business communication. It just takes the discipline of recording those events when they happen. Imagine being able to say, "David is 16 now, right? Has he started driving yet?" The questions show much more awareness and sensitivity than remarks like these: "Your kid is already in high school? No! But it seems just yesterday that you were home with the baby."

Add to your calendar the holidays and holy days, if applicable, of your associates in other countries. See the "Recommended Resources" section for resources that will help you to acknowledge special days with email greetings and to avoid expecting a response on days when your associates are away from their offices.

When you receive positive feedback or thanks, add those messages to a special paper or electronic folder. When you are feeling discouraged, you can open this folder to brighten your day and improve your relationship with yourself! In her comment on Business Writing blog, nurse practitioner Mary K. Parker described the dual value of saving such messages:

> I've saved all the thank-you notes I've received from patients. Not only does it comfort me on those Sisyphean days, it is an opportunity to show tangible customer-service skills to future employers.

An added benefit is that reviewing thanks-yous and other positive messages provides an important reminder to send the same kinds of valuable messages to others.

Add the dates of deaths to your calendar so you can remember their anniversaries with associates who are friends and family members of the deceased. See the chapter "Convey Condolences to Connect With Others" for sample messages.

Add to your calendar a note to review the chapter "Share Constructive Feedback to Improve Performance—and Relationships" at the start of the performance evaluation period at your company. The chapter will remind you of the purpose of feedback and the language to do your job well.

When you add a conference or professional meeting to your calendar, add time after the event as well to follow up with new contacts with whom you have made a meaningful connection. After the event, add each contact to your smartphone, your Outlook contacts, or the system you use. Then send an email or handwritten note or request a LinkedIn connection with the individuals you met. Avoid sending generic messages such as "It was a pleasure talking with you this morning." Instead write something like "I enjoyed our conversation about diversity programs and how to make them meaningful."

If you are looking for a job, add to your calendar a note to update your contacts on the progress you have made in your job search. Then send those updates so your network will remember your search and will recognize ways to continue to help you.

When you have a networking meeting or a job interview, add time to your calendar to send follow-up thank-you messages.

If your profession involves learning about milestones such as weddings, anniversaries, significant birthdays, bar mitzvahs and bat mitzvahs, first communions, and first home purchases—for example, if you are a minister, priest, rabbi, florist, baker, caterer, dressmaker, limo driver, travel planner, or real estate agent—send your own greeting to the person or persons of honor. If appropriate, add the date to your calendar and acknowledge it in coming years.

Seattle real estate agent Jayne DeHaan takes a similar step, calling clients on their birthdays. I have received a birthday call from Jayne each May for over 20 years, ever since I purchased my first house with her help.

If your profession brings you into contact with people whose family members (including pets) have died—for example, in medicine, veterinary medicine, law, nursing homes, hospice, brokerage services, insurance, and mortuary and executor services—add time to your calendar to send condolence notes or sympathy cards. If you do not know the family well, a printed sympathy card with a brief message such as "I am very sorry for your loss," along with your signature, is all you need to send. This small but gracious gesture shows you appreciate the other person as a human being, not just as a client or a customer. Also remember bereaved individuals at other times of the year. This sample message remembers someone's loss:

> Dear Mr. Jenner,
>
> As the holidays approach, I think of the clients I worked with this year, and you come quickly to mind. I know you will be spending the holidays without your wife, Kathryn, for the first time. Know that I am thinking of you during this time of continued loss.
>
> Warm wishes,
> Anita Robbins

If your profession involves helping people through life transitions—for example, adoption law, life coaching, and personal training services—send your clients notes of congratulation when they move through a transition or achieve a personal goal.

If you work for a nonprofit organization, when you schedule an auction or a similar fund-raising initiative, add time to your calendar to write thank-you notes and letters. Donors, sponsors, and volunteers may grumble when they are contacted a year later with a "Thank you for your support. It's time to give again" message. Acknowledge contributions specifically rather than generically whenever possible. For instance, rather than "Thank you for your generous donation," write, "Thank you for your generous donation of a week at your condominium in Belize."

If you are in a profession in which you regularly deal with adversaries—such as law, politics, and the military—add a note to your daily calendar to remind yourself to communicate positively and nurture your professional relationships. A reminder such as "Be kind in writing" or "Have you included positive language in that message?" can help you counteract your profession's focus on defeating the enemy or opponent.

If you are a student, start early building professional relationships. At the end of a class, send an email or thank-you note to professors and guest lecturers who have been especially helpful to you or who have worked hard to make your class engaging. Normally send the note to your professors after they have submitted grades, so your communication does not suggest an attempt to inspire a higher grade. Write a note of thanks or positive feedback whenever someone has exceeded your learning expectations.

If you are a blogger, make time to visit the blogs of others in related and unrelated fields. Leave comments expressing appreciation and praise for great content. Blog about the specific posts of others when you can. By doing so, you will enrich your work life with "virtual friends."

Take any of the actions in this chapter, and you will be using business writing to create and sustain great work relationships. As with the professors at Tulane and Cornell who sent memorable messages to student applicants, your efforts will be noticed and remembered, perhaps even many years later!

Personal Reflection

- ▸ How many of the action steps in this chapter are you already taking? Which steps will be easy to add to your routine?

Next Step

- ▸ Take a moment to congratulate yourself for everything you are already doing to create and sustain great work relationships. Enjoy the satisfaction and success those relationships bring.

For Your Reference

Recommended Resources:
Learn More About Building Relationships

Learn More About Etiquette

Books

Use *Emily Post's Etiquette,* Eighteenth Edition, by Peggy Post, et al. (HarperCollins, 2011), to learn more about manners in our quickly evolving world. The "Life in the Workplace" section covers the job search, office challenges, workplace relationships, and business socializing.

Use Robert Hickey's book, *Honor & Respect: The Official Guide to Names, Titles, and Forms of Address* (The Protocol School of Washington, 2008), to have answers to your momentous "how to address" questions at your fingertips. In the United States, the comprehensive volume is used at the White House, Supreme Court, and Department of State, among many other institutions.

Blog

Visit Robert Hickey's blog on names, titles, and forms of address, at www.formsofaddress.info/faq.html, when you are unsure how to address, greet, or list an important person. If Mr. Hickey, Deputy Director of the Protocol School of Washington, has not already answered your question online, he will do so.

Learn More About International Communication

Books

Gather more information about writing for people who read English as a foreign language in Edmond H. Weiss's *The Elements of International English Style: A Guide to Writing Correspondence, Reports, Technical Documents, and Internet Pages for a Global Audience* (M.E. Sharpe, 2005). The book offers 57 communication tactics with vivid examples and many helpful insights.

Learn more about the cultures, customs, and communication preferences of people in more than 80 countries in *When Cultures Collide: Leading Across Cultures,* Third Edition (Nicholas Brealey International, 2006), by Richard D. Lewis. This book provides excellent detailed guidance to help you lead, sell, and build relationships across cultures.

Websites

Learn about the national holidays celebrated in countries around the world, from Åland to Zimbabwe, on the Q++ Worldwide Public Holidays site, at www.qppstudio.net/publicholidays.htm. The site covers 198 countries and 48 semi-autonomous territories such as Hong Kong and Gibraltar.

Consult the University of Kansas Medical Center's diversity calendar to learn about religious and national holidays of various cultures and countries, at www3.kumc.edu/diversity/january.html.

On Wikipedia, at www.en.wikipedia.org/wiki/workweek, find out when your associates in other countries celebrate the weekend. Learn, for example, which Islamic countries celebrate the weekend on Thursday–Friday and on Friday–Saturday.

Use the websites www.worldtimeserver.com and www.timeanddate.com to learn what time it is around the world. Both sites include a time-zone converter and a time-zone map.

Get Help Solving Interpersonal Difficulties

Books

Pore over *Peer Power: Transforming Workplace Relationships,* by Cynthia Clay and Ray Olitt (Jossey-Bass, 2012). The book provides clues, strategies, and principles to help you identify and work effectively with nine challenging personalities including the attacker, the whiner, and the slacker.

Take your interpersonal skills to the next level reading *What Got You Here Won't Get You There: How Successful People Become Even More Successful,* by Marshall Goldsmith with Mark Deiter (Hyperion, 2007). Learn how to eliminate 20 bad habits such as making destructive comments, refusing to express regret, and failing to express gratitude.

Get Better at Building and Sustaining Relationships

Books

Dip into any chapter of Keith Ferrazzi's *Never Eat Alone and Other Secrets to Success, One Relationship at a Time* (with Tahl Raz, Doubleday, 2005) to get great gems on building business relationships. Mr. Ferrazzi promotes audacity, authenticity, passion, "pinging" (getting in touch briefly and often), and many gratifying ways of connecting with others.

Read *Brag! The Art of Tooting Your Own Horn Without Blowing It,* by Peggy Klaus (Warner Business Books, 2003), to learn how to comfortably and confidently share information about yourself. Although the purpose of the book is to "teach you the art of bragging," Ms. Klaus's strategies help you open up in ways that launch and build relationships.

Find out more about how giving to others builds success in *Give and Take: A Revolutionary Approach to Success,* by Adam Grant (Viking/Penguin Group, 2013). Professor Grant tells many stories that will inspire you to give to others in your professional life the way you do naturally in your personal life.

Learn More About Apologies

Book

Enjoy Aaron Lazare's *On Apology* (Oxford University Press, 2004), which provides everything you ever wanted to know about apologies in a fascinating read. Dr. Lazare's true examples of pseudo apologies, non-apologies, and excuses, often in rich historical contexts, give you a deep understanding of what can go wrong in apologies—and how to do it right.

Learn More About Giving and Eliciting Feedback

Book

Read Rick Maurer's short but powerful *Feedback Toolkit: 16 Tools for Better Communication in the Workplace,* Second Edition (Productivity Press, 2011), to learn more about what Mr. Maurer calls "telling each other the truth." This concise gem of a book offers insights and easy-to-follow plans.

Gain More Confidence in Your Writing

Book

Get *The Gregg Reference Manual: A Manual of Style, Grammar, Usage, and Formatting,* Tribute Edition, Eleventh Edition, edited by William A. Sabin (McGraw-Hill, 2011), to gain confidence about the correctness of your business writing. *Gregg* covers virtually any question you may have on grammar, punctuation, formatting, and related topics.

Ways to Render Names and Titles in Greetings and on Envelopes

❧

When you have taken the time to choose the perfect card or write a thoughtful note or letter, you don't want to worry about how to address someone. Nevertheless, questions may come up: Should you use a title such as *Mr.* or *Ms.*? When you write to a couple, whose name comes first? This section provides guidance so that you can confidently address your readers and render their names on envelopes. For information on greetings and how to punctuate them, see the next section, "Greetings (Salutations) for Letters, Notes, Emails, and Text Messages."

Guidelines for What Follows "Dear" and Appears on Envelopes
When you know your reader and your relationship is friendly, use his or her first name in the greeting. On the envelope, use a courtesy title or just first and last name.

Greeting:
Dear Kim,

Envelope:
Ms. Kim Batcher [OR]
Kim Batcher

When the relationship is formal, use a courtesy title or a professional title and a last name. Examples of formal relationships are student to professor and nonprofit employee to donor.

Greeting:
Dear Mr. Alfano:

Envelope:
Mr. Albert Alfano

Greeting:
Dear Professor Cook:

Envelope:
Professor Amanda R. Cook

When you write to someone who is much older than you or highly esteemed, use a title and a last name.

Greeting:
Dear Reverend Carlock,

Envelope:
Reverend Anita Carlock

Greeting:
Dear Dr. Mak:

Envelope:
Dr. Ronald D. Mak [OR]
Ronald D. Mak, M.D.

When you write to someone you do not know or do not know very well, greet the reader using a title and last name, or use both first and last names without a courtesy title.

Greeting:
Dear Mrs. Yang: [OR]
Dear Monica Yang:

Envelope:
Mrs. Monica Yang [OR]
Monica Yang

Be sure not to switch between a first-name and last-name basis with someone. If you do, Salma may wonder what she did to suddenly become "Dr. Bishara." If you have an assistant who prepares your correspondence, be sure he or she knows which approach you want to use.

Unless you are certain that a woman prefers the courtesy title *Miss* or *Mrs.,* use the title *Ms.* or leave the title out. Pay attention to women's signature blocks and online bios and profiles to see whether they communicate a preference.

Know which titles to spell out. Never spell out the titles *Mr., Ms., Mrs.,* and *Dr.* Do spell out these titles and similar ones: *Professor, Dean, Sister, Rabbi, Imam, Senator, Governor, Admiral,* and *Judge.*

Do not use an academic degree (*M.S., M.D.*) or professional designation (*SPHR, Esq.*) in the greeting. On the envelope, if you include an academic degree or professional designation after a person's name, do not use a courtesy title that indicates the same achievement (for example, do not use *Dr.* and *Ph.D.* together). You may use a title and a degree on the same line if doing so is not redundant.

Greeting:
Dear Dr. Pelley:

Envelope:
Olive Pelley, Ph.D.

Greeting:
Dear Mr. Lowe:

Envelope:
Jason Lowe, CPA

Greeting:
Dear Dr. Abramson, [OR]
Dear Rabbi Abramson,

Envelope:
Rabbi Sydney Abramson, D.D.

Jr., *Sr.*, **and roman numerals such as** *III* are normally included on the envelope, unless a message is informal. However, do not include them in your greeting.

Greeting:
Dear Nicholas,

Envelope:
Mr. Nicholas Parson Jr.

Greeting:
Dear Mr. Noss:

Envelope:
Mr. Jonathan Noss III

The traditional way to greet male-female married couples is with the man's title first, then the woman's title followed by the last name. On the envelope, only the man's first name appears.

Greeting:
Dear Mr. and Mrs. Wright,

Envelope:
Mr. and Mrs. Bruce Wright Jr.

Greeting:
Dear Dr. and Mrs. Terry,

Envelope:
Dr. and Mrs. James Terry

Greeting:
Dear Senator and Mrs. Smith,

Envelope:
Senator and Mrs. Gordon Smith

The modern way to address male-female couples and same-sex couples is to render both individuals' names the same way, with or without first names and titles. On the envelope, render the names either on the same line or one beneath the other, listing first the name of the person with a special title or the primary recipient (for instance, the person you know better).

Greeting:
Dear Anne and Bruce Wright,

Envelope:
Ms. Anne Wright
Mr. Bruce Wright Jr.

Greeting:
Dear Anne and Bruce,

Envelope:
Anne and Bruce Wright

Greeting:
Dear Mr. and Mrs. Wright:

Envelope:
Mr. Bruce Wright Jr. and Mrs. Anne Wright

Greeting:
Dear Mses. Carlson:

Envelope:
Ms. Nadine Carlson
Ms. Danique Carlson

When a woman marries, pay special attention to the name she uses. For instance, if Dawn Harden marries Ron Wice, she may remain Dawn Harden. Or she may be Dawn Wice, Dawn Harden Wice, Dawn Harden-Wice, or something else. If you are not certain which name a woman uses professionally, ask. She will welcome your interest.

In messages to two people (coupled or not), include the name of the person with a special title first, or list the main recipient first. Whenever you know your readers well and want to communicate in a friendly way, use first names in the greeting. But avoid using an abbreviated form of a person's name unless he or she uses it. For example, do not call a Juan Carlos "JC" or an Emily "Em" unless the individual does so.

Greeting:
Dear Ms. Donne and Mr. Trujillo, [OR]
Dear Drenda and Alex, (only if he uses the name *Alex*)

Envelope:
Ms. Drenda Donne
Mr. Alessandro Trujillo

Greeting:
Dear Dr. and Mrs. Ellis:

Envelope:
Dr. Moises Ellis (or replace *Dr.* with *M.D.* at end)
Mrs. Renee Ellis (or replace *Mrs.* with *Ms.*)

Greeting:
Dear Drs. Gerber and Singh: [OR]
Dear Dr. Gerber and Dr. Singh:

Envelope:
Dr. Robin Gerber
Dr. Gaurav Singh

Greeting:
Dear Drs. Moody:

Envelope:
Dr. Claire P. Moody
Dr. James M. Moody

Greeting:
Dear Captain Klein and Professor Klein:

Envelope:
Captain Erika I. Klein
Professor Roger K. Klein

Greeting:
Dear Reverend Paul and Mr. Green: [OR]
Dear Tim and Dan, (only if they use these short forms)

Envelope:
Reverend Timothy Paul
Mr. Daniel Green

Greeting:
Dear Mr. Lee and Ms. Roy-Lee, [OR]
Dear Anthony Lee and Susan Roy-Lee,

Envelope:
Mr. Anthony Lee Jr.
Ms. Susan Roy-Lee

Greeting:
Dear Messrs. Stone and Raj, [OR]
Dear Mr. Stone and Mr. Raj,

Envelope:
Mr. Joseph Stone
Mr. Alain Raj

Greeting:
Dear Mses. Woodard, [OR]
Dear Loretta and Chanel,

Envelope:
Ms. Loretta Woodard
Ms. Chanel Woodard

Greeting:
Dear Mrs. Hain and Mrs. Pham, [OR]
Dear Mesdames Hain and Pham

Envelope:
Mrs. Marie Hain
Mrs. Lu Pham

Messrs. is for more than one man with the title *Mr.* Its use is quite formal and traditional. You may use *Mr.* with each man's name instead.

Mesdames is for more than one woman with the title *Mrs.* Like *Messrs.*, it is formal and traditional. You may use *Mrs.* with each name.

Mses. is for more than one woman with the title *Ms.* You may also use *Ms.* with each name.

When You Have a "Mystery Reader"

If you are writing to a stranger and don't know a person's gender, do a bit of research on the Internet before leaving off courtesy titles such as *Mr.* and *Ms.* Type the individual's name into your browser's search box and see what you find. Or call the company and ask which courtesy title is appropriate. If your research doesn't reap a helpful answer, use the person's full name without a title, like this:

Dear Dana Simms:

Dear T.K. Spinazola:

Dear E. Hassan,

If you don't know and can't get the name of the person who will read your letter—for example, when applying for a job—use a targeted greeting with an appropriate job title, like this:

Dear Recruiter:

Dear Hiring Manager:

Dear Claims Adjustor:

You may use "Dear Sir or Madam," but that greeting feels more anonymous, as does the cold "To whom it may concern." Do not use "Dear Sir," "Dear Sirs," and "Gentlemen" because those greetings assume your readers are male.

If you are writing to a company rather than any specific individual, you may use the company name. This approach is considered slightly informal.

> Dear Syntax Training:
>
> Dear XYZ Company:
>
> Dear ABC Agency:

Answers to Common Questions About Names and Titles

The challenge of how to render names and titles correctly in greetings and on envelopes has raised many questions on my blog and in my email. Here are answers to some common questions.

Sometimes I am undecided about using a courtesy title. The message may be friendly—for example, a congratulations, but the relationship is more formal. Is it better to err on the side of friendliness or formality?

You will virtually always be correct if you use a courtesy title or a professional title such as *Ms., Mr., Dr., Father,* or *Dean* for your recipient. You may choose to leave out such a title when your message is more personal than professional or more informal than formal. For example, if your congratulatory note celebrates a new baby, that message qualifies as personal. If your congratulations marks a promotion or an honor, it is professional. Similarly, your invitations to a barbecue lean toward informal, but invitations to a gala are formal. You decide whether you want the communication to feel personal or professional, informal or formal.

If the person I am writing to uses two last names, do I use both or only one of them in the greeting?

You use both names in the greeting. For example:

Dear Professor Garcia Lopez,

Dear Ms. Gaertner-Johnston:

I have seen "Dear Sir" and "Dear Sir or Madam." Is "Dear Madam" ever correct?

"Dear Madam" would be correct if you knew your reader was a woman but did not know—and could not learn—her name. When your goal is to build relationships, doing the research to learn someone's name comes across as more thoughtful than being satisfied with a lack of information.

When I write to a man or a woman who has a Ph.D. or another doctorate, do I use *Dr.* as the title?

Use *Dr.* if you know the person prefers it or it is standard in your industry. If the individual is in academia or science in the United States, it is more likely he or she uses *Dr.* than in other industries (and perhaps countries). Otherwise, use *Mr., Ms., Mrs., Miss,* or *Professor* depending on any known preferences. If you have access to the person's bio or professional profile, pay attention to which title appears there.

If I am writing to a recently widowed woman, how do I address her?

At work, a woman rarely uses her husband's first name to identify herself. However, if you write to donors, constituents, members, patients, or customers who are widows, pay attention to the way they refer to themselves (in the traditional way, Mrs. Alfred J. Sherrard, or the modern way, Ms. Alicia Sherrard). If a woman uses her husband's name, write to her that way even if he dies. When and if she decides to stop using his name, you can follow her lead.

At the beginning of your business relationship with a widow or at the time she becomes a widow, you can ask her tactfully how she would like to be addressed.

Is it acceptable to use *&* (the ampersand) between names in the salutation?

No. It is traditionally not acceptable to use the ampersand for *and* in the salutation.

If I am writing to a family and each person has the same last name, what is the proper greeting?

The easiest way is to use first names.

> **Greeting:**
> Dear Don, Julie, and Julian,
>
> **Envelope:**
> Don, Julie, and Julian Burke

If you must be more formal, use this approach:

> **Greeting:**
> Dear Mr. and Mrs. Burke and Mr. Burke,
>
> **Envelope:**
> Mr. Donald Burke, Mrs. Julie Burke, and Mr. Julian Burke

When writing to an entire family, should everyone's name be on the envelope and in the greeting?

Rather than crowd envelopes and greetings with many names, you can use the parent's or parents' names with "and Family." For example, address the envelope to "Ernest and Kate Elgin," with a greeting to "Dear Ernest, Kate, and Family." Or use just the last name in both places: on the envelope "The Robinsons" and for a greeting "Dear Robinsons."

Should I use *Miss* or *Ms.* for a young girl?

Emily Post's Etiquette suggests the use of *Miss* until age 16 to 18, then *Ms. The Gregg Reference Manual* recommends addressing teenage girls as *Ms.* or *Miss,* following the girl's preference when you know it. For younger girls, *Gregg* indicates that you may use a title or omit it.

For boys, *Emily Post's Etiquette* recommends the title *Master* until age 6 to 7, then no title until age 16 to 18 years, then *Mr.* In contrast, *The Gregg Reference Manual* recommends addressing a boy as *Mr.* when he becomes a teenager. *Gregg* notes that *Master* is rarely seen.

If I am sending a letter or an email to many people, may I use a greeting such as "Dear Joshua et al."?

Et al., which is Latin for "and others," is not appropriate in a greeting. Many people will stumble over it, detracting from your message, and it seems too distant for a relationship-building message. If you need to greet up to five people, use all of their names. If you have more than five readers, try a group greeting such as:

In a letter:
Dear Chamber Members,

In an email:
Hello, Marketing Team.
Greetings, everybody.

If you regularly write to a group, why not ask group members which greeting they prefer?

If you have more questions about names and titles and how to render them, search my blog at www.businesswritingblog.com, or consult *The Gregg Reference Manual* or *Emily Post's Etiquette,* Eighteenth Edition, by Peggy Post et al. (Note: That's a correct use of *et al.*!)

Greetings (Salutations) for Letters, Notes, Emails, and Text Messages

After the date and a possible subject line, the first thing your reader sees is your greeting, also known as a salutation. Sometimes greetings set the tone of the message like a friendly smile and a handshake. At other times, they rest unremarkably on the screen or page and make little difference. This section offers guidance and answers common questions about salutations, so you don't need to worry about your greetings and what they may unintentionally communicate.

Greetings in Business Letters and Notes

The standard way to open a business letter is with *Dear,* the person's name with or without a professional title (Dr.) or courtesy title (Ms.), and a colon, like this:

> Dear Louise:
>
> Dear Patrick:

Dear Ms. Chu:

Dear Mr. and Dr. Paige:

Dear Professor Amato:

Dear Drs. Zhu:

Use a colon after the greeting (rather than a comma) when your message is more business focused than social—for example, when you are writing to explain a policy or say no.

The standard way to open a social business letter or a note is with *Dear,* the person's name with or without a professional or courtesy title, and a comma, like this:

Dear Nigel,

Dear Patty and Eric,

Dear Dr. Tarabi,

Dear Annette and Teri,

Dear Reverend Jans,

Dear Dr. and Mrs. Lewis,

A social business letter or note focuses more on the social aspects of your relationship than the business aspects. Letters and notes of condolence, personal congratulations (for weddings, births, retirement, and other celebrations), and thank-yous fall into the category of social business letters.

The colon-comma distinction is alive and well in the United States and Canada. However, in the United Kingdom, often no punctuation follows the greeting.

Greetings in Emails

For formal email—that is, email used in place of a business letter— greet the reader as you would in a letter. Use *Dear* before the person's name with or without a title, followed by a colon or a comma.

To warm up less formal emails, use greetings like these:

> Hi, Eva.
>
> Greetings, Finance.
>
> Hello, Drs. Furtado and Cho.
>
> Hello, Kwasi.
>
> Good morning, Folks.
>
> Ciao, everyone.
>
> Greetings, Professor!
>
> Dear all,
>
> Hello to all.

Think twice about greetings that indicate the time of day, such as "Good morning." Time-of-day greetings do not work well if some of your readers live in other time zones or will read your message long after you send it.

Some people use *Hey* as a greeting, similar to *Hi*, but others object to it as too informal. If you do use *Hey,* save it for very informal messages.

Various ways to punctuate the email greetings *Hi* and *Hello* are acceptable. As a punctuation traditionalist, I prefer these ways, either on the same line as the first sentence or above the body of the message:

Hi, Han.

Hello, Han.

You will also see these styles above the message body:

Hi Han,

Hi, Han,

Hello Han,

Hello, Han,

Some people leave out the greeting, but the resulting tone can feel cool or cold:

Brooke:

Team:

Professor:

Sue,

Accounting,

Rather than using a greeting, you may use the person's name in the opening sentence, like this:

Yiota, you were right about the prices.

For messages back and forth in an email conversation, use the reader's name in the opening sentence rather than repeating a greeting several times a day. When you do omit a greeting, be sure you include positive language in the message to warm up your tone.

Greetings in Text Messages

Texts are informal messages, so follow the suggestions for less formal emails. You may be tempted to omit the greeting when tapping out a text, but do not omit it if your goal is to build or maintain a good business relationship.

Notice that the greeting warms up the tone in these pairs of texts:

> I'll be there in 10 minutes.
>
> Hi, Professor. I'll be there in 10 minutes.

> I'm waiting in the lobby for you to escort me.
>
> Hello, Guy. I'm waiting in the lobby for you to escort me.

Answers to Common Questions About Greetings

Over the years, readers of my blog and participants in classes have repeatedly asked two questions about greetings. Here are those questions and answers.

If I don't like someone, do I still have to use *Dear* in the greeting of a letter?

Dear is not the same as *Dearest* or *Darling*. It is simply the standard term for greetings in letters, so you need to use it. No etiquette experts recommend "Not So Dear" as a greeting.

One place in which you can skip *Dear* is the simplified letter, which has no greeting. It begins with the subject in all capital letters, like this:

WAYS TO BEGIN A BUSINESS LETTER

I am writing to share information about standard letter openings to . . .

Do not use the simplified letter if your goal is to build a relationship with your reader. It feels too anonymous.

If I use words such as *team* and *everybody* in the greeting, should I capitalize those words even though they are not people's names or titles?

You should capitalize all nouns. Words such as *team, group, department,* and *managers* are nouns. You should not capitalize pronouns. The words *everybody, anybody, everyone, anyone,* and *all* are pronouns.

If you have more questions about greetings, search my blog at www.businesswritingblog.com.

Complimentary Closes (Sign-Offs) for Letters, Notes, Emails, and Texts

The complimentary close, or closing, is the last words your reader sees before your name. Complimentary closes are straightforward, but you may feel confused by what you have learned and what you see in the messages you receive. Use this section to remove any doubts about the closes you choose.

Complimentary Closes in Letters and Notes

Complimentary closes are standard in business letters, except for the simplified letter, which omits them. (The simplified letter, with neither greeting nor close, is not a strong choice for relationship-building messages.) Complimentary closes also typically appear in typed and handwritten notes.

Like greetings, closes range from formal and professional to friendly and warm. These acceptable closes are listed by their degree of formality or friendliness:

←——— More Formal Closes ——— Friendlier Closes ——→

Yours faithfully,	Sincerely,	Cordially,
Very truly yours,	Best regards,	Warmest wishes,
Respectfully,	Kind regards,	Warm regards,
Yours truly,	With thanks,	Warmly,
Sincerely yours,	Best wishes,	Affectionately,

For sympathy messages, choose one of the above closes or one of these:

> In deepest sympathy,
> With sympathy,
> With our condolences,
> Very sincerely,
> Wishing you peace,
> Sincere regards,

Regarding "Yours faithfully," my colleagues in the United Kingdom tell me it is used there regularly when writing to someone you do not know.

Do not use your closing to communicate anger or frustration:

> **Not this:** With strong malice,
> **Not this:** In deep frustration,

Instead, use a professional-sounding close such as "Sincerely."

Avoid using the word *warm* in closes to people you do not know. Doing so may come across as overly familiar. Use *affectionately* only in a very close business relationship. Avoid it if your affection could be thought inappropriate by the reader or anyone else who reads the message.

Do not use *xoxo* (kiss hug kiss hug) as a close in any but the most familiar relationships. Read the discussion of *xoxo* in the chapter "Add Heart to Your Writing One Message at a Time."

In the United States and Canada, a comma follows the complimentary close. In the United Kingdom, often no punctuation follows it.

Only the first word of the complimentary close is capitalized.

Like this: With best wishes,

Not this: With Best Wishes,

Complimentary Closes in Email

When you use email in place of a business letter, choose a complimentary close from the earlier list.

A close is not required in less formal email, but it helps you end your message pleasantly. Choose from the closes listed earlier, or pick one of these to add a positive tone to your email:

Best,

Regards,

All the best,

Cheers,

Yours,

Ciao,

Thanks **is not technically a complimentary close** although it appears at the end of millions of emails. If you use *Thanks* at the end of your email, why not make it a sentence and follow it with a period, such as "Thanks for your help" or "Thanks again for your interest" or "Thanks for considering my request"?

In an email conversation of messages back and forth, repeating the complimentary close and signature block is not necessary and could seem silly. But when you start a new conversation or revisit an email string after a few days, use a greeting and a close again.

Complimentary Closes in Text Messages

The nature of texts is quick, short, and informal, so any close you use should match that style. Good closes for texts are:

> Best,
>
> All best,
>
> Cheers,
>
> Ciao,

It's acceptable to skip the close in texts. But as in any message, a friendly sign-off communicates warmth.

Despite the brevity of texts, the closes below do not communicate well. They keep readers guessing and can come across as lazy. Therefore, do not use:

> Rgds,
>
> KR, (for Kind regards)
>
> BW, (for Best wishes)

Answers to Common Questions About Closes

Is it ever correct to add "I am" or "We are" above a closing?

Expressions such as "I am" above "Sincerely yours" or a similar close are virtually never used in 21st century communication. They are not even recommended in a writing handbook I have that was published in 1914, *Handbook of Business English,* by George Burton Hotchkiss and Edward Jones Kilduff. Do not use them.

How about adding "I remain" after a closing, such as "With warm regards, I remain"? Is that acceptable?

That style does not appear in any business writing manuals I have seen in the last 25 years, so I can't recommend it.

If more than one person will sign the letter, are there two closes?

Use just one complimentary close even if two people sign the letter. Have them sign above their names. Your closing might look like this:

Best regards,

Patrick White   Michaela Best
Manager, Customer Service   Regional Manager

Or like this:

Best regards,

Patrick White
Manager, Customer Service

Michaela Best
Regional Manager

Is "Your loving student" or "Your loving coworker" ever appropriate as a closing?

"Your loving" is too intimate for the student-teacher or coworker relationship. If the relationship is close, use "Warm wishes" or "Warm regards."

Is it acceptable to use two complimentary closes together, for example, "Yours sincerely, with best wishes"?

One complimentary close is plenty. Using two would call attention to its oddity. If you want to combine sentiments, you might use "With sincere best wishes."

If the closes in someone's messages to me begin to change from "Thanks" to "Best wishes," does that mean something has changed in the relationship?

Don't read too much into people's closes. Writers who change closes may simply have learned something new about them, for example, that "Thanks" is not a standard close. Or they may simply want to bring variety to their messages.

Is it acceptable to refer to the reader's friends or family in the close?

It's fine to use a close such as "Best regards to you and your family."

Can a simple "From" be used as a close, for example, "From [followed by a blank line] Your Friends at ABC Company"?

"From" is not a complimentary close. Replace it with a more standard close such as "Best wishes."

Is "Kindly" an appropriate close?

"Kindly" does not work as a close. Its meaning is different from "Sincerely" and "Cordially." It is too closely associated with "Please," as in "Would you kindly confirm the time of our meeting?" If you like "Kind" in your complimentary close, use "Kind regards."

Search for answers to more questions about complimentary closes on my blog at www.businesswritingblog.com or in *The Gregg Reference Manual*.

Index

Acknowledgments

My heartfelt thanks go to many people who supported me on this book-building journey.

Susan Daffron inspired me with her enthusiastic response to my first two chapters and outline. Marcia Yudkin coached and challenged me with her brilliant logic and deep understanding of what works in nonfiction books. My friend Doe Coover, whose support goes all the way back to our first year of college, cheered me across the finish line with her insightful advice and fine eye for grouping chapters.

My friends and colleagues Deb Arnold, Jerry Schlagenhauf, Ron Scott, Lynn Takaki, and Richard Wilkinson granted me interviews that brought several topics to life. They also took time to review and fine-tune their sections.

Many generous, smart people provided examples, suggestions, and stories that made the book practical and authentic. I list them here alphabetically: Deb Arnold, Mary Bennett, Gilda Bonanno, Pete Busacca, Keith Chapman, Cynthia Clay, John Cline, Dennis Dennis, Cameron Deuel, Lisa Dodge-Johnson, Hanna Ekström, Margaret Elwood, Charlie Gadzik, Kathy Goughenour, Carolyn Grimm, Doris Jeanette, Tim Jones, Marie Kelly, Joanne Masterson, Sten Olsen, Lesley Peters, Alice Risemberg, Mary Rolston, Jerry Schlagenhauf, Valerie Shields, Russ

Taylor, Steve Teixeira, Melissa Thirloway, and Marcia Yudkin, along with the staff at Hiers-Baxley Funeral Services.

These astute blog commenters expanded the book's points of view: Claudia Amaya, Anne Boardman, Jeff Chamberlain, Matt Charles, Ben Curnett, Alfredo Deambrosi, Paula Diaco, Nancy Doerhoff, Roger Green, Robert Hickey, Josh Hinds, Cornelia Luethi, Cyndy McCollough, Jeannette Paladino, Mary K. Parker, and Neil Wheatley.

The talented associates of 1106 Design transformed my manuscript into a professional book of which I am proud. Special thanks go to Michele DeFilippo and Ronda Rawlins.

Thanks and a shout out to Christi and the gang at the Island Country Inn on Bainbridge Island, Washington, where I wrote most of this book while enjoying a room of my own.

I thank my 100-year-old cousin Eleanor for inspiring me with a life well lived. Eleanor, you've always had heart!

My cherished daughter, Eva, accepted the absence of Mom and meals while I was away working on this book. She graciously replaced her question "What's for dinner?" with "How is your book?"

My deepest appreciation and love go to my husband, Michael Johnston. Without his support and repeated encouragement to go away and write, this book would still be an inadequate Word document tugging at my soul.

About the Author

Lynn Gaertner-Johnston has helped thousands of employees and managers improve their business writing skills and confidence through her company, Syntax Training (www.syntaxtraining.com). In her corporate training career of more than 20 years, she has worked with executives, engineers, scientists, sales staff, and many other professionals, helping them get their messages across with clarity and tact.

A gifted teacher, Lynn has led writing classes at more than 100 companies and organizations such as MasterCard, Microsoft, Boeing, Nintendo, REI, AARP, and Kaiser Permanente. Near her home in Seattle, Washington, she has taught managerial communications in the MBA programs of the University of Washington and UW Bothell.

Lynn's influence extends far beyond the corporate classroom. Her free monthly newsletter, *Better Writing at Work,* reaches many thousands of subscribers around the world. Her popular Business Writing blog (www.businesswritingblog.com) attracts more than 3 million annual visits from readers on six continents. A recognized expert in business writing etiquette, Lynn has been quoted in *The Wall Street Journal, The Atlantic, The Chicago Tribune,* and other media.

Lynn sharpened her business writing skills at the University of Notre Dame, where she earned a master's degree in communication, and at Bradley University, with a bachelor's degree in English.

CPSIA information can be obtained
at www.ICGtesting.com
Printed in the USA
BVHW071128200520
579862BV00001B/62